GUESTS OF THE EMPEROR

ALLIED POW'S OF WWII IN RANGOON BURMA

JEAN NEWLAND

authorHOUSE®

AuthorHouse™
1663 Liberty Drive
Bloomington, IN 47403
www.authorhouse.com
Phone: 1-800-839-8640

Published by AuthorHouse   11/08/2012

ISBN: 978-1-4772-8113-0 (hc)
ISBN: 978-1-4772-8114-7 (sc)

Library of Congress Control Number: 2012919702

DEDICATION

This book is dedicated to my uncle, Richard Brooks, Karnig Thomasian and all those gallant men who were imprisoned in Rangoon. Those who came home and those who did not.

CONTENTS

FORWARD

In 2004, my uncle, Richard Brooks, died in California. He left behind his army trunk filled with letters, reports, pictures, ribbons, medals as well as his complete uniform with boots! My uncle had survived imprisonment in the Rangoon Jail by the Japanese in 1944 Burma and saved the contents of his trunk for over 68 years. When I came into possession of the trunk and reviewed those contents I quickly realized that someone had to keep alive the memories that were emblazoned in each document. Thus the genesis for this book arose. The trunk was a true treasure trove not to be measured in money but by human suffering and survival. My uncle had kept together the individual letter records of survivors; these papers were called "circumstances of capture and liberation." I knew that I could not do justice to these records if I changed or modified the stories in any way because these stories were told by the men themselves. I have tried to identify the source for each story and in the process of writing this book, I have located other accounts outside the trunk and have included them!

As you read their narratives you will begin to know these men as I do. Not only will you hear them talk about their experiences, but those of their fellow prisoners. They weave an extraordinary story.

The men imprisoned in the Rangoon Jail were from all over the Allied world but they all held one thing in common: **They were invariably young and incredibly brave.**

PART 1

China-Burma-India
"The Forgotten Theater"

On December 7, 1941, the Japanese bombed Pearl Harbor and America was at war. Millions of American men thronged to recruitment stations to enlist. Their country had been attacked and they were ready to avenge this "dastardly attack" as President Roosevelt called it. America had become partially involved with the war already raging in Europe. President Roosevelt had been held from direct involvement because many Americans felt that America should remain neutral. In his election campaign, he had promised the American people that he would never send "our boys" to die on foreign soil again.

The First World War and tough economic problems were foremost in the minds of the American public. However, President Roosevelt felt the need to help our allies with the threat from the Axis powers. He proposed a plan to "Lend-Lease" supplies and arms to countries whose security was vital to the defense of the United States. These supplies would be repaid or returned to the United States after hostilities ended.

On March 11, 1941, bill H.R.1776 was passed by Congress a year and a half after the outbreak of the European war which started in September 1939 and nine months before the United States entered the war officially on December 8, 1941. Because of that bill, America would begin the production of arms, planes, ships and other war materials. Upon conclusion of the war, Russian Premier Stalin would go on record saying that without the Lend-Lease program, the Allies would not have won WW II. A staggering 50 billion dollars was appropriated by Congress and it was designated for 38 countries. The breakdown for these funds was 31.4 billion to Britain, 11.3 billion to the Soviet Union, 3.2 billion to France and 1.6 billion to China.[1]

Chiang Kai-shek, the leader of Nationalist China, would retain control over the funds and supplies appropriated by Congress for the war effort in his country. While he had almost unlimited manpower in China, he desperately needed help in training them. He would also need arms, planes and supplies. Having been involved with a civil unrest, his ability to defend China was questionable. He planned (unknowingly to the

---

1   About.com Military History

United States) on stockpiling these supplies to help him later on to keep the communists at bay.

American men lined up to enlist because they wanted to defend and protect their country and families - they were not thinking of what might await them. Many would die, be wounded, or become prisoners of war. This story is about the men who fought and became prisoners of war in Burma. It was referred to as the China-Burma-India (CBI) Theater. It has also been called, many times, the "Forgotten Theater." These men and boys (yes, boys) bravely flew supplies and men from India to China over the Himalayas, after Burma was lost. This mountain range was the highest and most deadly known to fliers. Pressurized planes were still in the future; therefore, these planes had to carry oxygen tanks which made it more perilous.

They would also bomb Japanese strongholds in Burma to try to free Burma of Japanese control and to regain the very important seaport of Rangoon.

Many factors were involved, creating even more difficulties for these fliers. And China's political problems would play a big part in their mission.

In March of 1925, Sun Yat-sen, the leader of the Kuomintang (Nationalist Party), died. He was a well-liked leader and respected by the Communists as well as the Nationalists. Sun Yat-sen was followed by Chiang Kai-shek, who eventually emerged as the leader after a struggle with Wang Ching-wei. Chiang Kai-shek tried to purge the Communists from China by spearheading the Northern Expedition in an attempt to unify China and force the Communists out. He imposed a blockade and the Communists were forced to evacuate to Northwest China.

Chiang Kai-shek was socially conservative, promoting traditional Chinese culture. He rejected western democracy and democratic socialism and was in favor of an authoritarian, nationalist government.

While he oversaw a modest reform, he was focused on fighting internal opponents and the Communists within China. When Japan invaded Manchuria in 1931, Chiang was still concentrating on his controversial campaign of systematical eradication of political opponents, namely the Communists.

In 1926, he controlled the three biggest cities in China: Canton, Beijing and Nanking. In 1928 under Organic Law, he was given what amounted to dictatorial powers over China. But because of the vastness of the country, he never had complete control.

On December 1, 1927, Chiang married Soong-May ling after divorcing his wife and vowing to be become Christian. Soong May-ling would become known as "Madame Chiang Kai-shek." In 1937, Japan invaded China. His critics complained that Chiang was more concerned about maintaining control of his party than he was of putting together a coordinated campaign against the Japanese aggressors that would become a major problem for the Allies.

In December 1885, Burma was established as a province of the British Empire. The British began to permeate the ancient Burmese culture with foreign elements and customs, often weakened by the imposition of British traditions. In the 1930s anti-British riots led to the Government of India Act, and in 1937, Burma became a British crown colony with a limited amount of self government.

Out of these Burmese protests by the "Intelligentsia" and the monks, a law student at the University in Rangoon, Aung San, emerged. He launched a national movement for Independence for Burma. In 1941, Aung San along with twenty nine others (Thirty Comrades as they were known) left Burma and went to Japan for military training. They were promised that if they helped defeat the British that they would gain Burma's freedom. When Aung San realized that the Japanese would not honor their promises, he negotiated an agreement with the British to help defeat Japan.

On January 15, 1942, Units of the Japanese 55th Division moved into Burma. They also came through 3 Pagoda Pass into Moulmien; this is where they would later retreat to when abandoning Rangoon in 1945.

This conflict goes a long way in understanding the animosity held by some of the Burmese people in regards to the POWs. Not only were they terrified by the cruelty of the Japanese, but also loss of their dream of independence. In 1947, after the war the British did negotiate an agreement that Burma would be granted total independence from Britain. Tragically, Aung San was assassinated in 1947 and Burma has been, to this day under a dictatorship.

A very good depiction of the relationship between Nationalist China and Communist China was made by Louis Jones as he told his story at the 40th Bomb Group Association reunion in 1986. It was printed in their publication of March 1987, Issue #14 called "Memories." (Excerpted below)

THE 'DIXIE' MISSION TO THE COMMUNIST CHINESE

I was an intelligence officer in the 45th. Nothing either interesting or important ever happens in the life of a squadron intelligence officer. However, I was lucky. I got a call one day from Col. Foss at Bomber Command headquarters who informed me that I had been selected to represent the XX Bomber Command on a fact-finding mission to communist Chinese headquarters. My primary assignment was to act as liaison between the communists and the XX Bomber Command. I was to determine to what extent they could be of assistance in recovering B-29 crews that might be down in areas they controlled.

At this period in history, the United States Government recognized Chiang Kai-shek as the political and military leader of all China. His nationalist forces were defeating the communists in the civil war that was underway at the time China was invaded by the Japanese. The communists were driven back into the mountainous and hilly region of North China. Their headquarters was located in Shensi province of Yenan.

Both the nationalists and the communists agreed that the common enemy was Japan and each waged war against the Japanese but in their own way. There was no attempt at coordinating efforts against the common enemy. The big difference was that the nationalists got military aid from the United States but the communists did not.

I joined the other members of the mission in Chungking, China and learned for the first time that our mission was to be known by the code name "Dixie Mission." The mission was composed of approximately 20 people, both officers and enlisted men under Col. Barrett, an old China hand. We had signal corps personnel, infantry officers, Navy officers, medical personnel, weather observers, two O.S.S. officers, two California Nisei who acted as interpreters of the Japanese prisoners, as well as two high ranking State Department men, and of course me.

At Yeana we lived in a walled compound area guarded by the Chinese and buttressed by a hill approximately 1,500 feet high. Our rooms were actually caves in the hillside. We bunked two to a cave. A wooden frame doorway covered the entrance to the cave. The doorway openings were covered with rice paper. There was a four foot overhanging that sheltered the entrance to all caves.

In meeting with the communist leaders, I emphasized that we were going to bomb Japan from bases in nationalist China and there was a probability that American flyers might come down in areas they controlled. They were eager to help.

Col. Barrett ordered eight of us to make field trips to evaluate the communist military forces. Of course, I spread the word that (1) all downed American flyers were to be harbored and kept safely together. (2) That Yenan was to be notified and everyone, crew members and rescuers, were then to wait for instructions. On these evaluation trips, we usually traveled in pairs. My fellow officer was Johnny Colling, a

Captain in the infantry who spoke fluent Chinese. His specialty was demolition. We rode horseback and each of us had a pack animal for belongings. Two Chinese attendants were assigned to each of us. Due to the nature of the countryside and condition of the trails, we did quite a bit of hiking. On those occasions we led the horses. We wore American uniforms unless we were crossing Japanese controlled territory and then we dressed in Chinese communist uniforms. On the flats, we rode. We would be mixed in with approximately 15 other riders. We crossed flat areas at a trot and would have a company of infantry surrounding us moving at double time. In the mountainous regions, we traveled single file and again led our horses. The company of Chinese troops would be spread out about a mile in front and behind us. Immediately in front of me, running ahead on the trail, was a German shepherd dog that hated Japanese. He would never let us out of his sight. When the trail curved, he would sit and wait until we caught up to him before running ahead again. I was impressed by this dog and the Chinese let me keep him when we completed our travels. The dog usually slept at the foot of my bed. We knew that if we got in a "fire fight" with a Japanese unit and the Chinese were unable to protect us, we would be killed as spies since we were out of uniform. Nevertheless, both Colling and I thought we would be killed if captured, whether we were in or out of uniform. So, we had no hesitancy or misgivings about wearing Chinese communist uniforms. We lost one officer to the Japanese, he was captured, his hands were tied behind his back and his legs were tied at the ankles. He was made to kneel and was shot in the back of the head. A sword was also used. We later recovered his body.

Rescue materials other than medicines in survival kits were of little use if you were downed. Once in communist hands, you would be fed, clothed and you followed their instructions. Usually it wouldn't be too many days before word got to Yenan and we would begin arranging a pick up. The method of rescuing downed B-29 crews was to move them to an area where there was an airstrip. They were to stay concealed near the strip and wait. We came as soon as we thought the conditions were right. Many things were considered besides weather: Japanese troop movements, Japanese fighters, etc. We used a stripped down B-25, which was actually General LeMay's personal plane, to attempt pickups.

The rescue of George Varoff's crew was an example of how painfully boring it was to remain concealed near an airstrip sometimes from 10 days to 2 weeks. When the first attempt was made Varoff's crew was not there. They had gone to a neighboring village to be wined and dined as guests of the communists. Once it was determined the crew was not at the strip, the rescue plane took off immediately. They could not afford to stay on the ground any length of time because Japanese fighter bases were too close. There was nothing but pleas over the communist network to come again. The second attempt went smoothly. The entire crew of 11 got out safely.

General LeMay authorized a delivery of a plane load of medical supplies to the communists to show our appreciation for the rescue help they had given the XXBomber Command. (End of excerpt)

On December 11, 1941 when the Japanese invaded Burma, there were only a few units of the British Army and a locally recruited 1st Burma Division to defend Burma against 35,000 Japanese soldiers. So the Japanese had little difficulty in making early gains.[2] The Burmese people were not happy being under British rule and were hoping that possibly the Japanese would allow them self rule. They found out that not only would this not happen, but that they were in for some very cruel treatment and unfortunate times. In their invasion of Burma, the Japanese closed the Burma Road which was the only overland supply route stretching from Northern India through Burma and into China.

General Harold Alexander was sent to Burma in January 1942 to command British and Burma forces. He related that "It was clear that the retention of Rangoon was impossible with the forces at my disposal, dispersed as they were with half of them already encircled. The day after my arrival I therefore ordered the evacuation to begin at daylight the following morning and the demolition of the port and its installations to be carried out thereafter as quickly as possible. I could not save Rangoon but I could save the Army, with luck. The loss of our base would be a most serious matter, as we had to depend on the scattered stores and dumps spread

---

2   www.spartucus.schoolnet.co.uk/22WWburma.htm

about in central and northern Burma. When these were used up, the Army would be crippled unless supplies could be sent over the mountains from India, but apart from a few mules' tracks, communications with India was non-existent. It seemed that we must do the best with what we had. With Chinese assistance, however doubtful, we should be able to at least make the Japanese advance into Burma slow and costly. Such were the thoughts in my mind when I ordered the destruction and evacuation of Rangoon."

There were virtually no roads in Burma; that was because it served the purpose of the Burma-India Steam Navigation Company which wanted to preserve a monopoly of carrying trade between Calcutta and Rangoon. The British believed the disease-ridden jungle that covered the mountains formed a natural barrier that made an offensive military campaign impossible. Unfortunately, for them, the Japanese had been trained to fight through the jungle and did not require long supply lines, as they carried with them their own food and ammunition.

As Rangoon was evacuated, the Lend-Lease stores were destroyed. Destroyed were 972 unassembled trucks, 5000 tires, 900 assembled trucks and Jeeps and 1000 machine guns with ammunition. However, the British and Americans were able to save some of the guns and ammunition that were transferred to them just before the fall of Rangoon.

On March 8, 1942, as the last British train left Rangoon, the Japanese marched into the undefended city from the west.

In March1942, General Joseph Stilwell was sent to Burma by President Roosevelt to take charge of the Allied Command. He had asked for a command in Europe, but was sent out to the Asian theater.

He not only had an Engineering Degree, but he spoke Chinese. What General Marshall and the President had conveyed to General Stilwell regarding his command was not exactly what he found. General Chiang Kai-shek said that General Stilwell might have "Executive Control" but that he, Chiang Kai-shek, would retain control over the Chinese

Armies as well as Lend-Lease supplies. This was to greatly restrict General Stilwell's ability to fight the Japanese. His first visit to Chiang Kai-shek was on March 7 1942.[3] He began to see what an uphill battle he was in for. Chiang Kai-shek had complete control of supplies that were part of the Lend-Lease program. General Stillwell had little left to command. He was faced with the invasion of China and Burma with India in direct line to be next. He met with Chiang Kai-shek and Madame (as she insisted to be referred to). Time and time again when Chiang agreed to plans placed before him by General Stilwell, he would then reverse himself the next day or week. General Stilwell became so frustrated dealing with him that at one point he asked to be relieved, but was refused. He was asking that the Chinese divisions be released to him for combat which Chiang Kai-shek refused to do -and the Allies were unable to move him.

By the beginning of March the Japanese had four divisions in Burma, and General Stilwell was unable to get any real cooperation from Chiang Kai-shek. On May 6, 1942, General Stilwell sent his last message from his position in Burma, ordering his radios and vehicles destroyed and he and his group headed west on foot into the jungle toward India while the Chinese forces headed East toward China. With him were 114 people, including what was left of his own staff, a group of nurses, a Chinese General with his personal body guards and a number of British commandos, a collection of mechanics, a few civilians and a newspaperman. Leading by example, Stilwell guided the mixed group into India, arriving there on May 15, 1942 without losing a single member of the party.

The Japanese knew that rubber was one of the few militarily vital resources that the United States was not self-sufficient in producing. The Japanese thought it critical that the Allies be denied access to Southeast Asia rubber supplies they believed the Allies would not accept peace terms favorable to Japan.

The United States was concerned that if Nationalist China was not supported by the Allies that Chiang Kai-shek might make a separate

---

3   Stillwell Diaries

peace with Japan. This would enable Japan to use the armies that were under the control of Chiang Kai-shek to expand their army.

This was probably not going to happen, since Chiang Kai-shek realized that Japan would strip him of his power in China. He was using the Americans to further his control and was actually more concerned with the Communist threat.

Washington was still trying to decide how to best supply China from India. As the Burma Road had been closed by the Japanese, other means had to be developed to insure that supplies would reach China.

One plan was that a new road be developed. A new road was going to be built and it would be called the Ledo Road. Winston Churchill called the project "an immense laborious task unlikely to be finished until the need for it had passed." The proposed route went through some of the toughest terrain in the world. Northern Burma included jungle covered mountains and swampy valleys. The mountains were formidable land barriers reaching heights of eight to ten thousand feet. The valleys were tropical rain forests where clearings were really swamps covered with elephant grass eight to ten feet tall. Add to that leeches, malaria-bearing mosquitoes, typhus-carrying mites and a six month monsoon season averaging 140 inches of rain; all complicated by the presence of a veteran Japanese force.

Another method had to be found. A.V. Soong, Chiang Kai-shek's brother-in-law (and Madame's brother) was the Chinese representative to Washington. A map was sent to Washington showing a route marked in red that extended from India, thru Burma and ending in China. It started from the Persian Gulf by rail to the Caspian Sea and then by boat to a railroad that would cross Russian Turkestan to the China border and then travel 2000 miles by road to Chunking. This course was a total distance of 5000 miles and would be very expensive as well as time consuming to build.

A.V. Soong suggested that an airline was the answer, as it would be more effective and only 700 miles flying over comparatively level stretches. The area that he alluded to of Saduja was at the top of Assam in N.E. China stretching to Kumming in China. He conveniently forgot to mention that between those two points rose the Himalayan Mountains considered to be the most treacherous flying environment in the world. He estimated that 100 DC3 Transports could fly 12,000 tons a month into China. The plan was to use Calcutta as the entry point, then forward supplies and troops by rail to Assam where DC3s would await them. As soon as the Airline was functioning they could begin to build the Ledo Road. Thus Stilwell's engineering background would come in handy for that project.

S.I Hsuing, biographer for Chiang Kai-shek noted:

"Many great men would have been considered greater if they had had the sense to die earlier for Example:

Napoleon before Waterloo, Wilson before Versailles, Chiang Kai-shek before the recall of General Stilwell.

Burma Road – Courtesy of US Archives

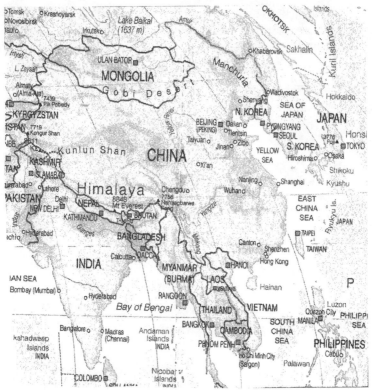

China, Burma, India Himalaya Mountains

Japanese Empire – Courtney of US Archives

PART 2

Becoming Airmen

In August 1943, the 40th Bomb Group became the first bombardment unit of the Air Force to be assigned the B-29 aircraft. It was one of four pioneer bombardment groups of the XX Bomber Command that would be given the task of proving that the B-29 was capable of long-range attacks that would carry the war to the Japanese homeland.

The need for Long Range and Heavy Duty Bombers to be developed and built was essential. This was to be a crucial element in the fight for the Pacific as they were needed to fly long distances over vast areas of water and land.

In June 1944, a total of 97 B-29s were built in Witichata, Kansas, but only 16 were airworthy. There were numerous problems. The engines were overheating, window seals didn't seal properly and there were sighting problems. These were just some of the problems that Boeing was facing. Even as planes were finally coming off the factory lines, they were still making modifications and were being re-designed.

The 40th Bomber Group was under the command of the 58th Bomb Wing; they would be assigned to fly the new B-29s. Airmen could not believe their eyes at the first glimpse of the B-29. It was the largest and heaviest mass-produced airplane in the world up to that time. Its wing span seemed endless at 141 feet. It had pressurized compartments for the 11 man crew and remotely controlled gun turrets, four 18-cylinder engines, the most powerful engines in aviation history, and it carried the largest propellers of any aircraft at more than 16½ feet in diameter. The B-29 could carry up to 20,000 pounds of bombs and supposedly could hit targets from an altitude of 31,000 feet.

The crew compliment of the B-29 was standardized. It consisted of 11 men: aircraft commander, pilot, bombardier, navigator, flight engineer, radio operator, radar specialist, central fire control gunner, left and right gunners and a tail gunner. They would train as a team and training was centered on crew concept. They were to remain together as a team, to be changed only in the event of wounding or death.

Because of the many problems of the B-29, crews were forced to take their training on B-17s and Martin B-26 Marauders. Most aircrews were lucky to get one B-29 flight a month.[4] This was to be the beginning of a love-hate relationship between crew and airplane.

However, the relationship between the pilots, their crews, and ground crew grew to be very close. In the months of training that were to follow, working under extreme cold temperatures in Pratt, Kansas and then in the extreme heat of India, created unusual relationships between ground crews and the flight crews. These men had been trained to fill multiple roles and often worked side by side. This made it easier to understand the emotional impact of the Group's first combat loss had on these men. The group paid a heavy price for its first mission.[5] A Catholic Priest, Father Bartholomew Adler, wrote for the 40th Bombardment Group (very heavy [VH]) Father Adler's history published by the Turner Publishing Company tells the following story:

FATHER ADLER'S STORY

The night before the mission, he took note of a subtle, yet noticeable change in the way the men played cards. The boys were not thinking much about the cards. He observed there was not much joking and at the end of the game one of the men came to him, handed him his wallet and said "keep this for me Padre." He had never done that before.

The next morning, Father Adler joined the ground crews to watch the huge planes wait their turn to thunder down the dusty runway and disappear in the distance. You could tell what the men flying the planes were thinking as one after another raises the thumb on his right hand into the air. That signal means "This is it." It is hard to control your emotions. Now the planes are lined up one behind the other, their huge propellers turning. There is going to be a minute interval, two minutes at most, between takeoffs. You drive over to the side of the east-west runway, and you wait and sweat. Your mouth feels dry when you try to speak and you can feel your heart beating faster. Here comes the first

---

4   www.historynrt.com/world-war-ii-40th-bomb-group.htm
5   40th Bombardment Group (VH) History, Turner Publishing

plane; it is taking its position. Slowly, majestically, it wheels into place. A few seconds are spent in the final warming up and then the plane begins to move. You are thinking of the short runway with the ditch at its end. You yell, "Give her the gun." Faster and faster she moves. By the time she passes you she is going 90 carrying tons of metal, bombs, traveling on six wheels with 11 human beings aboard.

The mechanics who have labored long hours to get their planes ready; long hard hours with the sun blistering their backs. Some of them have worked 36 straight hours preparing their planes for this morning. Now they stand on the sidelines, tired, dirty and hungry but happy. Not only the mechanics are there but the weather men, the medics, the bomb handlers, the cooks, the fuelers, the clerks, we all stand watching the last word in heavy bombers take to the air. We are in the nose with the bombardiers, or back with the tail gunners or sitting in the waist watching the engines. And then it happens. Maybe the pilot figures because of the cloud of dust at the end of the runway that the plane ahead of him hasn't cleared the runway so he is trying to lift his plane as early as possible. The plane doesn't respond. Instead, her tail skid drags the concrete causing bluish flames to leap up from it. The pilot puts her nose down again, but by dragging the skid the plane has lost precious speed. The end of the runway is coming up fast; he will have to raise her now. Again, Johnny (Father Adler uses fictitious names to keep the enemy from identifying these men in war time) tries to lift her off the concrete; she rises slowly and is airborne. He is now away and got out of that nicely, but, he isn't out of trouble yet. He rises to about 150 feet and the plane is slipping toward the left. His left wing is down. Bring her up, bring her up, you pray, or you will crash. "Dear Mother of God help him," you murmur. And then as the plane slips down behind the trees that lie west of the runway, you raise your hand in absolution. Ego vos absolve in nomine patris, et filii, er Spiritus Sancti. The words are hardly out of your mouth when a huge column of flames shoots into the sky, and then over the sound of your racing car you hear the dull thud of the explosion as the plane blew up.

Frantically, Father Adler drove down the road toward the wreck. He could hear the popping of ammunition set off by the terrific heat of the fire. Suddenly you are thrown on your face by the impact of a bomb which "cooks off." Bullets whistle overhead. For a minute, you hug the ground. Finally you circle and come to the wreck in another direction. It is a gruesome scene. Sadly, you make out the various forms among the scattered, burning debris. John is there, and Willie. Your scarcely recognize them, so bend down to look at their identification tags. They are Burt and Al, co-pilot and flight engineer. Burt is still strapped in his seat. He was thrown clear by the explosion with his safety belt still fastened. His legs are broken and he has a deep gash over the eyes, but he is still breathing. You look more closely at Al. You can tell he doesn't have much of a chance. But, he is still living. In no time at all the doctor and his assistants are giving both men morphine and injecting plasma. Frantically they work over both of them, even while the stretcher-bearers carry them tenderly to the ambulance, a slim chance. Having paid the price of freedom, they have gone to the reward promised to men who lay down their lives for their friends.

The final planes to takeoff on the mission pass directly over the wrecked plane, ... a once majestic bird with glistening silver wings, now broken and shattered in a smoldering heap. Back at the field you run into Johnny's crew chief. He is the man who was in charge of maintaining Johnny's airplane. He has a dazed, hurt look in his eyes. It is the first plane he ever had charge of that crashed. You can't think of anything to say to him, so you just pat him on the shoulder. The ground personnel then waited nervously for the return of the planes. (End of Excerpt).

A base was established in Chakulia India and its code name was B-4. A forward base was established in Hsinching China named A-l. These bases were to be used not only for bringing supplies to China but to facilitate the bombing of the Japanese homeland. This was accomplished in May 1944. The runways had to be built and extended to accommodate the Super fortresses. This work could not have been accomplished without the help of the Chinese population. Parts of China were already under Japanese occupation. The Chinese having witnessed the brutality already perpetrated upon them in places like Nanking, had no illusions as to what was in store for them.

The Chinese civilian population was very different from the Burmese civilian population. The Burmese wanted independence from the British; they considered American intervention as just an extension of British rule. Therefore, men captured in Burma were treated as enemies. The Chinese civilian population perceived Americans as saving them from the cruel domination of the invading Japanese.

As landing fields were being built in China and runways extended, men, women and children of the villages would help by carrying such basic materials as rock and sand in woven baskets. They used their livestock to pull equipment. Sometimes with little more than picks and shovels they worked alongside of the American Army engineers. The western road engineers estimated that it would take many years to build the Ledo Road which was going to be used to send supplies overland from India to China. With the help of 90,000 Chinese civilians, it was completed in two years. Not only were these astonishing feats completed in record time, but under unimaginable circumstances. They would come not only under Japanese attack but suffer in a jungle plagued by disease and monsoon seasons.

The Chinese early warning network consisted of Chinese guerillas and civilians in the field, who at great risk of capture or death, called in information on Japanese aircraft movement. The greatest comfort of all, was the knowledge by the American pilots that if they were shot down and crashed and were later picked up by the Chinese, they would have a good chance of escaping the Japanese and returned to their base alive. Unfortunately, this was not the case of those airmen that were captured over Burma.

In the beginning, the B-29 crews were required to fly 25 combat missions to qualify for going home or to go on leave; this would soon be escalated to 30 and finally 35. A B-29 combat mission could be extremely long in duration, anywhere from 13 to 16 hours, and that was not taking into account pre- and post-flight times for the pilots and crew members. They usually spent 2 hours pre-flight and 2 hours post-flight. Some combat missions could be 17 to 20 hours. The crews considered these flights to be a series of long boring periods, punctuated by short bursts of adrenaline and fear.

The Japanese were desperate to take down the B-29s. They decided, like their Kamikaze brothers, they would give their own lives by ramming into the B-29s. They were to call it "Taiatari" (body crashing). They put attack groups together and stripped the planes of all armor and armament. This would lighten the plane and allow it to get up to the altitude of the B-29. Even when those planes made it to the required height and position, it still required a great deal of skill. At this point in the war they were lacking this expertise due to the heavy losses of pilots they were experiencing, but they still managed to sometimes accomplish their missions.

The ramming tactics were terrifying. They B-29 crews could not understand any pilot who would deliberately crash their plane into another one. The B-29 crews that witnessed these atrocities never quite recovered from the shock of that for the balance of their missions.

In 2005, the air crews and pilots that flew the Hump during WWII (the Himalaya Mountain range between India and China) where invited to be the guest of the Chinese Government back in China. They and their families were given a hero's welcome. The Chinese Government wanted to thank these men for what they had done for the Chinese people. It was a very emotional time for both the fliers and their Chinese hosts. At the banquet held in their honor, Larry Jobe, President of the Flying Tiger Historical Organization, spoke of the bond between these Airmen and the Chinese people. He related the following stories:

"We all know the story of Jimmy Doolittle's raid on Tokyo and what a devastating blow it was to Japanese moral and what a huge boost to Americans. But did you know that after bombing Tokyo, all the planes were slated to land in China? When they arrived over China they could not find their intended landing strips and all the crews crash landed or bailed out. Eight pilots were captured by the Japanese and the rest were rescued by the Chinese and returned to American bases. The Japanese, in retaliation, killed every man, women and child in any area that those bombers could have landed, in all 250,000 Chinese civilians were murdered, many in barbaric methods.

"The Chinese soldier depended on this airlift for all his arms and supplies. Always short of what he needed to fight a well-armed and equipped Japanese army, he none the less performed heroically in the defense of his country. A story told to me by one of the Hump pilots demonstrates just how much the Chinese Soldier was willing to sacrifice for his country. General Chaing-Kai-shek had finally released some of his army to be under the command of General Stillwell. This Hump pilot was flying a C-47 full of Chinese soldiers from India, where they had trained, back to China over the Hump. They hit bad weather and the plane iced up making it impossible for the pilot to maintain altitude. On board was an English-speaking Chinese officer whom the pilot told to have his troops prepare for a crash because they were too heavy and could not maintain altitude. Not long thereafter, the plane began to climb. The Chinese officer came forward and when the pilot looked back, the cabin was empty. All the troops had jumped out to lighten the load and when questioned by this pilot, the officer's simple reply was that the plane and the material that it could supply to the Chinese army was more important to China's survival than the troops. With that he went back and also exited the plane.

"These rescues often put the Chinese at great risk. I met a man in Shedadawang who helped rescue ten airmen from a bomber crew that was forced down over enemy territory. He had a picture of himself and the ten airmen. He wanted to know if I could tell what had become of these men. Of course I could not. He then told me the story of their rescue. They were picked up and dispersed in the countryside near the Chinese village where the bomber crashed. The Japanese came into the village and attempted to discover the bombers crew's whereabouts by torturing the villagers. First the Japanese took the old women of the village and cut their fingers off one by one. They did not talk. Then the Japanese took babies from Mother's arms and threw them down wells. Still they did not talk. Then the Japanese began bayoneting the men of the village and still no one talked. All ten airmen made it back to their base because of the sacrifice made by those Chinese villagers."

The Chinese population considered all American fliers to be Flying Tigers, whether they were from the Bomber Groups or Transport Hump pilots, they were all to be revered as saving China.

The following speech was given in 2011 in Xian China by Larry Jobe at the dedication of Flying Tiger Heritage Park:

"Ladies and Gentlemen: Never have so few done so much for so many with so little. I speak of course of the Flying Tigers as defined by the Chinese. Many books have been written about the Flying Tigers and the pilots who flew the Hump, but for the most part the story and record set by these combatants has been passed over when reporting on and recording the larger history of the Pacific War in WWII. The Chinese contribution has all but been ignored and yet these unsung heroes sacrifices are what allowed our American flying forces to achieve the success they did. So I would like to tell you some of the Chinese side of the story. During the ten years that I have been visiting the great city of Xian, I have witnessed its phenomenal growth. Seemingly to have sprung up overnight, it is an example of just how much the Chinese can accomplish in a short period of time. In WWII the Chinese also accomplished the seemingly impossible. Western road engineers had estimated it would take many years to build the Ledo road. The Chinese working alongside American army engineers, built it in less than two years using nothing more than picks and shovels.

"In just three months, with up to 90,000 Chinese working on a single airfield, the Chinese built all the airfields General Chennault needed for the 14th Army Air Force. This allowed General Chennault to take the war to the Japanese very early on in the conflict.

"The early warning network consisted of Chinese guerillas and civilians in the field who, at great risk of capture and death, called in information on Japanese aircraft movements. Most of these calls came into the command cave you visited in Guilin.

"But the greatest comfort and aide of all was the knowledge by our pilots that if they were shot down and picked up by the Chinese, they had a good chance of escaping the Japanese and returning to their base alive. I had two Flying Tigers who accompanied us to China in 2005 who were shot down and they related the story of their escape to me. I want you to hear them now.

"The first pilot was picked up by the villagers near where he crashed. They took him to their village and took his boots away. He spoke no Chinese and they no English. His thought was 'Oh great, they are going to strip me of anything of value and turn me over to the Japanese.' Two of the villagers took him to their home and when the Japanese came, they hid him in a chamber below their bed. It is a chamber used for hot coals in the winter to keep warm. Two Japanese soldiers entered the home and began to beat the two Chinese unmercifully in an attempt to discover his whereabouts. At one point, he could have reached out and touched the boot of the Japanese soldier. Then another Japanese soldier came and all three soldiers left the home and the Japanese left the village. Only then did the pilot discover that the villagers had given his boots to a young man who had left a trail out of the village which the Japanese fell for. Later a missionary came to guide the pilot back to his base and he asked him to ask the two villagers why they risked their life to save his? They said 'when the Japanese come we see fear n the eyes of the Chinese, when the Flying Tigers come we see fear in the eyes of the Japanese.'

"The second pilot was also picked up by villagers and hidden underground with a young mother and her baby. As the Japanese snooped around the village, the baby began to fuss so the mother put the baby to her breast and held it there until the Japanese left. When she removed the baby from her breast it was dead. Because of the young mother's sacrifice that pilot was alive today to tell me the story.

So I think we can say of the Chinese 'never have so many done so much for so few and paid such a dear price.'

"When I hear stories like this, I often wonder how many American children were conceived after the war and are alive today because of the help and care given by the Chinese villagers, often at great risk to their own life? Could any of the sons and daughters with us today at this dedication of this Memorial owe their existence to the cooperation and friendship between the Chinese and Americans in WWII?"

Larry Jobe ended his talk on that day with "As we progress into the 21st century, I hope that our two countries continue to build on the friendship and harmony left by our finest generation, to make a better and safer world for all people."

There was no such thing as a "typical" Hump trip even as routes changed. The monsoon season from late June to mid-September made most of the flights very unlike those before and after that time. Monsoon storms claimed many lives, presenting a greater psychological hazard than either earlier or later flights.

A young pilot, George Lowry of the 395th Squadron relates that he made 34 Hump flights with his crew carrying supplies from India to a very grateful China. In 1986 when the 40th Bomb Group asked him to relate his experiences, he related one that he remembered well. As he explains, there were no typical flights.

"The scenery was most spectacular along the northern route, if it could be seen. A Wonder of the World, not known to western civilization, was a hazard on the northern route near Likiang, a turning point. Still not identified on maps sixty-five years later, the hazard is a spectacular shard of rock split down its length in nearly equal proportions. It seemed to be anchored near a distinctive turn in the Yangtze River. It overlooked a large valley and extended a couple of miles above the level; it seemed to be anchored. It reached an elevation estimated to at 18,000 to 20,000 feet. It was not a cliff, since it did not seem to be supported by anything except the mountain ridge to which it was anchored." Lowry, referred to it as "The Rock" because its extreme height caused severe turbulence for a long distance. Lowry continued, "I, for one did not venture close to it. Those who flew only the more southerly route over the Hump (Himalayas) did not see it. These flights were regarded as 'operational hours' and no combat hours were accredited." Later combat hours were accredited and George Lowery's crew were given 9 combat mission hours for their 34 Hump flights.

Lowry continues: "The monsoon season was in full swing. The average rainfall from June through August was 300 inches. My most memorable flight over the Hump was about to begin. It was my fifth flight and it was July 2, 1944. To beat the heat in Chakulia, we got an early start. Everything worked well, so we were off with a roar and a full load of gas, curving around to the north while climbing out over the jungle. At only several hundred feet, we leveled off to delay climbing until part of the load had been burned. Mostly, there was a dark grayish green jungle for mile and miles, but now and then a small village flashed by with no apparent road in or out. After about 45 minutes of jungle, we crossed the Ganges River at flood stage, a broad torrent of dark brown foaming water. By the end of the first hour, we were confronted by a long mountain across our path, and soon afterward we made the first change in our course near Cooch Behar. We were headed up a wide canyon with the Brahmaputra River on our right, snaking down through its own flood plain and bringing a lot of mud with it. The mountains were closing in on both sides. The light green color along their base became bluish and then dark, indistinct blue, ending abruptly at the overhanging cloud bank above. Suddenly, the bank had become solid, no longer white, just marbled with ominous gray.

"It was time to start our climb. The air transport base near the river at Tezpur was the first friendly thing I could see. There was a large storm. We were flying into a trap! Suddenly we were on instruments; there was no choice. And we saw no more checkpoints. Jorhat and Chabua disappeared from the world.

"During the next half hour, our navigator, Tony Lacko, gave me a couple of changes of course to follow, but they had no more meaning than just numbers on a compass. We had reached 16,000 feet and leveled off, but the storm was getting worse. We had heard about "The Rock" up ahead (not on the map, but rumored to be 20,000 feet), so we agreed that the smart thing to do was to climb above all we could see. We didn't even know exactly where that rock was!

"Up we went. Headed for 21,000 and some sunlight. Minutes went by. Then our rate of climb and altimeter ceased to respond. We weren't getting anywhere! We stayed at a little less than 18,000. Then came the worst news. We were iced up on as much of the wings as could be seen, and we had to face it: This was going to be a low-level, high-sweat mission.

"Tony re-figured our position and gave us a change of course to go further south than he thought the Rock might be. We settled into our second hour on instruments and waited. And waited. Then the air got rough and rougher, and I was sure I could hear some rivets popping. I must admit that I felt clammy cold. Could we be just downwind from the Rock? (I felt my toenails digging into the soles my shoes!) Nobody on the crew said a word, so I can only guess what all of them were thinking. **Was this to be the day?**But then the rough air began to smooth out.

"Tony clawed his way up out of his navigator's hole, like a groundhog in February, and came out to blink at the world. There it was – nearby, all around, and white. While he crouched there and just blinked, I noticed that numerous little streams of sweat kept rolling down his face and dropping off his chin. That seemed unusual because I was <u>cold</u>! In a couple of minutes, though, he turned to me and said, 'I think we must be past it by now, so probably we can turn north and start letting down a little. If we break out pretty soon there ought to be a little lake up there ahead a few miles and a little to the right.'

"Even without knowing what would be coming next, I was glad to get down out of there. We started our descent on the new northerly heading and in a few minutes and a couple of thousand feet we began to break out. Sure enough, there was the lake, almost exactly where it was supposed to be; not on the prescribed course, but on the course that got us around The Rock! We were southeast of Likiang, but from there on to Ipin, 16,000 feet would get us through.

"By the time we reached Ipin, it could not be seen. Clouds hovered in the Chengtu valley to infinity, so I thought 'Here we go again,' and we did. Luckily the radio operator got prompt approval for us to descend to A-1 (our landing field), so we started the dogleg to Loshan and plunged into it on instruments. It seemed no time at all to Loshan and the next leg to our base, but I was increasingly concerned about how high the overcast was down there. I just did not like at all that hill sticking up right off the end of the runway, and I kept wondering who was the dumb one who put the runway there in the first place. Finally, we were down to less than a thousand feet above field elevation, but still nothing in sight. Then our luck improved. I caught a glimpse through a small hole which showed a piece of river bed and the tip of a runway. Now I knew where we were, so I quickly corkscrewed down so as not to lose it. We broke though at possibly less than 500 feet, but were headed the wrong way, so we had to circle back, back around, past that damnable hill and come in over the river bar.

"Getting past the hill was a short approach, but clear enough to be safe. On the final turn, though, something unexpected! The first half of the runway was covered by thousands and thousands of people, but the tower never mentioned them. What to do? Back around the pattern and maybe the soup, or ahead into those people. We kept coming in and at the end of the runway the crowd miraculously parted and ran to each side, barely beyond the wing tips. Then they closed right back in behind us. Certainly they had more faith in my ability to stay in the middle of the runway than I had. These were the Chinese who had worked so hard to make these runways and airfields so that they could also accommodate the big B-29s.

"We talked and listened to those air transport crews in and out of the patter, hauling gasoline in drums. What a tough time they must have. No heat, no oxygen. Can't even climb up safely above the mountains. And those fellows have to come down in here on instruments all the time. I wonder how many trips they have to make before they can go home?

"The next morning we were taken by truck to our plane for our return trip. After we climbed off the truck, there to meet us was one of those five feet four inch Chinese GIs with his six-foot Czechoslovakian WWI rifle with bayonet, stamping his bare feet on the ground to keep warm, yet grinning from ear to ear and not understanding a word we said. How was it that, even when they were blue in the feet and in the face too, they could still smile, stick up their thumb, radiate enthusiasm, and say 'Ding Hao!' in a exuberant voice? They were rugged little men with far more capability than their appearance suggested.

"On to the business of flying home! Our gasoline cargo had been unloaded during the night so, with the usual pre-flight preparation of inspection, starting, run up, and closing of doors, we were ready to go. There was heavy overcast, thin patches of mud and water were on the taxi strip, and at the end of the runway, that blue denim crowd of thousands of laborers carrying gravel from the river bed, placing it just so in the muddy spots on the runway, and apparently mixing in some tung oil to stick together. Nobody paid attention to us. We ran up the engines and did our final check at the end of the runway, cleared with the tower, and pulled into place for takeoff. Only when we began to roll did anyone seem to acknowledge our presence, and then only slowly. Suddenly, though, a big V right down the middle split open to our wing tips, and we soon left the ground and a wet China behind us. The smooth roar of the engines, the landing gear, the flaps, the instruments, the compass heading and the weather demanded all our attention and immediately we were in the soup again. For close to two hours we flew on instruments interspersed with short broken stretches between the clouds–with no icing up this time. While crossing those short clear areas, we could see just enough of the terrain below to decide that it was not merely awful, it was awful awful. Not even Genghis Khan could have found his way out of there. We finally came to the Irrawaddy, but the terrain began to improve. What we had seen in barely 150 miles, the massive water distribution system for China, Laos, Thailand and Burma. Who but Hump fliers ever could see anything so vast, so great, and so unimaginable; we were in the homestretch to Chakulia. I felt warmth from both sun and the prospect of soon being back to home base. I was tired, but it didn't bother me now. Instrument work was done for the day. Then there it was B-4, the runway. Home!

"Call the tower. Into the pattern. Check list: props, landing gear, flaps. Engineer's check OK. Full flaps. Flare it a bit, and then ease the throttles back. Touchdown! Well-yes, but it was only a little bounce. Roll to the end and taxi back to the hard-stand. Shut'em off. Fill out the logs. Tell the crew chief that all was OK. No problems. Ran great! 6:05 hours. 2:00 hours instruments.

"How was it? 'Oh, great. No trouble at all.' (Now comes the ticklish part and inevitable question) 'How much gas did you drop off over in China?' 'Barely a thousand gallons.' 'Only a thousand gallons? That's all?' 'Yeh-that's all. Quite a headwind going up, I guess. Maybe better next time'."

Captain Sam Burton was also one of those Hump pilots. He flew with the Air Transport Command and was the pilot that would be requested by General Stillwell when he needed a ride. He felt General Stillwell was a dedicated, no nonsense man. He flew the Hump numerous times taking supplies, troops and sometimes ferrying aircraft to China. He related that as part of his preflight plan, he always was very careful to check his cargo and how it was loaded. He also invariably checked the manifest. The loading of these planes was crucial because they flew under the worst of flying and combat conditions. The updrafts and downdrafts over the mountains were sudden, unexpected and unpredictable. Severe weather existed on the Hump almost year around. The monsoon season with heavy cloudiness, fierce rain and embedded severe thunderstorms with turbulence severe enough to damage aircraft. Winter winds aloft were sometimes extreme, often exceeding 100 MPH. Northern Burma was largely uninhabited except for wild native tribes. Uncivilized headhunter tribes existed on the southern rim of the main Himalayas in China. Always in your mind while flying over those areas!

Before one of his flights, Captain Sam approached his plane to begin his pre-flight checks, as he always did, when he noted that the plane was virtually empty except for some boxes. He asked the ground crew when the loading would be completed and he was told that it was complete. He had never had a load like this before so he checked the manifest and found that he was carrying 7,500 pounds of gold. He was flying the gold to China. It had come from the United States Government. The gold was undoubtedly destined to go to General Chaing Kai-shek.[6]

The success of this operation did not come lightly. Their final records showed 509 crashed aircraft records "closed," and 81 lost aircraft still classified as "open." Three hundred and twenty-eight of lost aircraft were ATC (Air Transport Command), 1314 crew members were known dead, 1,171 walked to safety and 345 were declared still missing.

Having two bases to maintain for the B-29s, the B-4 in India and the A-1 in China, there were major concerns for the ground crews. Runways had to be built and extended beyond what had been required to be able to accommodate the Super fortress.

A total of 33 B-29s were lost during the first seven months of operation, four, possibly six, were due to enemy action and the remaining planes were lost due to operational problems.[7] One Flight Engineer recalled having to bail out over the "Hump." The route was littered with downed aircraft and often referred to as "The Aluminum Trail."

In early August 1944, the command of the 40th Bomb Group was given to Col. William H. Blanchard. By the end of 1944, the 40th Bomb Group had participated in over 22 missions covering 12 primary targets. Pilots had formed into teams of fighting units. There were many confrontations with Group Commander Blanchard over his command style.

---

6   Interview with Captain Burton 5/5/11
7   40th Bombardment Group (VH) History Turner Publishing

The most disastrous mission came on December 14, 1944. Over the protests of almost everyone involved, Col. Blanchard insisted on a mixed bomb load. There was an unofficial contest between group commanders to see who could drop the most tonnage; however, this would require a mixed bomb load. His orders from General LeMay were to have a maximum bomb load over the target. Each plane was loaded with twelve 1, 000 pound bombs and six 500 pound demolition bombs. The armament officer, Capt. Frank Reeder of the 44th squadron, informed his commander, Lt. Col. Ira Cornett, that "this is a bad load," and pointed out the dangers of a collision of the bombs of different weights. Lt. Col. Cornett went directly to Col. Blanchard with the facts and strongly advised him to reconsider the orders for a safe and more efficient distribution of the bomb load. Cornett pointed out the unusual characteristics of stacking 500-pound and 1,000-pound bombs one on top of the other to get that "all important" maximum bomb load. He stressed the orders for a safe and more efficient distribution possibility of the bombs hitting each other after release from the racks and detonating just below the formation. But to no avail! The colonel ordered the lead bombardier to carry out the mission or face a court martial. The mission was to proceed as planned. To this day, the men on those planes still hold Col. Blanchard responsible for that December 14th fiasco when so many planes were lost along with their crews.

Their primary target that day was to be the Rama V1 Bridge in Bangkok, but heavy cloud coverage restricted their view. So they proceeded to their secondary target, the Rail Yards in Rangoon, Burma. Seconds after they released their bombs, there was a tremendous explosion just below the formation. Many fliers speculated that the heavy flak hit some of the bombs causing them to detonate prematurely Many pilots blamed the bomb load mixture. More than 50 bursts of flak were observed about the time the bombs were dropped. Rangoon was always considered a dangerous target by the flyers because it was defended by gun installations with both heavy and accurate fire.[8] This is when a B-29 named "Queenie" went down.

---

8   Karnig Thomasian.

One of those men on Queenie was an 20-year-old radio operator from Hartford, Connecticut, named Richard Brooks. When he enlisted in the Army on December 29, 1942, he had no idea what awaited him. He and his siblings were first-generation Americans. His Father, John Brooks, had emigrated from Quebec, Canada and his mother, Catherine Sullivan was a devout Roman Catholic from Kenmare, Ireland; she arrived in the United States as a teenager. Richard had a twin brother, Raymond, who had enlisted in the Navy. His older brother, Roderick, was an Army pilot. On that fateful December 7th, another older brother, Randall, also in the Army, was stationed at Pearl Harbor. When the Japanese attacked, he would always remember being on a hillside with only a rifle, shooting at a grinning Japanese pilot, with a scarf around his neck, screaming out of the plane and laughing at him, as he strafed the air base, killing soldiers and the civilians.

December 7th would also always be remembered by a young Army doctor, Joseph B. Pomerance, who was being discharged that day, his tour of duty completed. He walked down to the docks where his belongings were all neatly deposited to be loaded onto the ship that was to take him home, when he saw the first Japanese planes approaching. As the planes began strafing the piers and docks, he saw the Arizona, Oklahoma and other ships hit, he began a dead run back to the hospital. He knew he would not be going home that day. In fact he did not return home until 1945.

Richard had two sisters. His sister, Phyllis Lee, would be like most women at the time, going into a business that would aid the war effort. She would be providing leather interiors for the submarines being readied at New London, Connecticut. His younger sister was in a cloistered convent at that time. His Irish Catholic childhood would serve him well in what he was about to endure.

Like most of the young men during that time, he had done little traveling outside of his hometown in Connecticut. So when he was sent to Miami Beach, Florida for basic training, he was overwhelmed. There he marched in the sand with a broomstick because there were not enough guns for them. Guns were in short supply and the available ones were being sent to our troops that were already deployed. Soldiers were lodged in hotels or wherever there was space.

In March of 1943, he found himself at Scott Field in Illinois. This was considered to be one of the best Army Air Forces Technical Training Commands. They had an intense and exceptional radio school. After attending several other schools, he was transferred to Salina, Kansas and then on to Pratt Air Force Base where he joined the 25th Bomb Squadron. Pratt was designated to be the exclusive training post for B-29s. At Pratt he received classroom instruction on the B-29, covering maintenance, navigation, bombing and gunnery. After Pratt, he went on to Clovis AFB New Mexico where he completed his training in July.

The assembled group would now become the 45th Squadron attached to the 40th Bomb Group. He and the crew were now ready to be sent to Herrington, Kansas to pick up their new B-29. At that time they were assigned to the crew of 1[st]Lt. Wayne W. Treimer. Richard's story was just beginning.

The crew soon departed to India via Florida, Puerto Rico, Georgetown, Guiana, Belem, Brazil, Natal, Accara, Gold Coast, Khartum, Adne, Misera Island and Karachi. As soon as they landed, their plane was taken from them and they flew a number of missions over the Hump in gas- carrying B-29s. They were assigned to C-109s at Kalikunda from where they made quite a few trips to Hsinching (A-1) in China.

Richard relates "on one of the earlier trips we detected smoke coming from the bomb bays, but couldn't locate the source. The pilot, Wayne Tremier, decided we had to go down or bail out as the smoke was quite heavy. I sent out a message indicating immanent abandonment of aircraft, but we finally made it to Myitkyina, Burma where we landed on a strip which was still under Allied control, but was suited for C-47s and C-46s. We ran out of runway very shortly and slid through a mud field for some distance. No one was injured and we off-loaded the gas cargo we were carrying. With the aid of personnel and trucks they managed to drag the aircraft back to the runway.

"No one in operations took the time to notify Kalikunda that we had landed safely so as far as our OPS were concerned we were missing. While there, we went swimming in the Irrawaddy River. The Japanese were on one side and the British on our side. Snipers were trying to pick us off so our swimming didn't last too long. When we flew back to Kalikunda, OPs wouldn't believe us when I called in with my assigned call sign. They sent up fighter aircraft to intercept us and escorted us to the base. When I returned to my basha (a small hut), all my clothes and personal effects were gone and I had a time of it to recover them.

"As far as combat missions were concerned, I flew on three of them. On November 27, 1944, I went to Bangkok; on December 7, 1944 to Mukden and my final one was December 14, 1944 to Rangoon via Bangkok."

Eleven B-29s took off that day. Four of them would be lost and the remaining seven would be severely damaged. Seventeen men would lose their lives and 29 would become prisoners of war.

Sam Burton waves from his B-17 before heading over the hump
– Courtesy Sam Burton

Queenie's crew – Courtesy of Richard Brooks

Queenie's flight and ground crew – Courtesy Richard Brooks

The B-29 – Courtesy US Air Force Archives

The Chinese with their primitive carts building airfields
– Courtesy Karnig Thomassian

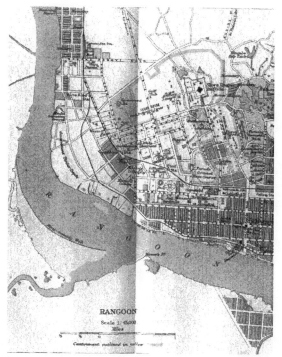

Arial view of Rangoon indicating location of POW prison in the city
– Courtesy Karnig Thomassian

Interior of B-29 showing tunnel escape route from rear of plane
to bail out door. – Courtesy US Archives

HEADQUARTERS, TWENTIETH AIR FORCE
OFFICE OF THE COMMANDING GENERAL
WASHINGTON 25, D. C.

AAF 201 - (G-1258) Brooks, Richard M.
31276601

January 2, 1945

Mr. John B. Brooks,
26 Congress Street,
Hartford, Connecticut.

Dear Mr. Brooks:

The Adjutant General notified you that your son, Sergeant Richard M. Brooks, has been reported missing in action since December 14, 1944.

A communication has just been received indicating that Sergeant Brooks was a crew member of a B-29 (Superfortress) which participated in a bombardment mission to Bangkok, Thailand, on December 14, 1944. The report does not reveal the time and place of the loss of this bomber, although it states that the craft sustained damage and fell out of the formation.

The Missing Air Crew Report concerning the disappearance of your son's Superfortress has not reached this headquarters. However, immediately upon receipt of that report we will furnish you any additional data it may contain.

We know that you may desire to correspond with the families of the other men who were in the plane with your son when he was reported missing. However, because of military security requirements, we are unable at the present time to furnish their names and addresses. As soon as the release of this information is permissible we will communicate with you again.

Please be assured that a continuing search by land, sea, and air is being made to discover the whereabouts of our missing personnel. As our armies advance over enemy occupied territory, special troops are assigned to this task, and agencies of our government and allies frequently send in details which aid us in bringing additional information to you.

Very sincerely,

LAURIS NORSTAD,
Brigadier General, U.S.A.,
Chief of Staff.

Letter #1 Received by Richard's father after plane was lost.

HEADQUARTERS 40TH BOMBARDMENT GROUP
ARMY AIR FIELD
APO 631

8 January 1945

Mr. John R. Brooks,
26 Congress, Street,
Hartford, Connecticut.

Dear Mr Brooks:

I know you are anxiously awaiting news in regard to your
son, Sergeant Richard M. Brooks, 31 276 801, and I want you to
know as much as I have been able to find out.

Richard was reported missing from a mission over Rangoon
on 14 December 1944 and immediately ships from my command in-
stigated a search over the probable areas where his ship was
last seen. We were unable to locate any trace of the plane or
crew members.

Since that time we have renewed our searches and though
we have found no trace of him there is still the thought that
he may have parachuted. This of course has not been definite-
ly determined.

I will keep you informed of any later developments that
may arise.

Sincerely,

William HBlanchard,
WILLIAM H. BLANCHARD,
Colonel, Air Corps,
Commanding.

Letter #2 Sent to Richard's father from Col. Blanchard
who most of the crews considered responsible for the bad bomb loads
that caused the planes to go down.

C. 215

The Capture of the Assam Province is Near

The City of Imphal!

Imphal, the most important advance base of the Anglo-Indian Forces, was completely captured by the Indo-Nippon Units. What the Britishers called, The Impregnable 4th Army Corps was annihilated to the very last soldier. The Indo-Japanese Units without resting are again advancing toward Ledo, Dimapur, Silchar, Dacca from 5 different directions. The Assam railroad line will be intercepted within a few days. Then before the monsoon arrives, the capture of the Assam Province will be completely executed. You are now in the very verge of life or death since your life-line, retreating roads are now in our hands. You are now placed in such a position that you could never acquire nor hope for any help, food, or supply of arms from outside. In concert with the Indian National Army, the Indian Masses at various parts of India are now revolting against the British. Numberless Indian soldiers are running from the British Army and are joining the Indian National Army. With sticks and stones, the Indian Masses without arms are killing the Britishers.

Again we proclaim. DEATH OR SURRENDER?

Nippon Army.

Japanese propaganda leaflets dropped in Burma.

Japanese Propaganda Leaflets Dropped in Burma

The Capture of the Assam Province is Near

The City of Imphal !!

Imphal, the most important base of the Anglo-Indian forces, was completely captured by the Indo-Nippon Units. What the Britishers, called The Impregnable 4th Army Corps was annihilated to the very last soldier. The Indo-Japanese Units without resting are again advancing toward Ledo, Dimapur, Silcher, Dacca from 5 different directions. The Assam railroad line will be intercepted within a few days. Then before the monsoon arrives, the capture of the Assam Province will be completely executed. You are now in the very verge of life or death since your life-line, retreating roads are now in our hands. You are now placed in such a position that you could never acquire nor hope for any help, food or supply of arms from outside. In concert with the Indian National Army, the Indian Masses at various parts of India are now revolting against the British. Numberless Indian soldiers are running from the British Army and are joining the Indian National Army. With sticks and stones, the Indian masses without arms are killing the Britishers.

Again we proclaim. DEATH OR SURRENDER !

NIPPON ARMY

Leaflet Imphal – Translation of above letter.

Japanese leaflet

Japanese Propaganda Leaflets Dropped in Burma

To You The English Soldiers!

You are like fished caught in a net, without an outlet. The only faith left for you is Death alone. When we think and give consideration about your loving wives ,parents and brothers we would never carry on inhuman like actions. Therefore stop your useless resistance. Throw down your arms and surrender. It is then that we will guarantee your lives and will treat you according to the International Law.

How to Surrender to the Japanese Forces

1. The surrenders are required to come hoisting some white cloth, or holding up both hands.
2. Carry the rifle on the shoulderupside down.
3. Show this bill to the Japanese soldier.

Nippon Army

Japanese Translation

Leaflet to English Soldiers – Translation of above.

WHEN MY BROTHERS FELL FROM THE SKY

Christopher W. Morgan, 311th Fighter Group, 529th Squadron

Home City: Yonkers. Home State: New York.

When I was a POW, the only thing of beauty to behold from the Rangoon Central Jail was the sky at night, the Southern Cross constellation, and during the day, the magnificent B-29 formations. You fellows didn't know it, but we were down there rooting for your success and praying for your safety.

The bomb runs always came over the prison, because your targets, either the railroad marshalling yards or waterfront shipping, were on each side of us.

You cannot believe the sound of the bombs as they fell—like the continuous crashing of a not too distant surf. We thoroughly respected your marksmanship; nevertheless we had made zigzag trenches for protection from errant five-hundred pounders.

On December 14, 1944, you had started your bomb run, and I had started mine (for the trenches) when a sudden tremendous cracking explosion from above caused me to dive headlong into the nearest hole. "Oh, my God, look!" One of our invincible B-29 Superforts was in a flat spin; two others were smoking and peeling off in opposite directions; opening parachutes were beginning to appear. What an unexplainable tragedy.

Forty years have passed since that day, and as I recall the many experiences of my 560 days of captivity, none is more vivid or painful than the memory of that day when some of you, our heroes, fell from the sky to join us in our misery.

Jean Newland

(Christopher Morgan details his experiences in the following pages of this book).

This narrative was obtained from the 40th Bomb Group Association, "Memories" Issue #6

PART 3

We Are Prisoners of War

This first narrative is by Sgt. Richard Brooks, a Radio Operator on the B-29 "Queenie." His story in that old trunk along with his fellow prisoners' stories had to be told. To forget the men who fought, died and suffered and became Prisoners of War in the China, Burma and India theater would be unforgivable.

Richard Brooks, Sergeant, 20th Air Force / Radio Operator B-29 (QUEENIE), XX Bomber Command, 40th Bomber Group, 45th (VH) Squadron.

Home City: Hartford. Home State: Connecticut.

Date of Imprisonment: 12-14-44 thru 04-30-45.

It all began on the 13th of December 1944; base somewhere in India. My crew and I along with 13 other crews were being briefed on the mission which was scheduled for the next day. We were told that our target this time was to be the marshalling yards at Bangkok, Thailand. We were given all the latest data pertaining to anti-aircraft defenses and the number and types of fighters the Japanese could throw against us. Our secondary target was Rangoon, Burma. Our tertiary target was to be Bassien, Burma. As we filed out of the briefing room, we shared the feeling that this was to be an easy mission, so without giving much thought to the dangers involved we went to our "bashas" as our native dwellings were called. And to bed very early that evening as we would need all our strength and energy for the coming eleven hour mission early the next morning.

We were awakened about 0300 in the morning, ate a wonderful breakfast of fried fresh eggs and then driven to our ships.

We (our crew) lined up for our pre-flight inspection by the pilot. I will take this opportunity to name the crew. They were as follows: Pilot: 1st Lt. Wayne W. Triemer, Hartley, Iowa; Co-Pilot: 1st Lt. Chester E. Paul, New York, New York; Navigator: 2nd Lt. Norman Larsen, Brooklyn, New York; Bombardier: John B.McGivern, Minnesota; Flight

Engineer: David B. Parmelee, Guilford, Connecticut; Top Gunner: (CFC) Vernon L. Henning, Concordia, Missouri; Left Gunner: Sgt. Karnik A. Thomssian, New York, New York; Right Gunner: Sgt. Leon I.McCutcheon, Groves Texas; Radar Operator: Robert Dalton, Chicago, Illinois; August Harmison, Pittsburgh, and myself, Radio Operator: Sgt. Richard M.Brooks, Hartford, Connecticut. A man could not ask for a better or more pleasant crew. We had eaten, worked, gone on passes with one another for the preceding eight months, and now we were to fly and bomb and harass the enemy together. Yes, we were indeed close to one another, so close we were like brothers.

There was no time to waste, so after pre-flight inspection we climbed into the Superfortress and started our engines and taxied out of our revetment to the end of the runway to await our turn to take to the air. We were airborne about 0445 and climbed on course to our rendezvous point some three and one half hours away. We quickly left India behind and were over the Bay of Bengal and at the prescribed place, time, and altitude we were to meet the other 13 planes. We circled twice and were off as a formation to our target at Bangkok. We found our target readily enough, but we also found that it was obscured by clouds as we were at an altitude of 22,000 feet. We made two bombing runs over the marshalling yards amidst black and white bursts of anti-aircraft shells. The formation leader seeing that we could not fulfill the job adequately ordered us to head for our secondary target: Rangoon. Little did we know what lay ahead for us at the capitol of Burma.

We came over the city of Rangoon at 21,000 feet; the time being approximately 1100 hours. As in the case of Bangkok, here at Rangoon the target was the marshalling yards. We began our bomb run without interference from anti-aircraft fire or interceptors. We had caught the Japs flat-footed this time and we were going to make the best of this opportunity. Our bombs were salvoed upon the target and all was well–so we thought.

"Bombs away," shouted the bombardier, Lt.McGivern, and as I scanned the forward bomb bays for any "hangers," an explosion shook the aircraft and the forward bomb bay bulk head door was torn from its hinges and struck me in the chest at such velocity, it threw me between the upper and lower turret shrouds. My headset cord had been pulled from its receptacle, so I lost communications with the rest of the crew. Within the forward section of the aircraft there was a very bright light and being slightly stunned and disoriented, I didn't know what happened. While lying on my back entangled in my headset cord and oxygen hose, I noticed our navigator, Lt. Norman Larsen, scrambling on all fours toward the front section of the aircraft. Immediately I got to my feet and looked out into the bomb bay and noticed that our auxiliary fuel tanks were on fire and the bomb bay doors had been blown away. There was no doubt in my mind that the plane was doomed. I stripped off my flak jacket and helmet and squeezing through a lattice work within the bay dropped free of the aircraft. Later in prison camp, our left gunner, Karnig Thomasian asked me who had gone through the forward bomb bay? I answered I had, he asked me if I was aware that my chute was open as I left the plane. I had pulled the rip cord before I had cleared the aircraft. I must have passed out for a few minutes after the chute opened as the next thing I saw was several aircraft departing the area, some smoking and others (ours) I believe, crashing below me. I looked down and saw a number of chutes below me and recognized my left gunner, I yelled out to him and he heard me and waved back. When my chute blossomed, it was then and there that I began to realize the gravity of my position. I thought the world had come to an end as I hung my head down and began to say prayers I knew. I was descending right over the City of Rangoon and at approximately 10,000 feet the enemy opened up on me with machine guns. I immediately took evasive action by slipping my chute to the north across Rangoon (Irrawaddy) River. Fortunately there was a brisk wind at that height which carried me to the south of town and over some open rice fields.

At such a height, the objects on the ground appear to be very small and it wasn't until I was 800 feet or so that I noticed just how quickly I was descending. I had never made a parachute jump before and the ground seemed to come right up and hit me. I had forgotten to keep my mouth closed and somehow my tongue had gotten between my teeth, so consequently I came very close to biting it off.

Once on the ground, I quickly took off my chute and hid it in the foot high rice. Instantly, I noticed a Burmese native not more than 50 feet from me. He was on his knees looking at me and somehow from his mumbling in Burmese I gathered that he was begging me to spare him. I turned my pistol on him and asked in English just how I would get out of these open fields and into the jungle. I might as well have saved my breath as he could not understand me and I couldn't make out what he was saying. I imagine I was somewhat fierce-looking to him as my hair was disheveled and the blood from my cut tongue had gone down my neck and onto my flying suit.

I let him go and that was my big mistake. I know now I should have killed him or at least left him unconscious. I let him take off and waited until he was out of sight before I started on my way. I stopped a few minutes later as I remembered I had a few papers on my person which had the names and address of my parents as well as many of my friends back in the states. I dropped down to a kneeling position and buried them and then decided to crawl on my stomach to a shelter not too far from me. After moving along on my knees and my elbows as I wanted to leave my hands free with a trench knife in one hand and a '45 in the other. I stopped for a minute to rest when I looked up from my hiding place in the rice; I saw eleven Jap soldiers approaching me. They all had rifles and were coming my way; not as a small group but in a semi-circle fashion. It didn't take much thought to know that they had me spotted and were coming toward me very slowly so they could observe me and my next move. When they were 50 yards from me they halted and spread out so they could get me in a cross-fire. I knew then that my next course of action would decide whether I was to live, to die or be taken prisoner. I also knew that my pistol was no match for their rifles at long range. Surely if I started firing they would open up, and then if by some miracle I should survive they would have a regiment after me in a short while. I had heard many stories about the Japanese and their treatment of prisoners of war. At this moment I was living and perhaps if I gave myself up I would live a few more days or maybe I could escape and then again, the war was going well in our favor in Burma as well as in the rest of the world and I might be recaptured by Allied forces. I would give a try, so, I got up on my knees and raised my right hand in token of surrender, i.e., if there was to be surrender. I turned the left side of my body to them as I wanted to be as small a target to their guns as possible and all the while I held my small gun in my right hand. Yes, I was afraid; afraid that the next moment would find me riddled with bullets; afraid of what they would do to me when they had their hands on me. It was a strange sensation; one that cannot be described in writing or narrating. It was a feeling that could be made only by experiencing a situation such as I was going through. One of the enemy soldiers motioned for me to get to my feet and raise my arms. I did as I was instructed and then walked up to my capturers, who were only too happy to receive me. I was then informed by a soldier who spoke broken English that I was now a prisoner of the Japanese Imperial Army. I had my choice of actions and I was beginning to wonder whether I had chosen the wisest one. I knew that I wouldn't have to wait too long before I received an answer to that thought.

The Japanese soldiers then took the belt off my flying suit and used that to tie my hands securely behind my back. It was then that I saw the native whom I had let go free. It was very obvious that it was he who had led the Japs to my hiding place. I regretted very much then that I had been so trusting and careless. The next time, if there was to be a next time, I would know better.

The soldier who had spoken to me first asked where my parachute was. I replied by saying that I did not know and perhaps I left it on the plane. Just then a native came running with the parachute dangling from his arms. That didn't go too well with the little man. I could tell he was fairly angry. He noticed my empty soldier holster and asked where my gun was. I told him that I left that in the plane also. Much to my surprise and dismay another native came trotting up to him with my 45. He really got angry then and slapped me twice across the face. This is a new experience for me, to get slapped without being able to fight back, although it was not to be my last.

After that incident, they turned me around and we started to march off. I had no idea where they were taking me or what was in store for me. I could only hope and pray that if they were going to execute me that my death would come quickly and that they would not torture me to make me reveal military secrets. I was expecting to be put to death and never once did I entertain the idea that I would come out of captivity whole both in body and mind unless I could escape. I then began to wonder just what happened to the remaining crew members. Had they been killed or wounded in their chutes; did the Japs kill them when they captured them or had a few of them escaped and were heading north to the jungle? Only five crew members besides myself had been so fortunate or unfortunate, as the case may be, to bail out of the B-29 that had been turned into a burning inferno. I didn't know then or for a long time to come just who the lucky ones were; those who had taken the "silk" or they that rode their plane down to a quick and painless end.

There were times after that surrender that I wished I hadn't. They took me to a village where there were a number of soldiers. I was stripped down to my shorts, tied to a tree and worked over. It was obvious to me many of the soldiers had been drinking as they were trying to use me for bayonet practice. Several times when they came lurching at me on unsteady feet, they came close to pinning me to the tree with their bayonets. I believe that the only thing that saved me was an officer who came along and stopped their fun and games.

I was taken to a small launch and was moved across the river to the city. I was still clad in nothing but my shorts, hands tied behind my back, a rope around my neck and marched down the main thoroughfare with crowds lining the street cheering my captors. I was thrown into a wooden barred cell and left to ponder my fate.

Later that evening, two guards came and dragged me out of the cell and into an interrogation room. Sitting behind a small desk was a Japanese officer who was to question me at great length. He spoke perfect English with no accent. (He had graduated from Columbia University in New York, and knew my home town, Hartford, Connecticut almost as well as I did.) Questions and evasive answers went back and forth with guards taking turns bashing me with the butt of their rifles when the officer was displeased with my answers. I tried the name, rank and serial number routine with them but that was not the answer they wanted. The only way to stop the treatment was to tell them a pack of lies that they would believe. I was thrown back in the wooden barred cell. This went on for several days. I was tired, hungry, sore and, of course, very apprehensive about my future. Near the end of that day, I was then taken back to the Japanese interrogating officer. He said he had made his decision. He said 'in view of the number of civilians we had murdered on this raid, he sentenced me to death.' I told him I accepted that but had only two requests: One that I see a Catholic priest and the other that after the war he would tell my father what had happened to me. He said he would grant both requests. The nights were long and lonely except for the cockroaches. Daylight came and the cockroaches disappeared, but what would this day bring? Near the end of the day, two guards appeared tied my hands behind me and hustled me out of the cell to a courtyard enclosed by a high wall. I was told that I was a war criminal and would be executed. I was forced to kneel in front of a soldier who had an unsheathed sword with the tip of the weapon resting on his boot. There were at least six or seven Japanese officers and men…it looked ominous… in my heart I knew I had not too long to live. I waited for awhile and I heard footsteps of a number of people behind me, but I dared not look up. They were told to kneel and lined up abreast That was when I saw that they were the survivors of our crew… five plus me was six out of a crew of eleven. They were Lt. Chester Paul, co-pilot, Lt. Norman Larson, navigator, Lt. James McGivern, bombardier, Lt. David Parmalee, flight engineer and Sgt. Karnig Thomasian, gunner. The wait was agonizing and I thought that we were all to be beheaded. Finally an English speaking officer stood up in front of us and read from a sheet he was holding. His announcement was that the Japanese Imperial Army would spare our lives; however, we would be sentenced to seven years in prison at the end of the war. Our crime was murdering of defenseless civilians during our bombing raid. This seemed fair to me as I knew we were going to win. They got us up and out of the courtyard to the street and into a waiting open truck. We arrived at the Rangoon Jail in the dark of night. They warned us that of we tried to escape there was only one penalty…death. After outlining the rules and forced us to sign a document that said we would not try to escape. We were then taken to a cell block that turned out to be solitary; I was beaten every day for 30 days, as were a number of B-29 crew members. The enemy just hated anyone who was a B-29 crew member because the raids were hurting Japan. After thirty days, we were put into the general population, but never allowed to forget we were B-niju-ku (B-29) personnel.

While in the cell, I saw their medic cutting off the arm of Richard Montgomery several times. As they had no adequate antibiotics it would re-infect itself. They had no pain killers and I don't know how Richard could stand the pain. If memory serves me right, I can recall them throwing the severed parts from his arm to the Commandants pet cat. Incidentally, we got the cat later and he was delicious.

I am sure you have heard of camp conditions and what went on. Perhaps there is one incident I can relate. About 4 months after capture the Japanese decided to interrogate the B-29 personnel again to see if their stories were the same. I had read an article sometime before back home about the Japanese taking Hong Kong and an item stuck in my mind. It was that the Japanese fear crazy people. I could not remember in detail what I had told the interrogator earlier so I feigned insanity giving him answers to questions that were totally unrelated. After 15 minutes of this they took me back to the yard. Then Lt. Joseph Levine was brought in and he tried the same thing and of course they couldn't believe that both of us were that far gone and really worked him over. When he returned to the yard, he came to see me and asked what I had told the enemy. I told him I acted crazy and he remarked that was his role. I guess we both read the same article.

On April 25th, one day after my 21st birthday, all able bodied prisoners were rounded up (there were 424 of us) and were put on a forced march to Pegu. For four days and nights we marched carrying supplies and dragging ox carts without food or water. The Japanese were trying to evade the advancing British 14th Army. All this time we were strafed by British Typhoon fighter bombers whose pilots thought we were a Japanese column as we were dressed in enemy uniforms. That was all we had as the clothes we were left with after capture were reduced to loin cloths. (They didn't realize they were killing their own people.) Those who fell by the way side were bayoneted.

On the 5th day (April 29th), I escaped during an intensive strafing run. I went into the jungle and hid, and then I met up with some Burmese guerrillas (now they were on our side) and actually went on several ambushes with them. A few times I was almost recaptured; however, I was able to elude the Japanese patrols. A few days later, a native came into the village and reported that the British army was nearby. I waited until dark and was able to infiltrate their lines that evening and finally made contact with a couple of Sihk soldiers who took me to the battalion commander. I identified myself and reported the presence of a number of POWs in the area. He was unaware that a group of prisoners were in his sphere of activity. The British also rescued the remnants of the surviving prisoners on the march.

The next day, wearing a British uniform, I was taken to Akyab and flown to Calcutta and then on to the 142nd General Hospital. When I entered the ward, there was the rest of my crew waiting for me. They didn't know what happened to me nor did I know if they survived the Rangoon Jail after we left on the march.

It was a happy reunion, but also a sad one as we had lost five out of eleven of our crew.

OUR LIVES ARE OURS AGAIN . . . . .

After a visit home to see family and friends, Richard relocated to Honolulu, Hawaii and continued his career as a radio operator. He remained on active duty except for a one-year absence to attend school. In September of 1946, he returned to China with the MAG and was finally routed out of that country in December 1948 by the Communists. He then became a member of SAC (Strategic Air Command), the 576th SAC Missile Squad. He worked on the Atlas "F" ICBM.

He was aboard the Redstone as a radio operator for the recovery of the Apollo Astronauts. This included the first Lunar Landing on July 20, 1969. He ended his military career at Vandenberg Air Force Base.

He joined ITT World Wide and in 1981, was named one of ITT's 13 Employees of the Year. He retired from ITT to California.

He wanted the world to know that he held no hatred for the Japanese people. He thought the average Japanese person was a decent human being. He said "there were good people and bad people in every race." He never had dreams or nightmares of what happened to him. Tears only came with the memories of those who did not come home. His beloved wife Teru, a Japanese woman, died Christmas Eve 1992. He expired 07/14/03. He and his wife are interred together at the

National Memorial Cemetery of the Pacific in Honolulu, Hawaii.

Every year, until he died, he brought her family to Honolulu from Japan on the anniversary of her death for a Memorial Service

Richard Brooks

City Jail – New Laws Court

Rangoon Prison – Courtesy Pegasus Archive

Entrance to Rangoon Prison – Courtesy Karnig Thomassian

RANGOON OCCUPIED. THE WATERFRONT AT RANGOON. PHOTO TAKEN
FROM AN RAF AIRCRAFT FLYING VERY LOW OVER THE CITY SHOWS
WRECKED PIERS AND SUNKEN SHIPS.

AFPPA-12

CASUALTY QUESTIONNAIRE

1. Your name **Brooks, Richard M.**   Rank **S/Sgt.**   Serial No. **31876801**

2. Organization **40th** Gp Commander **Blanchard** Rank **Col.** Sqn CO **Shaef** Rank **Lt.Col.**
   (full name)   (full name)

3. What year **1944** month **December** day **14** did you go down?

4. What was the mission, **Bombing(Hi-Alt.)** target, **Rangoon, Burma** , target
   time, **1030 hrs.** , altitude, **21,500** feet, route scheduled, **Secondary**
   target , route flown **Bankok** **to Rangoon**

5. Where were you when you left formation? **Over target (Rangoon, Burma)**

6. Did you bail out? **Yes**

7. Did other members of crew bail out? **Yes, Nav, Co-Pilot, Bomb, Eng. Left Gnr, and myself (Radio Op.)**

8. Tell all you know about when, where, how each person in your aircraft for whom no individual questionnaire is attached bailed out. A crew list is attached. Please give facts. If you don't know, say: "No Knowledge".

9. Where did your aircraft strike the ground? **In target area**

10. What members of your crew were in the aircraft when it struck the ground? (Should cross check with 8 above and individual questionnaires)
    Four or five men Tail Gnr. Rt. Gnr Top (C.F.C) Gnr. Radar Op. and probably Pilot

11. Where were they in aircraft? **At their Respective crew positions**

12. What was their condition? **No knowledge**

13. When, where, and in what condition did you last see any members not already described above? **I saw only the pilot at the beginning of the mission.**

14. Please give any similar information on personnel of any other crew of which you have knowledge. Indicate source of information. **No knowledge**

(Any additional information may be written on the back)

6-3862, AF

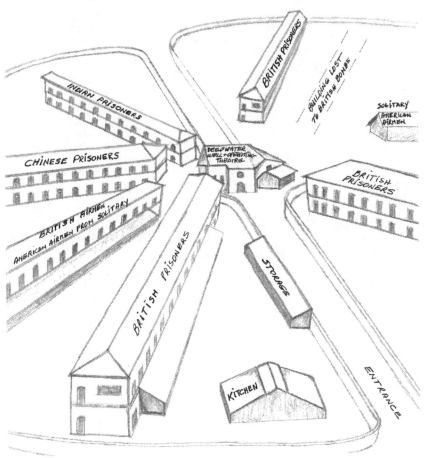

RECREATION BY Bob NEWLAND
VERIFIED BY
KARNIG THOMASIAN

INDIAN PRISONERS

CHINESE PRISONERS

BRITISH AIRMEN
AMERICAN AIRMEN FROM SOLITARY

BRITISH PRISONERS

KITCHEN

STORAGE

BRITISH PRISONERS

DEEPWATER
WELL·OPERATING
THEATRE

BRITISH PRISONERS

BUILDING LOST
TO BRITISH BOMBS

SOLITARY
AMERICAN
AIRMEN

ENTRANCE

Layout of Rangoon Prison – Courtesy Karnig Thomassian & Bob Newland

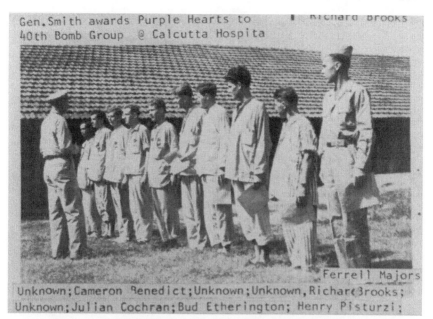

Gen.Smith awards Purple Hearts to ★ Richard Brooks
40th Bomb Group @ Calcutta Hospita

Ferrell Majors

Unknown;Cameron Benedict;Unknown;Unknown,Richard Brooks;
Unknown;Julian Cochran;Bud Etherington; Henry Pisturzi;

Purple Heart awarded to Richard Brooks.

"Our First Pair of Shoes" – Courtesy Richard Brooks

Our crew training at Clovis with B-17 – Courtesy Richard Brooks
Top row left to right: Wayne Treimer, Chet Paul, James McGovern, Norman
Larsen, David Parmalee. Kneeling left to right: Richard Brooks, Vernon
Henning, Leon McCutcheon, Karnig Thomasian, August Harmison (not
pictured Bob Dalton).

Usual arrangement for interrogation with POW sitting on floor to reinforce
lowly rank – Courtesy Karnig Thomassian

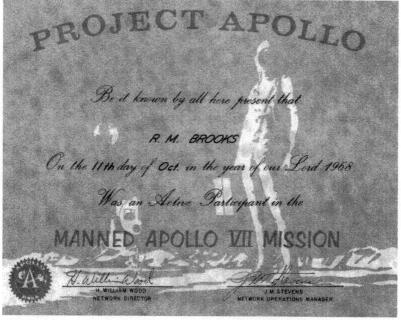

Apollo Project – Courtesy Richard Brooks

USNS Redstone – Apollo 8 recovery – Courtesy Richard Brooks

ITT Worldcom Employee of the Year
(Richard Brooks second from the left).

Chester E. Paul, 1st Lieutenant, 20th Air Force / Pilot (Queenie), XX Bomber Command, 40th Bomber Group, 45th (VH)Squadron.

Home City: North Hills. Home State: New York.

Dates of Imprisonment: 12-14-44 thru 05-03-45.

December 14, 1944- Target- Bangkok Bridge- Bomb load mixed load of 1,000 pounds plus 500 pound bombs with instantaneous fuses. Target cloudy and since this primarily a training mission, photos were required. Went to secondary target- Marshalling yard at Rangoon. Apparently some bombs crossed trajectories and detonated under the Squadron.

Our plane, number 831, was in a flat spin with both inboards on fire. Neither manual efforts by Lt. Treimer and myself, nor automatic pilot could regain control. An alarm was sounded but failed to activate. Bail out was ordered over the intercom and was heard. Nose wheel was lowered (bomb bays were still open) and all bailed out of the cabin except Lt. Treimer whom I last saw at the wheel well ready to jump. He did, however, have blood on the side of his head. I never saw him again.

We were fired upon while descending and Lt. M. Larsen and I compared bullet holes in our chutes days later in POW. camp. He won with many more than I had. I landed in a circle of Burmese natives and Japanese soldiers and was taken at once to the City Lock-up for questioning and several days later transferred to the POW. compound. My best recollection of the City Lock-up was a sign giving rules to be observed and ending with the admonition: "THOSE WILL BE CLEANLINESS EVERYWHERE."

Liberation: We marched (pulling Ox carts) 60 miles north to Pegu. Japanese abandoned us when they ran into the British 14th Army. A Burmese runner made his way through Japanese lines (falling back toward us) to the British who sent a contingent to bring us out. While waiting for them, spent a night in Burmese village which was infiltrated by Japanese- some of whom were asleep right beside us (ask Lt. Larsen.) Flown back to Calcutta and several weeks later- HOME.

OUR LIVES ARE OURS AGAIN . . . . .

Chet Paul returned to New York City to become a jewelry shop owner and designer.

This narrative was obtained through a "Circumstances of Capture and Liberation" report written by 1st Lieutenant Chester E. Paul and given to Harry Changnon the 40th Bomb Group Historian and "RICHARD BROOKS TRUNK."

Norman Larsen, 2ⁿᵈLeutenant, 20ᵗʰ Air Force / Navigator B-29 (QUEENIE), XX Bomber Command, 40ᵗʰ Bomber Group,45ᵗʰ (VH) Squadron.

Home City: Baldwin. Home State: New York.

Dates of Imprisonment: 12-14-44 thru 4/30/45.

Our B-29, No. 831, Queenie, had been very hard hit when some of the bombs we were carrying exploded under the formation. We were flipped over on our back and then right side up again and went directly into a flat spin for which there was no recovery. It took me a little time to crawl to the nose well and when I got there I found that the hatch had slammed shut on somebody's foot. I managed to get the cover opened enough for the foot to disappear but that was as far as I could open it. (I later found out that the foot belonged to our bombardier, Jim McGivern, who spent some rather trying moments hanging upside down, trapped in the nose wheel well.)

Our pilot, Doc Treimer, was still in his seat trying to pull the plane out of the spin when I yelled at him to come back and help me get the hatch open. He did this and between the two of us we got it opened and hooked up. He then told me to jump, which I did, and at this point I glanced at the altimeter and saw that it was zapping past the 4,000 foot mark. I never saw Doc again and assumed that he had returned to his seat in a heroic but vain effort to try to get the plane out of the spin.

I delayed pulling my rip cord as long as I dared in order to try to slow up to no more than the terminal velocity of gravity. I opened my chute when I was about 900 to 1000 feet. A machine gun on the ground immediately opened fire, but I wasn't in the air very long. Shortly, I landed in the middle of the Rangoon River. I could see a bunch of Jap soldiers on shore shooting at me, which continued until I drifted down stream out of range. Finally, a launch came out and fished me out of the water.

It was late in the morning on December 14, 1944 and I found myself in the not so enviable position of having my hands tied securely behind my back and being transported by Japanese soldiers in a truck to the New Laws Court Jail in downtown Rangoon. I was soaking wet after having parachuted into the Rangoon River.

I was questioned briefly, actually no more than name and rank and then brought to a room which had a shower in it. The guard motioned for me to get under the shower. I was glad for the chance to wash off the muck of the river. After a few minutes, the guard had me stripped naked and left with my clothes. I resumed my shower without, of course, soap or towel. But still it felt good. I didn't realize it was to be my only shower, aside from standing out in the rain, during my stay at Rangoon.

After the shower, I was marched, still naked, to a cell on the ground floor of the jail. It was two cells to the left of the doors to the inner courtyard. It was a large cell with a tiny wattage bulb in the ceiling which burned continuously. The only object in the cell was a small, tin-lined British ammunition box which I was told later was called a binjo box and served as a toilet. On the back wall was pasted a piece of paper. It was headed "Rules for Prisoners." I recall last of the eight or nine rules was: "THOSE WILL BE CLEANLINESS EVERYWHERE." Ah so.

There wasn't anything about that cell that I particularly liked, but there was one thing I came to hate. The entrance was only about three feet high so to get in or out, I had to crawl on my hands and knees. I always felt this put me at a disadvantage with the guards even though when I stood up I towered them. The bars were made out of wood about three inches square (teak I think) and were as hard as steel.

I was alone, scared, and down in the dumps. I didn't know who on the crew had made it and who had not. I saw no one except the odd guard going by. The cuts under my chin and on my wrist were minor, but my ribs ached.

That evening I had my first taste of POW cuisine. A tin dish was shoved into my cell. It held a small portion of rice liberally mixed with small pebbles and dead bugs covered with a thin watery liquid which I subsequently found out was called "soup."

I wasn't given a spoon or a fork so I drank the liquid and shoved some of the rice in my mouth. The rest of it went into the binjo. It actually takes a day or so before you get hungry enough to eat swill like this.

That night, when the doors to the courtyard were closed and the jail quieted down, I tried to get some sleep. I lay down on the bare wooden floor, but sleep was out of the question. It was cold and worst of all, I was being eaten alive by a swarm of mosquitoes. I've never been so miserable in all my life. I remember saying what I suppose could not be considered a prayer, but more a petulant complaint to the Man Upstairs: I'll take care of the Japs by myself, but these damn mosquitoes are yours, and they are driving me nuts. Little did I know that in a few days, I would really desperately need help.

The next morning, I had the first of many interrogations during two days and nights of the 15th and 16th of December. I still had no clothes; I found it rather difficult to act like a proper soldier when facing my enemy naked. I refused t go beyond name, rank and serial number and tried to invoke the Geneva Rules of War. I heard for the first of many times that "Here in Rangoon we go by the Japanese Rules of War." These rules were never spelled out for me, but I gathered that one salient feature was that to be granted POW status, you had to "prove" that you were a soldier. The fact that I had bailed out of an American bomber which had just bombed the Rangoon railroad station, that I was wearing a khaki uniform and had dog tags on didn't count. (I even had a 20th Air Force patch on my shoulder. I was not supposed to have it on but after all, the mission was only a milk run.) The proof they demanded was the number of my squadron and group and the name of the airfield I had come from. I refused to give any information and was given quite a hard time during the interrogations.

When I was escorted to my cell, I found some of my clothes on the floor. No flying suit, belt, shoes or socks, but I did get back my underwear and my shirt and pants. It cheered me up immeasurably to get my uniform (such as it was) back on. I ripped off the 20th shoulder patch and used it as a spoon. Also that night, when I tried to sleep, I wrapped my tee shirt around my face and tucked my hands in my pockets. This only exposed my ankles and feet to the mosquitoes. The quality of life was improving.

I remember one interrogation which I enjoyed. The interrogator was a young Jap who had been brought up in the United States. He told me that he had been back in Japan visiting relatives when the war started and had been drafted. I asked for, and he gave me, the first cigarette I had smoked since being captured. We also learned that we had both been students in New York University, he in the daytime and me at night. It was an interesting session. He pleaded with me to give him any kind of information, even if it was meaningless, so he could show his superiors that he was doing his job. He said he didn't think these superiors really trusted him. I regretfully declined but did thank him for the cigarette and said I hoped we could get together sometime in New York.

Back in my cell, I was reading Rules for Prisoners for the hundredth time when I noticed that the top left side of the paper was away from the wall. I looked in back of the paper and found the most astounding document I have ever seen. I read it on the sly a little bit at a time. Once I had to slip it in my pants pocket when I was taken out for an interrogation.

It was written in pencil on small pieces of paper which had been carefully pasted together, presumably with paste made from rice and tea. The story was horrifying, heart breaking and filled with despair. Yet it was also tender and loving. The writer said his name was Lt. James Gray from Philadelphia. He had been a navigator on a B-24 when he was shot down. He described the brutality, the beatings, the starvation and the many deaths. I read with horror about the pitiable cries of the untended, badly wounded, who lay in their own filth until mercifully died.

Of course I never met him, but I felt that I got to know Jim Gray rather well. I learned he was married and that his wife gave birth to a boy after he left for oversees. He wrote longingly of his son, and I recall that he wrote a poem which he lovingly dedicated to the little boy he was never to see or hold.

I don't remember the dates of the diary entries, but there was a long stretch when no words were written. When the entries resumed, Jim explained he was heartbroken when the Japs discovered his pencil and took it away from him. It was a long time before he got another. As I recall, he said it was from a new prisoner.

A rather odd thing happened on the afternoon of the 16th. There was a small hole in one wall of my cell at floor level. Several times I had seen a tiny mouse come in from the next cell into my cell. I had not reached the stage where I talked to a mouse, but I did try to make friends with it. I had put several little mounds of rice on the floor, and I had seen the mouse occasionally take a grain of rice before running off. I was sitting on the floor watching the mouse hole hoping my buddy would come in. Instead of the mouse, I saw a small stick with a tiny piece of cloth attached to the end poking through the hole and waving back and forth.

I got excited thinking that perhaps it was a member of my crew trying to make contact. I hurriedly checked to see if any guards were around and then leaned over a whispered a hello into the hole. It wasn't a member of my crew, but instead the voice identified himself as a Burmese civilian who had been put in jail for stealing and who said he hated the Japanese. He then asked me if I would like him to help me escape. I took this with a grain of salt, but I said, "Sure, that would be very nice." He then said he had to make sure I was an American soldier and would I please tell him the number of my bomber group. Same old baloney I thought. And of course it was so superficial that only an idiot would have fallen for a gag like this. I moved away from the hole and when the flag came back inside I quickly shoved it back through the wall. A little later, I saw a guard take the guy out of his cell, and I saw he was indeed a Burmese. At the time I could not help but wonder why it was so important for the Japs to find out the number of a B-29 group. It just didn't make any sense to me.

A half hour or so later I was taken out for yet another interrogation. It was the same old stuff until surprisingly the interrogator said, "OK I will tell you the number of your squadron. You are in the 45 squadron of the four 0 group." I neither confirmed nor denied it, but I felt a tiny sense of disappointment because at that point I thought only my crew had been shot down and so it had to be someone from the crew who had given the Japanese the information that they seemed to want so much.

In the very early hours of 17th December I was awakened and taken out for what turned out to be my last interrogation at the New Laws Court jail, and it was a dandy. At each session I had tried to size up the interrogator. Some were worse than others. I quickly decided that this guy was a real mean one. In no time, he was screaming at me and, I will admit, that it could get very intimidating. At one point he stopped, took out a pack of cigarettes and lighted one up. And he carelessly left the cigarettes on his desk.

By now I had reached the point where I just didn't give a damn. I was sitting in a chair on the left side of the desk. I suppose it was rather foolish, but I got up, reached across the desk and helped myself to one of his cigarettes. I took his matches, lighted the cigarette, stuck it in the corner of my mouth and sat down again. I gave him what I hoped was a wide-eyed innocent look that tried to convey the message that, after all, we are still all soldiers in this thing together. Eh?

I don't think he got the message because he suddenly jumped up and hit me a stunning blow to the right side of my jaw. I went flying off the seat across the floor just barely conscious. I managed to get up on my hands and knees, looked around the room and found my cigarette. I crawled over to it, stuck it in my mouth and crawled back to my seat. I lifted myself up on the chair and sat down and resumed smoking the cigarette. Remembering "Rules for Prisoners" and the importance of cleanliness, I pulled his ashtray closer so I wouldn't have to dump the ashes on the floor. The Jap sat there glaring at me and I could see the blood rising in his face. I thought the son of a bitch will have a stroke, and I'll probably be blamed for it. He never said another word but incredibly let me sit there and finish smoking the cigarette. He then shouted for the guard who came and escorted me back to my cell.

As I said earlier, the doors to the inner courthouse of the jail were two cells to my right. This was important because when the doors were open I could hear the temple bells in town tolling the hours. It was shortly after 10:00 a.m. that I was again taken out of my cell. Only this time, instead of one guard with a club for an escort, there were two Japanese soldiers armed with rifles. Instead of going left where I knew the interrogation rooms were, we went to the right and up a flight stairs. We entered a room in which there were two people. One was a civilian who turned out to be an interpreter and the other was immaculately dressed Japanese army officer. I remember noting that he was wearing a shirt which looked like silk. He was sitting behind a huge polished desk. There was nothing on the desk except a neatly stacked sheaf of papers. The interpreter said this is major so and so. I immediately came to attention and saluted. I decided this was really serious, and I better try to act like a real soldier, even though I had a stubble of beard, my shirt was dirty and bloodstained, I was barefooted, and worst of all I had no belt. This caused my trousers to slip down when I sucked in my stomach. But I gave it the best shot I could.

I recited my name, rank and serial number, and then the major went into the all too familiar routine "proving" I was a soldier and again he told me about the Japanese rules of warfare. I tried to reasonably explain to him that he was an officer in the Japanese army, and I was an officer in the American army and that if he were in my position he would simply obey the Geneva Rules of War the same as I was trying to do. He coldly replied that Japanese officers don't surrender but prefer to die fighting. So much for my argument.

He then abruptly changed the subject and told me that morning I had been charged, tried and found guilty of the murder of innocent women and children in Rangoon on 14 December, 1944. I can quote the rest verbatim:

Lt. Larson: "I demand the right to an attorney."

Japanese Major: "You were represented at the trial by an attorney."

Lt. Larsen: (To himself, the bastard couldn't have been very good.) Out Loud, "I demand the right to appeal the sentence to his Imperial Majesty Emperor Hirohito of Japan."

Japanese Major: "Appeal denied." He paused and then continued. "Now would you like to hear sentence Leftenant?"

(I didn't particularly want to hear the sentence so I said nothing.)

Japanese Major: "I hereby sentence you to die tonight at 7:00 p.m. by beheading with Samari sword." He paused again then leaned forward and sort of leered at me. He said, "Now Leftenant, do you have anything else to say?"

I relaxed my military bearing, hitched up my pants, and planted my dirty fists on his clean, shiny desk. I leaned across the desk, and I said to him, "Yeah, fuck you Major." The civilian duly translated this, and I guess it must have sounded a little funny in Japanese. One of the soldiers let out a laugh. This infuriated the major. He shouted something, and two guards grabbed me by the arms and started pulling me out of the room backwards. The room had a bare wooden floor, and I was worried that I would get splinters in my heels, so I was trying to bounce up and down. We got into the hall and the guards hit me with their rifle butts and kept beating me until we got back to my cell.

The rest of the day is somewhat of a blur. I tried to put the thought of execution out of my mind. They are only trying to scare me, I thought. Any minute now they will be back and take me out for another interrogation. But as I listened to the temple bells in town, I began to realize that was probably only wishful thinking on my part.

Two positive things did happen that day. First, my shoes and socks were thrown into my cell. And I thought, at least I will die with my boots on. Early in the afternoon, the first American that I had seen was put into my cell. He said he was Captain Bud Meyers and that he was a B-29 aircraft commander who had bailed out on the same mission I was on. He also told me that many or all of the planes in the formation had been hit. He said he was able to keep his plane aloft for only about five minutes before his crew bailed out, and he also told me the radio operator had been severely injured.

I told Bud about my session with the Japanese that morning. I also asked him to try to contact my parents if and when he got out alive and explain to them what had happened. He was only in the cell for a short time when a guard took him out again.

Once more I was alone. I don't know how I got through that day but suddenly I heard the 6:00 o'clock bells and I really started to sweat. I had come to terms with the thought of dying, but I had this overriding fear that I would break down before the enemy and show them how terrified I was. Gone was the tough-guy front I had put up before the Major that morning. Instead I was just plain scared silly.

Finally two soldiers armed with rifles with fixed bayonets showed up to take me out of my cell. I crawled out the door, stood up and suddenly my knees collapsed completely. The guards grabbed me by each arm. And I said the most desperate prayer I'll ever say in my lifetime. "Help me to die like an American soldier, without blubbering." Strength seemed to surge back into me, I was once again in complete control. I pushed the guards away, cursed them and told them I damn well could walk out by myself without any help.

When we got into the courtyard, I saw a scene that was strictly out of a grade B movie. There were armed Japanese soldiers ringing the courtyard which was lighted by many burning flares. There were four Americans kneeling on the concrete who had their legs tied to each other. All with the exception of Bert Parmalee (engineer on my crew) had their hands tied behind their backs. I was made to kneel down next to Bert and was similarly tied up. I saw that Bert had his right arm in a sling, and I whispered to him to ask how bad it was. He said it was pretty bad. At that time Richard Brooks (radio operator on my crew), was brought out and tied up like the rest of us. He was tied to me. In a short time, there were seven people from the 40th Bomb Group lined up on the concrete. Bill Walsh and one other person were from Captain Meyer's crew. In addition to Richard, Bert and myself from our crew was also Chet Paul (co-pilot) and Karnig (Tommy) Thomasian (left gunner). I glanced in back of me and saw a very muscular little Jap who was stripped to the waist and who was waiving a sword over his head. I idly thought, he looks like a baseball player warming up in the on-deck circle. Richard whispered to me, "What do we do now Lieutenant?" Since I assumed he knew he was about to be executed, I thought that was rather an odd question. So I sort of growled at him, "Say your beads, Sergeant. Say your beads."

It wasn't until many years later when Tommy and I got together that I came to realize that in all probability I was the only one sentenced to death that morning. It is, of course, pure speculation, but I think it is possible that when I cursed at the Major and Japanese soldier laughed, that the Major lost face, and may have simply ignored telling the other victims about their impending execution. I remember the pile of papers on his desk.

The officer in charge of the execution was very neatly dressed and was wearing shiny black boots. After what seemed like an eternity, I saw a soldier come running out of the jail with a piece of paper in his hand. He went to the officer and they conferred briefly. I kept thinking, it's getting awfully close to 7:00 p.m. The soldier with the paper told us in English to stand up, and we struggled to our feet. He them started reading from this document.

I didn't hear, and have long forgotten, most of what he said. But I do remember two things. Our sentences had been commuted to life in prison, and we were transported immediately to the POW camp and any untoward action on our part would be dealt with severely on the spot. Wow .....

Closely guarded by enemy soldiers, we were brought out of the jail to a small beat-up old Chevrolet pickup truck. We were loaded in the back and joined by the other B-29 people who came directly out of the jail. Among them was Jim McGivern (bombardier on our crew), so now I knew who the sixth and last survivor on the crew was.

At the POW camp, after some nonsense about "voluntarily" signing a statement giving our promise not to escape, we were brought to the cell block and placed in cells on the second floor. In my cell were Bert Parmalee, Karnig Thomasian and Richard Brooks. There was nothing in the cell, which was about 9½ feet square, except the inevitable binjo box. We were issued two burlap rice sacks which had been opened and which were full of holes, two tin dishes for our food (one of mine was a rusty old sardine can) and a prison-made spoon. We were issued a small piece of cloth and a pin. On the cloth was written our POW number. It had to be worn at all times.

It was dark when we reached the cell which was to be our home for the next month and a half. There was no electricity in the cell block building, nor was there any in compound 8 which we were transferred to later. There was a window in our cell which had no glass in it, but it only contained bars. There was also a full-length set of bars in the door opening which for me was a notable improvement. We bedded down the best we could although it was bitterly cold, and two skimpy rice sacks didn't provide much warmth. But at least now I owned a pair of shoes again so I tucked one into the other and used them as a pillow.

In the morning I got my first look at Bert's wound. A piece of steel had gone into the underside of his upper right arm, severed the bone completely and went out the top. The wound on the bottom was about

2½" to 3" long, almost an inch wide and ugly as sin. The exit wound was about the size of a silver dollar and looked considerably neater. Bert told me many hours after he was captured, he was taken to a medic. This medic took a couple of swabs, dipped them in a bottle of some kind of liquid and pushed the swabs completely through the arm. He did this three or four times and then put a bandage on the wound. He then fashioned a device made out of two pieces of wood in an "L" shape and put this on his arm and put the whole contraption in a sling which was wrapped around his neck. This was the extent of his medical treatment. The wooden contraption was doing no good and was causing Bert needless agony. So I took it off and tightened up the sling so the arm was a little more comfortable. For the first few weeks Bert couldn't sleep lying down so I had him propped up in a corner of the cell with his head against the wall and he was able to get a certain amount of sleep. Although the pain must have been almost unbearable, Bert never once complained.

In the compound were a total of about 100 POWs mostly American and English. There were also two New Zealanders, one Canadian, one Aussie and one Dutchman. Grades and ranks went from Private (one) to Wing Commander (two). The biggest single contingent was the 29 people from the 40th Bomb Group. All the POWs had one thing in common. We had all come to Rangoon by air. The Japanese still considered us to be criminals, and we continued with the skimpy diet. But now things were much better. There was a cement trough in the compound about 25 or so feet long which was filled with water. We had the chance to dip this water out over ourselves and take a bath. This felt great. However, it wasn't long before allied bombers destroyed the water system of Rangoon, and that was the end of our bathing. From then on we could only run out in the occasional rain storm to clean up.

Medically speaking, we were a pretty sorry lot. Bouts of malaria were common as were cases of diarrhea and dysentery. Many of the guys had ugly looking ulcerous sores on their bodies and everyone had beriberi to some degree. One prisoner lost his mind and refused to believe he was a prisoner of war. Miraculously, both Bert and Monty were healing quite nicely. At one point, a scab formed over the wound in the lower part of

Bert's arm, but there was still pus inside the arm. The Jap medic took a pair of scissors, jabbed them into the arm and cut through the flesh for about a ½". Cruel and effective.

Life went on in compound 8. There was the ever present starvation diet, the disease and the deaths. But there was also a chance to freely move about, and the chance to associate with many different people. At New Laws Court and in cell block No.5, I somehow felt that I had been singled out for special attention. Why, I have no idea. But here in compound 8, I was just plain old No.1117 and largely ignored and this was fine with me.

As far as liberation, I did that the hard way, too. I was one of the 430 POWs who left Rangoon on a forced march with the Japs on April 25, 1945. They were using us as a work party to pull their bullock carts, which were loaded down with equipment. On the morning of April 29th, we made camp in an abandoned Burmese village a few miles north of Pegu. We knew the front could not be too far away as we could hear the sounds of artillery fire. The big Tai formally turned over command of the POWs to British Brigadier Clive Hopson, and the Jap troops left us. Shortly after, we were bombed and strafed by four Royal Indian Air Force Hurricanes, who managed to kill Brigadier Hopson. We subsequently were ordered to retreat to another Burmese village a few miles further south, which we did. The Burmese in this village fed us a huge meal of rice and tea. This was the first time we had anything to eat or drink since the morning of the 26th. After we had eaten, the word was passed around to spread out across the village and stay out of sight in case there were any Jap soldiers around. I was with a group of about 15 other guys when I laid down on a grassy spot and promptly fell sound asleep. It was pitch dark when a rescue party came into the village and evacuated all the rest of the prisoners leaving me peacefully sleeping on the side of the path. When I was awakened, I went back into the village, and ended up sleeping in a Burmese farmer's hut. In the morning, I was shocked to find that there was a Japanese soldier sleeping in the same room with me.

Later that morning, I met two other American stragglers and the three of us went to the edge of the village to watch a field, where we hoped the British would come. It was about noon when a line of Gurka soldiers arrived. A bunch of Japanese soldiers, who had been in the village with us, went out to meet them. It was a short sharp fight and when it was over, there were 23 dead Jap soldiers in the field including my roommate of the night before. Shortly after, we were taken to British Brigade Headquarters, but when we got there, we found that all other prisoners had already been flown out. The three of us finally decided that we would hitchhike our way (by air) and head for Calcutta. It took us three days, but we finally got to the 142nd General Hospital, and were reunited with some of our comrades who had given us up for lost.

This narrative was obtained through a "Circumstances of Capture and Liberation" report sent to Harry Chagnon, 40th Bomb Group Historian by Norman Larsen along with an additional narrative that was printed in the 40th Bomb Group Association newsletter called "Memories"

Karnig Thomasian, Staff Sergeant, 20ᵗʰ Air Force/Left Gunner, (Queenie)

20ᵗʰ Bomber Command, 40ᵗʰ Bomber Group, 45ᵗʰ (VH) Squadron.

Home City: River Edge. Home State: New Jersey.

Dates of Imprisonment: 12/14/44 thru 5/4/45.

Our crew consisted of Lt. Wayne "Doc" Treimer: Pilot, Lt. Chester Paul: Co-Pilot, Lt. Norman Larsen: Navigator, Lt. James McGivern: Bombbardier, Lt. Buton Paramalee: Flt.Engineer, Sgt. Richard Brooks: Radio Op., Sgt Vernon Henning: CPC Gunner, Sgt. Karnig Thomasian: L.Gunner, Sgt. Leon McKutcheon: Rt.Gunner, Cpl. Robert Dalton: Radar, Sgt. Augie Harmison: T.Gunner.

It all started very calmly in the late afternoon of December 13, 1944. "Mission for tomorrow… Bangkok, Thailand, target… the bridge that leads to railway yards;" we all followed the pointer as it went north to… "Secondary target…the railway yards and station in Rangoon Burma." (The following facts were common knowledge only to the lead commanders, bombardiers and pilots at the time of the mission.) The ballistics for the 1,000 pound bombs were to be entered into the bombsights. The six 500 pound composition B bombs were loaded beneath the twelve 1,000 pounders, this meant that the 500 pounders would be released first without any precision aiming. The destruction of the bridge required the 1,000 pounders. The 500s were obviously loaded to increase bomb tonnage. Lt. Col. Ira Cornett went immediately to Col. Blanchard with the facts and strongly recommended that he change the orders to a safer and more efficient distribution of the bomb load. But to no avail… the Colonel ordered the lead bombardier to carry on the mission or face a court martial. The bridge at Bangkok was heavily overcast so the formation leader ordered the change of course to Rangoon. Rangoon was in sight and we went directly into our bomb run. The ships were flying in a tight formation. The noonday sun was beating in through the window adding to my discomfort. I unhooked my safety harness and crawled over to the bomb bay hatch for the third time, and hopefully the last. I had to let our bombardier know, thru the intercom, that all bombs were dropped and none were hung up.

The bombs hung in the open bomb bays poised and ready to…BOMBS AWAY…..

The bays were cleared in an instant I turned away as I called "all clear" over my intercom when B-L-A-M. I couldn't move… I was glued to the floor of the plane. Everything was an eerie red as if I were looking through a red filter. The bomb bay hatch was blown open and my hand was bleeding and air was rushing all around. Moments later I was able to move more freely so I fully opened the swinging hatch and saw that we were in a flat spin with flames and smoke blowing past under the bomb bays. I looked around and saw Leon turning to get out of his right gunners seat. Vernon was climbing down from his CPC position and I could see that I had to get out of their way. I looked again through the bomb bay and saw what must have been a body whiz past beneath the plane, then another. Somehow through my stupor I was able to realize that I had to jump. None of us talked, we must have been in shock. I doubt that we would have heard one another if we did, because of the incredible rush of air blowing through the bomb bay. My chest buckle to my chute harness was still open and I tried to buckle it but for some reason my injured right hand made it impossible. I decided to clasp my arms across my chest and jump. I couldn't jam the hatchway any longer so I grabbed both sides of the hatch frame but couldn't fall out. The centrifugal force was keeping me in the ship. I gathered all the strength I could muster and finally popped out. My next recollection was a powerful jerk and strains in both my arms and shoulders. The force of the chute opening had snapped the upper part of my body out of my shoulder straps and there I was hanging upside down with only my leg straps holding me up there. I was still in a daze and my actions must have been instinctive. I don't remember thinking about doing or not doing anything. I just did what I had to do. No emotion, no fear, nothing.

I grabbed my pants leg and pulled myself up enough to grab the chute straps and kept climbing until I could get my one arm through the shoulder straps above me. I had to stop there, my shoulders and arms were hurting and the air was very thin at the height we were at, so I tried to relax and regain my strength. Brooks was above me and he yelled my name. Hearing my name brought me back to reality. I kept looking down below me praying for my guys to jump from our blazing ship. One more chute opened...Please God, let me see more chutes. Moments later time stood still, our proud B-29 hit and disappeared in a fiery burst of flame and smoke right near our target. There were no more chutes...the realization was numbing. I knew for sure I had lost some close friends. I remembered Vernon Henning's father had come to see us in Kansas just before we were to go overseas. I will never forget his look as he took Vern and me aside and looked us both straight in the eye with those honest mid-west eyes and told us to take care of one another. Suppose Vern didn't make it and I got home, what was I to tell this wonderful man.

The lower I got the more oxygen I was able to breathe and the more my mind started to think. It was extremely quiet...like another world. I had time to think of many things. Would I ever see home again? I heard a whizzing of what must have been bullets going by that brought me out of my dream world. Those bastards were shooting at me. At that very moment I noticed that one of the two main belts that hold the shroud lines had a "v" cut in it about a foot above my head. That was too close and I curled up into as small a ball as I could. The ground was coming up faster and faster. I flexed my legs up and down to loosen them up and then BUMP...I made a hard landing. I quickly got out of the leg straps, ripped my first aid kit off and harness off and ran away from the river that I had seen coming down. I ran across rice paddies until I realized that there was a whole army of peasants running at me from all directions. They were soon all around me brandishing knives and spears and anything else they could get their hands on. The Japanese soldiers were soon on hand and took control. They tied my hands behind me and searched for my 45 and got it out from under my flight jacket.

They marched me back over the rice paddies and to the river bank. We walked around a hut and there was my co-pilot Chet Paul sitting in the shade on the ground leaning against the wall. We checked each other out to see if we were OK. So far the Japs did not rough me up outside of poking and pushing me to go faster. Soon we were herded on to a little motor craft that took us to the city on the other side of the river.

While we were going across, some Japanese officers took pictures of us; I suppose to send home. Another man, a civilian type, shot some newsreel footage of us for the six o'clock Tokyo news.

The first thing they made us do was to take all our clothes off as they searched everything thoroughly, then we put them back on. My shoulders and arms were still hurting badly from my jump. The undersides of my upper arms were numb and there was pain when I reached back or up when I took my clothes off and on. My crew helped me when they could.

After the guards finished searching our clothing and our persons, they led us down a hall to a row of big dark cells with bars made of 4×4" teakwood set 3" apart. The doors to the cells were short, about 3½ feet square. There was a small box on the other end of the cell referred to as a Binjo box about 18 × 8 × 8". This was our toilet. We had to take our shoes off and crawl into our individual cells.

I looked around and wondered what was going to happen next. I was very tired. We started to have a parade of spectators looking us over. I soon learned that I had to be standing at attention when anybody passed our cells. I wondered if we going to be interrogated. What would they ask me? What would they do if I didn't answer them? My mind was racing trying to figure some sort of a plan so that I wouldn't stumble around when questioned. One-half hour didn't pass before the guard ordered me out of my cell and led me through a series of dark passages, finally entering a little room. The room was about 12 feet square with one 2½ foot by 4 foot simple table and two chairs. There was one plain light of some sort hanging from the ceiling. The Interrogator sat down on one chair and glared at me. He was a short, squat, fat man...almost bald with eyes as cold as ice cubes. His interpreter sat on the other chair. He was a fairly short man, wiry and had a sneering attitude. Seemed to be a crafty and sneaky type. He told me to sit on the floor, which I did...and waited.

"NAME?" I told him my name and spelled it out as well as my rank and serial number. "WHERE DO YOU COME FROM?" snapped the interpreter. I told him that I could not tell him anything. He insisted that I must tell him everything. I told him again that I could only tell him my name, rank and serial number. He laughed aloud and told me I must answer his questions. I wondered what the next step was going to be. "WHAT YOUR AGE?" There was no harm in that so I told him I was 20. They both smiled and the interpreter leaned towards me and said, "So young to die, isn't it?" I told him that I wasn't dead yet, then I realized what he was driving at. He was really irritated and told me that I would die if I didn't talk. They asked me a whole battery of questions: How many planes in our raid…Who was the squadron leader…where we came from..? I thought I'd try to reason with them. I pointed out the rules of war and that I was given certain orders. I couldn't go back on them. I had many friends still fighting and anything I might say could cause them to be killed. I asked him if he were captured would he talk? The interpreter translated all that I had said and came back to me saying that they wouldn't be captured, they would fight and die. I told them how well we treated our prisoners, but I could see that all this talk made no impression at all. It was all a hopeless stab in the dark.

They resumed their questions by asking me if I would like to see my folks again. Would I like to see my sweetheart again? I bristled at those questions and asked them if they wouldn't like to see theirs. They got angry and told me that if I didn't talk, I would be shot. At this point the interpreter picked up a teakwood club and went behind me. I didn't take my eyes off of him and it probably saved a bone from being fractured. He began hitting me on my back and arm, but I was able to ride with the blows. I still had my leather A-1 jacket on and it absorbed some of the hits. They told me that if I talked they would put me in a POW camp and after the war I would go home. A funny feeling came over me… I just didn't care what they would do. I reasoned that they would kill me anyway whether I told them anything or not. The shock and excitement of this day had affected me in strange ways. I had always thought of life as a very precious thing and at this moment I was willing to give it up. I had been brought up to respect principles and values. The war brings a person face to face with the cost of maintaining these values…..the cost may be your life. I wondered why these people were fighting so fiercely and why they were so cruel. How naïve I was.

The interpreter suddenly asked me why I was fighting. I answered that my country was attacked and that I volunteered to fight and do my part for my country. I told him that we were fighting for the rights of people and that they were trying to destroy those rights. They snickered and got pretty mad at hearing all this. They reminded me that I would be shot but they realized that I had made my decision. That was when the interrogator lost his control and took off his leather sandal and started to beat me with it. I warded off most of the blows so he went back and got his chair, then quickly put it down and grabbed the teakwood club from the guard who was in the room. I got off the floor quickly this time. He started swinging at me … I was scared. Again, having my leather jacket on probably helped me a great deal from not getting hurt more than I did. I asked him if he thought this was fair…he could do anything he wanted and I couldn't hit back… what kind of justice is that? The interpreter said that it was all fair since I didn't talk. For some reason he finally stopped hitting me and put the club down. I had bruises all over, but thank goodness he didn't hit me on the head. He sat down and motioned for me to sit on the floor again. He then asked me an odd question through the interpreter. Who did I think would win the war? I told him that we would win; because God was on our side and that we were right and right would win. They had a great laugh at that as tears were welling in my eyes. Even then, I was very emotional. I believed what I had said.

The guard poked me to get up and then directed me out the door and down to my cell. I breathed a sigh of relief and sat down to rest…but not for long. Apparently the guard had been ordered to have me always stand at attention and also not to feed me. After about an hour or so I was pretty tired and thirsty. Back at our base, we would have had our chow and gone to the clubhouse and finished our plans for a weekend in Calcutta. I'm not there, I'm here and I'd better make the best of it. Well, I stood up as long as I could and when the guard was out of sight, I'd sit down. Then get up fast when I heard him coming. This went on for a couple of hours and still I didn't get anything to eat or drink. I asked for water, but it was no use. They just ignored me. By now we were well into the evening hours and it was very dark except for a small light hanging from the ceiling.

I must have fallen asleep standing up and just slid to the floor, because I woke up the next morning with the guard banging at the thick teakwood bars of my cell. I quickly stood up at attention. He jabbered about something I couldn't understand, so I just stood still. He finally went off down the corridor. This wasn't all a dream after all…I really was a prisoner. Now what's going to happen? Did they forget about me? I just stood there facing the front of my cell, when a guard stopped and stared at me. He placed down a bucket he was carrying and started to put a few scoops of rice from the bucket into a tin he had brought with him. He shoved the tin through an opening in the bars made for that purpose. I was so hungry that I was grateful for anything. He didn't leave any utensils, so I dug into it with my fingers. I thought that I might just as well ask for some water; I was so thirsty. The guard must have understood because he came back and poured some into my tin. I was purely baffled by their change of attitude. Yesterday, they said they would shoot me… today, they fed me. I just didn't understand them. I decided to sit tight and see what happened next. Sitting alone in a cell gives a man a lot of time to think, and I did a lot of that. Christmas was just a couple of weeks away, and I prayed that they wouldn't notify my folks 'til after the holidays. I hoped that someone had seen our chutes…what did they know about us….who survived and who didn't? I wondered if the Japs really intended to kill us. I looked over the cell and noticed names and dates written on the walls. I wondered what happened to those that were here before me.

Chet was in the next cell to my right all the time. When the guard left, I went to the front right corner of my cell and taped on the wall. I told Chet of my interrogation the day before. He told me that if worse comes to worse, to tell them certain things they already know, but to think, then speak. We had to stop talking because the guard was making his rounds again. I guess we were all on edge; something had to happen soon.

After nightfall something did happen. The guards batted their guns butts on the wooden bars and ordered us out of our cells. We crawled out of the small door of the cell, and quickly put our shoes on. The guards then ordered us along a hallway which led to a small open courtyard. It was about 18 feet by 22 feet with a hard dirt ground. That's when I first saw Richard Brooks. It was good to see that "Brooksy" was OK. His face looked much worn. I could see that he was scared about something. I looked all around and all I saw were Japanese officers with their swords. They ordered us to kneel down in a row and not talk. My mind really started to race all over the possibilities. Was this the way it was going to end? I just couldn't believe this scene. The door we came through opened again and I recognized the rest of my crew, six in all. I saw Norman, my navigator, for the first time. I was so happy to see him but we couldn't talk... we winked at one another as he knelt down beside me. Parmalee was suffering with his shattered arm. He needed medical attention, but at this moment that wasn't uppermost in our minds. They ordered us to place our hands behind us as they handcuffed us together. They then all came around in front of us and the chief officer held out a sheet of paper and started to read it in Japanese. Was this our notice of execution?

The interpreter was there and he translated the message to us. It was the most surprising thing I could have heard. He told us that we were to be transferred to a Prisoner of War Camp. I almost melted right there. It could well have been our death sentence.

We were all led to one of the buildings in the prison. We entered and they started to direct us into cells by twos, threes and fours. Our crew was ordered to the second floor. One of the things we found was that this building was solitary confinement, Compound #5, and all airmen were placed there. Since we were all physically and emotionally exhausted, we related our individual experiences to each other and soon fell asleep.

It was about 7:00 to 7:30 AM when we got something to eat. It was more rice and some brown stuff that didn't look too good. We tried it but it tasted awful and left it. After the guards left the building for awhile, voices from some of the older prisoners gave us some more valued advice. They made a big point about the brown stuff. They called it Nucca, and it was the brown shell of the rice that was ground up and boiled in water. Since it was the only source of vitamin C in this place, we had to eat it. They made it clear if we didn't, we would get Beriberi. It was a disease of the nerves resulting in partial paralysis, swelling of the legs caused by the abnormal accumulation of body water or serous fluid. Eventually one could die from this without treatment. That was enough for me. About noontime on the first day, the guards came to our cells and told us to put on all of the clothes we had and that we had to stand just outside our cells. There were about ten to twelve of us that were caught in the first raid. They gathered us together and took us downstairs and out to the open ground next to the building. We stood there in this dirt yard wondering what was coming next. One of the officers came up to us and explained that they were going to take pictures of us. It seemed that we passed our propaganda screen test and they ordered us all back to our cells.

About six that evening, we got our second meal of the day: rice and maybe a vegetable mixed in. That was all we were to have every day. The old hands gave us more advice and helped us with some useful Japanese words and commands. They told us what the guards expected of us and that we had to bow to them when they came by our cells. We should never be caught sitting down or they would beat us. All this information was a great help to us at this time and probably saved us many a beating.

Then one of the men on the bottom floor asked for some quiet so that he could read to us from the Bible. Somehow he had managed to smuggle it in, and every night would read from it. This was a very emotional moment. No place of worship, however large, however adorned with statues of gold, could ever capture the sincere pureness of this religious experience. Each night it gave us hope and assurance that someday we would get out of this nightmare and go home. After the reading we were led in prayer and all joined in "The Lord's Prayer." Our first full day in solitary was at an end.

I found out that the air forces were singled out to be in solitary because we were "Indiscriminate Bombers" and they blamed us for the Doolittle raid. Therefore, we were not allowed any extra privileges such as being in a regular compound where you could walk around and talk to the other men…go on work details and get better food rations.

The little Jap guard looked at the nameplate on the outside of our cell and called out what must have been my name, "Tomaasan." I answered "Heit" which is the equivalent to "yes." He unlocked the gate and led me downstairs and outside to a small shack near the right front of our compound. He hadn't asked me to take all my clothes, so I figured this couldn't be too much. I entered the shack and saw two Japanese sitting at a small wooden table. I remember seeing one of them when we were taking pictures just outside this shack. He had a pair of thick blue tinged glasses over a pair of cold eyes. He was an interrogating officer. He told me to sit in the chair opposite him while the other Japanese, a civilian type, sat on one side of the table. The interrogator could speak a little English so he started to ask me a lot of the questions they had asked me at the New Laws Court. We exchanged many words in the next half hour. He wanted to know my home address. I asked him why he wanted to know that. He said it was to notify my parents I was alright. I told them he could send my serial number and my name to my government and that they would notify my parents. This is the regular procedure. He wouldn't listen to such a thing. I told him that I believed he planned to harm my folks. He blustered and fumed and finally blew up when I wouldn't tell him anything about the B-29 and other details. He got up and crossed over and picked up his rawhide whip. It was only two feet long but it hurt and I got up to better fend off the blows with my arms. A guard walked in to help by belting me with a teakwood stick that all the guards seemed to have. I pleaded with them that I couldn't tell them anything. He finally stopped for a breather. I sat down trying to think of what to do and I remembered what Chet had told me back in New Laws lockup. The interrogator asked me more questions and placed a sheet in front of me with a bunch of questions. There were a lot of questions and I thought that this may be the time to act smart and maybe I could get out of this. I started to answer the question that could be answered with an approximation, such as air speed, range, bomb load, etc. I gave numbers that were far from correct. When I finished, I told him I didn't know the answers to all the questions and he sort of believed me. They were done with me, but instead of going back to my cell, they put me in another one all myself. I suppose it was to keep me from telling the others what I had said or didn't say. I felt pretty lonely for the next couple of hours when suddenly they brought Parmalee and put him in the cell with me. They had beaten him also even though he was badly wounded. We compared notes and spent the rest of the day in this cell.

The next few days were more or less uneventful until a guard called my name; then unlocked the door and motioned for me to come out. I wondered what was going to happen now. "See you later, guys." He directed me downstairs and out the front gate, then turned right towards the little interrogation shack. Here we go again I thought. I stood outside until they got good and ready then the guard pushed me to go in. They told me to sit down in the same old wooden chair and we were off again. This time there was a new cast of characters. Right across from me was an East Indian in some sort of officer's clothes with sashes and braids all over him. I later found out that he was a Chandra Bose, a high ranking officer of the Indian National Army which was strongly and very actively anti-British. The Indian spoke English well with a bit of a British accent. He asked if I had ever heard of Ghandi. I said that I had. He suddenly got angry and asked me why they had imprisoned him. I looked at him and told him that as far as I knew Ghandi wasn't in prison and that somebody was fooling him. Then he started to ask me about my base in India. He said, don't lie to me, because if you do I will know. I have my men all over India. Well, I said, if that is so why ask me...why not just ask your men? I didn't think that was the most tactful thing to say, but it was out already. He told me not to act so smart and answer his questions. He gave me a sheet of paper and a pencil and told me to draw a diagram of the field that I came from. Right away I told him that I wouldn't, but that didn't get me far. I sat and thought for a moment and decided to do what they asked but in a generalized and deceptive manner as possible. I was always good at drawing, so I could make it look believable. I picked up the pencil and drew a runway then a road horizontal to it going quite a distance. Along the road I put a post exchange building...then some tennis courts...then a large area for a baseball diamond and an N.C.O clubhouse. The Indian and the Japanese started getting mad. They wanted to know where the hangers and planes were. I scattered a few hangers around and said that there were about sixteen to eighteen planes scattered around and not in one place. They didn't seem to question the validity of all the lies I drew. They asked be about other fields, but I told them that I never saw any of them, because I had just arrived in India and didn't know too much.

The Indian asked me where I went on my passes. I told him that I had not been there long enough to get a long pass. He said I must have gone to Karagpohr, it was so close. I figured that if I told him I have gone there it would be alright since the men from all the fields go there and wouldn't give him any lead as to which field I was from. He then asked me what I did there. I told him I usually got some ice cream or saw a movie at the British-American U.S.O. with some of the men. He asked me if I liked ice cream and would I like some. I said, sure, do you have any? He yelled, "You wise guy, eh?"...and the guard batted me around some more. They practically threw me out of there but not before I was made to bow before leaving. I was relieved to get back and see my buddies again.

Days passed with more interrogations. One stands vividly in my mind as one of the silliest encounters with the Japanese mind. They were always unpredictable and it was hard to understand their motives for doing some things, especially during these interrogations. There I was sitting in the familiar wooden chair again opposite the surly interrogator with the blue tinted glasses. He said they were impressed by my ability to draw and that he would like me to draw a B-29 with all its armament. I told him that would be impossible. I was glad that I had worn my leather flying jacket because they immediately started battering me. They stopped and he shoved the paper and pencil in front of me again. Somehow Chet's earlier advice came into my head again and I started to think as fast as I could...and decided what to do. I drew the silhouette of the B-29 and began placing 50 Cal. Machine guns and 20mm cannons all over the plane. I was either going to get away with this or get my head handed to me. At that moment in time I could not think of any other solution. When I was all done, it looked mighty impressive; I only wish I had it with me now. Apparently they liked it too, because I was sent back to my cell immediately. I was still very concerned because I don't know why they did not go to one of the crashed planes and take a look. I just could not believe that planes would burn so hot as to melt all trace of armaments.

One day, while idly kicking pebbles on my routine morning walk within the prison compound, I noticed a thin, delicate shoot of greenery pushing its way up from the stones and rubble of barren ground. For the past six months, I had been interned with hundreds of Allied Air Force personnel where days stretched into weeks and months. In their passing, the pain, hunger, suffering and humiliation continued. I stooped down and quickly cleared away debris from the tendril, aerating the soil around it. Here was a sign of hope---a new, fresh, living symbol of life. If only it could be kept alive, for Easter was nearly here.

As the routine of care continued, I told a few of my fellow prisoners and they came over to watch with growing anticipation. A bud soon appeared, and bets were made as to color and kind of flower. Easter morning dawned. After roll call, we went to see our flower—it had blossomed into a white Lily, pristine and so beautiful in all its glory. Was this a sign from God to give us hope that we would be freed soon? I carefully plucked it and took it to one of the men who was acting as our chaplain. No explanations; just a symbol of hope amidst all the suffering.

As the morning wore on, word was passed around that our chaplain would lead us in an Easter service. Great care was taken not to alert the guard to what we were planning. To this end, those of us of the Jewish faith volunteered to mill around and act as lookouts while our brief ceremony was in progress. Slowly we gathered, as we settled down and waited for the sermon to begin, all our eyes went to the makeshift altar, and there, in the middle of the table was a bamboo cup holding the lily. Unashamed tears fell. Hope does spring eternal as did that lily on that Easter morning.

For surely as that lily bloomed, we knew we would gain our freedom.

In the days following, the guards kept us on edge with their pointless beatings. One day, we were standing around in our cell waiting for the guard to come by. He was the drunken one. We snapped to attention, in the manner prescribed, and bowed as always. For some reason he didn't like something about Richard. Maybe his fingers weren't straight and rigid at his side. Whatever the reason, he unlocked our cell door and came right in and started beating Richard with his teakwood stick like he was swinging at a baseball. How and why he didn't turn on the rest of us is still a wonder. Luckily Richard was wearing my leather jacket or he would surely have had some broken bones. If any of us had intervened, it would have been the end of us for sure. We were convinced, after many such beatings, that these must have been the dregs of the Japanese soldiers…they were animals. History has shown that even our forces were not immune from having such types. We were in this sort of situation every day…some worse…some better.

We were informed by the Japanese that they were leaving our camp and taking the prisoners who were able to walk and carry equipment. They gave us the option of going or staying. I did not know if they would kill us before they left, but I decided to stay because I was afraid of not being able to walk and if I couldn't, of being killed and that is what happened. Along the way men were killed because they slacked back. I also thought that maybe I could help some of the guys who were really bad off.

When the Japs had left finally, we took over the place. My friend, a New Zealander, and I were sitting on the steps of the compound and I was smoking tea leaves. I never smoked in my life, but I started there. So we're looking out over the city and we see Boom…Boom…Boom. They are blasting things. It's late at night and we're saying "Hey, I haven't seen a guard come around, have you?" We walked around and went into the hut again, took a brick out, walked to the front and looked and we could see the main gates were open, and I didn't see any movement. We talked to the Wing Commander, and he said, "Alright, don't tell anybody because it'll be a riot here." So we hopped over the wall- it was only about eight feet, you hike a guy up and he gets up and over. We hopped over and went down there. Now we were taking a risk. Now we are in dead man's land, about seven of us. And some guys went to the gate and they saw a note. I have a copy of that note. "We meet you on future battlefields, and now you are free to go" ......Bullshit.......

We were still being bombed by the British, by mistake. We put up a sign that said "Japs gone." The British fighter pilots thought we were joking and so they bombed us. They missed and hit one of our outer walls. The British prisoners got up and wrote this "EXTRACT DIDGIT" In British terms it meant "take your finger out of your ass." So right away they came back and they waved their wings. Then they came back and dropped food containers. I mean would you believe it? It was just wild. What brilliance to come up with that.

The Prisoners were kept in separate compounds according to their nationality. I went over to the Chinese compound and I met this fellow. I can't remember his name now, but he was the one that doled out the rice when we were in solitary. He had a black skull cap, a white flowing shirt, short black pants and sandals. That's how he came around. He would always look to see if he could give us a little more if the Jap wasn't over his shoulder. We couldn't converse. But I will always remember him. So, I went over where the Chinese were and I found him and I said, "Does anybody speak English?" One of the fellows could speak a little English and I said, "Tell him that I want to thank him for his kindness, he made life more bearable for us and he was such a nice man." Then the guy who was interpreting said, "Could he give you his father's address and you write, tell him that you saw his son and he's all right?" I said sure, he gave me the address, and then the Chinese fellow got a coin, and he broke the coin. He said "When we meet again, we will match the coins." So I wrote to his parents. His father had a pharmacy in some town in China. But back in the States along came a letter, all in Chinese. One to me and one to his son. I showed it to a friend of mine in Art Students League in New York, a Chinese guy. I asked if he knew how to read Chinese? He said yes and I asked him to translate the letter. So he gave me the translation a few days later. He didn't translate the son's letter, because that was private. The father said he hadn't seen his son in all those years. That was the first time he'd heard anything about him. And it was so nice of you to write and his mother is happy to hear that he's okay. He asked "Do you think you could send him a letter?" I don't remember what he wanted to say but basically he wanted to get in touch with him. So I said, let me find out.

I called up the 142nd General Hospital, they were not operational any more, but they had an office in America. To make a long story short, I found that these Chinese were released from the hospital and they walked back to China. That meant that he had to walk over the Hump, possibly by the Burma Road which was still a dangerous place. The Japanese were gone but many other obstacles were in place. He was walking from Rangoon to China, thousands of miles, and that is probably was how he got to Rangoon in the first place. So I wrote back to his father and said "HE IS WALKING HOME."

OUR LIVES ARE OURS AGAIN. . . . .

A New Yorker, Karnig volunteered in the U.S. Army at the age of 18. After his liberation from the Rangoon Prisoner of War Camp and honorably discharged in 1945, he used the GI Bill to attend the Art Students League in New York. He worked for top advertising agencies and a graphic design firm for 44 years. Retirement in 1996 enabled him to pursue his artistic capabilities and returned to his love of portrait artistry and can be reached at www.portratsbykarnig.com.

However, his deepest desire was to help ex-POW/veterans in getting their disability compensation. He became an accredited National Service Officer in 1999 and to this day, has helped over 92 combat veterans.

He has written a definitive book "Then There Were Six" in which he describes his personal experiences as a POW in which he has honored family and his fellow prisoners. He and his wife were instrumental in producing and writing newsletters, Rangoon Ramblings, which has been a wonderful resource for this book. His generous help, encouragement and review of my writing are very much appreciated.

This narrative was sent by Karnig Thomasian to Harry Chagnon, the 40th Bomb Group Historian in a report called "Circumstances of Capture and Liberation." Karnig Thomasian also wrote a book regarding his capture called "Then There Were Six" from which he graciously allowed me to quote.

"Richard Brooks "TRUNK "

Karnig Thomassian then and now.

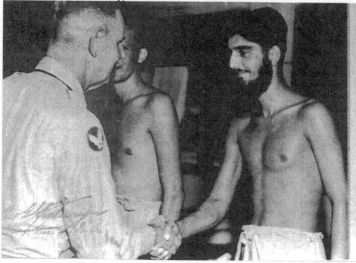

Karnig Thomassian after liberation with General Stratameyer.

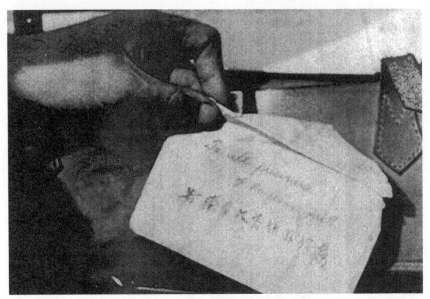

Japanese note found on gate by Karnig Thomassian
telling prisoners they were free.

"The Lily That Bloomed" – Courtesy Karnig Thomassian

QUEENIE'S CREW THAT WOULD NOT COME HOME

1ˢᵗLieutenant Wayne Treimer "Doc" Pilot B-29

With 3 engines in flames and no controls, the plane went into a flat spin. He stayed with the plane to try to give the crew time to bail out. It finally hit the ground in a burst of fire and explosions.

Corporal Vernon Henning, Central Fire Control Gunner on B-29
Vernon was unable to get out in time.

Corporal Leon McCutchen, Right Gunner/Engine Mechanic on B-29
Leon was unable to get out in time.

Corporal August Harmison, "Augie" Tail Gunner on B-29
Augie was unable to get out in time.

Corporal Robert Dalton Radar Operator on B-29
Bob was unable to get out in time.

A.l. Bearden, 1ˢᵗLieutenant, P-38.
Home City: Houston. Home State: Texas.

"I was the leading element of first flight. Dive bombed a bridge south of Mandalay (approximately 20 miles). After dropping the bomb, I circled the target in formation waiting for other flights to drop bombs. My room-mate Lt. E.L. Barnes, was leading element in third flight pulled up from his dive and rammed me from underneath. He may have been already hit by Ack-Ack which was extremely heavy. Both planes were demolished by the impact. I pulled the escape panel, released my safety belt and was torn out of the cockpit by a terrific slip stream. My plane exploded just after I cleared it. My parachute opened at approximately 4,000 feet and I landed close to a Burmese village. My leg had been hurt and I could not walk away from Burmese villagers who were very hostile. Held them off with a 45 until the Japanese came."

This narrative was obtained through "Circumstances of Capture and Liberation" report sent to Harry Chagnon, the 40ᵗʰ Bomb Group Historian by A.I. Bearden

Richard Brooks "TRUNK"

Joseph E. Wells, Staff Sergeant, 10th Air Force/Gunner, B-24, 10th Bomber Command,

7th Bomber Group, 9th Bomber Squadron

Home City: Boone. Home State: Iowa.

Dates of Imprisonment: 12/4/43 thru 5/4/45

We were lead plane of a 48 plane mission. Jap fighters jumped us before we reached our I.P. One engine lost over target, then fighters jumped us again. We lost one more engine. I was struck by fragments from an explosive shell in the left leg, arm and head. The aircraft caught fire, and I put it out mostly with my hands. We lost one more engine before we had to bail out. I then received a back injury. After landing, I was in the jungle until December 4th, when the Burmese picked me up and turned me over to the Japs, who then took me to Basien on December 5th. That evening we were loaded on a barge, sent to Rangoon and arrived on December 9th. Because I could barely walk, I was carried into the jail in the New Laws Courts Building where we were placed in cells 9' by 13'. In August 1944, we were taken to the Rangoon Central Jail and placed in cell block #5 (solitary) until about the middle of January 1945. We were then transferred to cell block #8 where we stayed until liberation.

On May 4, 1945, I was carried from the prison to a small ship that took us out to the harbor where the British ship (H.M.S. Karapara) was anchored. They took us straight to the 142nd General Hospital in Calcutta to be rehabilitated before being sent home.

This narrative was obtained through "Circumstances of Capture and Liberation" report sent to Harry Chagnon, the 40th Bomb Group Historian by Joseph Wells.

<u>Richard Brooks "TRUNK"</u>

Joseph Wells after release. Courtesy Pegasus Archives

**Frank H. Tilcock, 1ˢᵗ Lieutenant, 9ᵗʰ Photo Recon Squadron/
Pilot, P-38, CBI Theatre.**

Home City: Tallahassee. Home State: Florida.

Date of Imprisonment: 9/19/43 thru 04/?/45.

In September, 1943, I was on a photo mission over Rangoon, Burma. I was to photograph the Docks, Railway Station and Mingladon Airport. I had made two passes when I saw two Japanese fighters over my left shoulder. I fire walled the throttles on the P-38 and headed for home. After about 30 minutes, I couldn't see the fighters and throttled back to cruise. All of a sudden a noise like hail on a tin roof occurred and my instrument panel disappeared and smoke poured into the cockpit. My left engine was on fire. Time to bail out. As I climbed out of my seat, the plane exploded. I passed out. When I came to, I knew I was falling, how long I don't know. I pulled the rip cord and passed out again. When I came to, the fighters were circling my chute. They did not shoot. I went through some clouds then landed in a tree, which bent enough to allow my toes to touch ground. I got out of my chute and retrieved it by cutting down the tree with my machete, which was in the seat of my chute. I walked through the jungle following a stream for 2 days. On the 3ʳᵈ day, I was surprised by some Burmese. They acted friendly and appeared to be helping. We walked for several hours, by-passing many villages. At dusk, they led me to a hut on the outskirts of a village, where I was met by Japanese soldiers. They put me in an ox cart and drove onto a paved road. I was then put into a truck. They drove all night and we arrived at Rangoon. I was interrogated several days and was in solitary for 86 days. After which I was put into a compound with other prisoners.

In April 1945, the well prisoners marched out of Rangoon prison at night. I think the forced march lasted for 3 nights. The 4ᵗʰ day, we were resting in some trees and the Japanese guards left us. Some small Army recon planes flew over and attracted their attention. Soon after, we were strafed by British Fighters. We all split… That night I hid in a ditch covered with leaves and heard troops and tanks passing by. The next day, the British encountered us. I was returned to Calcutta by air and it was all over….. **Thank God.**

Our Lives Are Ours Again. . . .

Frank retired from the USAF after 29 years as Major F.H. Tilcock. He went to work for Eastern Air Lines as a meteorologist for 18 years, retiring in Tallahassee, Florida in 1983. He enjoyed his final days playing golf and enjoying the company of his loving wife, Mary, and many close friends. He always enjoyed the Rangoon Reunions.

This narrative was obtained through "Circumstances of Capture and Liberation" report sent to Harry Chagnon, the 40th Bomb Group Historian by Frank Tilcock.

<u>Richard Brooks "TRUNK"</u>

Leland H.W. Waltrip, Staff Sergeant, 15th AF/Tail Gunner, B-25, CBI Bomber Command, 12th Bomber Group, 434th Squadron. Home City: Cottonwood. Home State: Arizona. Dates of Imprisonment: 05/29/44 thru 05/03/45.

On May 29, 1944, on a flight over Burma, we were skip bombing the Railroad north of Pegu and were hit by ground fire. Ship started burning, was told to bail out over the mountains by Pilot John McClosky. Co-Pilot was killed on bailout. Captured within three days and taken to Rangoon City Jail. I was there approximately one month, put in solitary for approximately 8 months and then put into Block 5 until we were marched north, turned loose and liberated on May 3, 1945. No need to write about mistreatment, as everyone that was there knows all about it.

Six were in my crew, only four made it back.

This narrative was obtained through "Circumstances of Capture and Liberation" sent to Harry Chagnon, 40th Bomb Group Historian by Leland Waltrip.

Richard Brooks "TRUNK"

Robert Derrington, Captain, 20ᵗʰ Air Force/ Pilot, B-29, 58ᵗʰ Bomber Wing Command, 40ᵗʰ Bomber Group, 25ᵗʰ Squadron.

Home City: Sun City. Home State: Arizona.

Dates of Imprisonment: 12/14/44 thru 05/04/45.

December 10, 1944- a replacement crew arrived in Chakulia, India bringing a new B-29 to the 40ᵗʰ Bomb Group. I was the Aircraft Commander of the "new kids on the block." December 12—I was told that a mission was scheduled on the 14ᵗʰ and that new pilots would ride as observers on their first mission. Another pilot, Stacy Hall, had just arrived, so we were both assigned as observers to the mission. December 14ᵗʰ --- Upon arrival at the briefing, I noticed that I had originally been assigned to ride with Howard Gerber's crew and a change had been made. I was now to ride with Captain Bud Meyer's crew. No big deal at the time; I had not met either of them as yet.

Our flight to the primary target, a railroad bridge near Bankok, was routine. The bombardiers had been instructed to bomb visually only. After two dry runs over cloud cover, we turned toward Rangoon, our secondary objective. Again, a routine approach at 20,000 feet towards the railroad station; no flack, no fighters as our 11 plane formation neared the target. BOMBS AWAY...Seconds later, it sounded like somebody had thrown rocks against the plane. (We learned later that our instantaneous fuses, mixed load of 500 and 1,000 bombs had collided, and we had blown ourselves out of the air.) Fire everywhere....I opened the nose wheel escape hatch as Bud and Lional Coffin were trying to control the plane. Bill Walsh, the engineer, rolled out of his seat head first through the hatch. As I started to follow him, I saw Monty Montgomery, the radio operator, clutching his injured arm.

There I was at 30,000 feet on my back.....No, it was well below 20,000 feet as I tumbled down, and trying in vain to control my body spin. In my training days, somebody had said "Delay opening your chute, fighter pilots might use you for target practice." Finally, I pulled the rip cord and found myself floating toward a rice paddy. I carefully put the rip cord in my pocket, felt for my pistol and found that it had fallen out of the holster. Looking down and around, I saw several other chutes and smoke from the crashed plane. Upon landing, I was quickly captured by Burmese and tried to enlist their help. NO WAY.. An English speaking native said that if they did not turn me in, the Japs would kill them. Shortly thereafter, I was delivered to the Japs, beaten because I could not tell them what happened to my pistol. I was then taken to military headquarters at Judson College, now known as Rangoon University. The years have blurred some of the timing, but for a couple of days I was detained along with Walsh, Montgomery, Joe Levine and Marion Burke at the guard shack at the University entrance. We were tied together and forced to remain standing for almost 24 hours before being taken in for interrogation. Finally we were taken to the Rangoon Central Jail where all five of us were put into one cell in cell block #5. After several weeks in solitary, everybody in the building was moved to cell block #8, but not before Monty's injured arm had deteriorated to the point that it was necessary to amputate at the elbow with no anesthetic or pain medication.

Much has been written by others about our experiences while in prison; the beatings, illnesses and diseases with no medical attention, lack of food; so I will skip to late April when about 400 prisoners left the camp on a forced march. Most of us wore old Japanese uniforms they made us wear. Many with no shoes. The Japs had planned to cross the Salween River east of Pegu, about 50 miles north of Rangoon, and turn south toward Thailand and who knows where. After three days of being strafed by British fighters, we arrived at a small deserted village a few miles east of Pegu. Here, the Japs abandoned us and went on their own. The British, mistaking signals made by mirrors, strafed us killing only one man, an English general. With the help of a native boy, we made contact with British troops who bulldozed a landing strip for a C-47 to pick us up and take us to the 142nd General Hospital in Calcutta. I mentioned at the beginning that I had been transferred to another ship for this mission. We lost 5 planes over the target and one got back to the base in Chakulia. Captain Gerber's was on Meyer's right wing. Many of us were fortunate to survive. We only know that Gerber's plane was seen turning away from the formation after the blast never to be seen again.

Call it fate or whatever you want, but as I look back on my ½ mission, I often thank God for the switch that spared my life.

[A more detailed account regarding the "Walk Out" is detailed by Capt. Derrington in the special Walkout From Rangoon Prison chapter that he wrote 44 years later for the publication "Memories" later in this book.]

This narrative was obtained through a "Circumstances of Capture and Liberation report sent to Harry Chagnon, 40th Bomb Group Historian by Robert Derrington.

RICHARD BROOKS "TRUNK"

Richard A. Montgomery, Master Sergeant, 20th AirForce/Radio Operator, B-29,

58th Bomber Wing, 40th Bomber Group, 25thSquadron.

Home City: Riverside. Home State: California.

Dates of Imprisonment: 12/14//44 thru 05/04/45.

I was the Radio Operator on Capt. C.C. Meyer's crew (B-29); we were part of the ill-fated formation that flew over the railroad yards at Rangoon, Burma. Heavily damaged as a result of our or other B-29's bombs colliding as they left the plane, our aircraft was kept under control by the Grace of God and the flying skills of Capt. Meyer and Lt. Coffin, our co-pilot, until all hands bailed out.

Except for about an inch of flesh, my left hand was severed at the wrist by shrapnel. Grasping my left wrist with my right hand, I was able to stop the bleeding, letting go long enough to pull the rip cord. Landing in a dried up rice paddy, I was quickly captured by a group of irate Burmese, one of whom tried to shoot me with my own pistol. Fortunately, I never kept a round in the chamber and he didn't know about having to pull the slide back. After several unsuccessful attempts at firing the pistol, they took me to a nearby village. I succeeded in getting one of the Burmese to tie a tourniquet around my wrist. They led me into a small bamboo building and let me lie on a table, after I gave myself a shot of morphine from my survival vest, Joe Levine, our Bombardier, and Marion Burke, our Navigator were brought in. They were not injured. Joe removed some sulfur powder from his survival kit and sprinkled it on my wound. He them improvised a sling for my arm, using a piece of board and a length of parachute cord. He also gave me a shot of morphine.

A short time later, several Japanese soldiers arrived and took us into custody. We were taken by truck and by river boat to a Japanese Army post for interrogation. At regular intervals all during our journey, Joe Levine would loosen my tourniquet in an effort to avoid gangrene. Along the way we were joined by Bill Walsh, our Flight Engineer and Bob Derrington, a Pilot observer on his first mission. While others were interrogated, I was taken to some sort of field hospital, where orderlies severed my hand from the remaining piece of flesh, sewed up the stump and bandaged it. By this time (probably 10 or 12 hours after the mission), my wound looked pretty bad. They didn't even bother to wash their hands, so I knew infection was inevitable.

By now it was day break and we were loaded onto a truck and driven to the Rangoon POW Prison. After entering the gates, the five of us were lined up and a guard went down the line slapping each prisoner in the face. We were then taken to the second floor of Cell Block 5 and put into a small cell with a wooden platform to sleep on...no bedding... an empty ammunition box for a toilet, which leaked onto the concrete floor.

About every other day a medical orderly would come into the cell, undo the dirty bandage, look at my stump, shake his head and depart. Gangrene had set in. One morning he appeared and announced "Today...amputation." He then led me downstairs to the pump house, a small corrugated building where the prison well was located. There a Japanese Warrant Officer and the prison Medical Officer were waiting. I learned later he wasn't even a doctor. He spoke no English, but had no trouble communicating his contempt of me. He injected a syringe of what I assumed to be local anesthetic into my shoulder. Whatever it was, he apparently injected it into the wrong place, because instead of numbing my arm, it affected my breathing. He pinched my arm with tweezers to see if I could feel it; when I winced with pain that angered him. Tried again with the same results...he grew frustrated, slapped me in the face a few times and ordered me back to my cell. I was sure the Japs would have no more concern for me and would just let me die. Three or four days later, the little Jap orderly came into our cell and again announced, "Today...amputation" and made a cutting motion with his right hand across his left forearm. I was not overjoyed at the prospect of going through the same again, and I indicated my unwillingness. He said, "No-no, today good doctor-English doctor." We had been informed through hand signals at the cell window that there was a real doctor in the English compound. I was filled with hope at this development. Surely my prayers were being answered. We walked to the same building. Gathered inside were the Prison Commander and several of his officers, including the Warrant Officer who had botched the first attempt. There were also two British POWs: an older man in his late 50s and a younger man perhaps 30. I was shocked at their appearance. Each wore nothing but a dirty "G" string; their bodies covered with scabies and their legs were swollen with beriberi. These men had been POWs for over four years, since the fall of Burma. The older man introduced himself as Col. MacKenzie (I learned later he was a Scotsman...an admirable man who had the opportunity to be flown out of Burma with the rest of the high ranking officers when the Japanese overran Burma, but instead choose to be captured with the troops so that he could help with their medical problems.) He then explained that he was going to amputate my arm and the only anesthesia available was one syringe of Novocain. There would be a great deal of pain, but with God's help and that of his assistant, Lt. Ramsey (the younger POW, also a doctor), we'd get through it alright. He also said that there were few instruments at his disposal...nothing to cut through the bone. Therefore, he would have to sever the arm at the elbow joint. In a hospital he would have been able to cut lower on the forearm, so that I'd have the use of my elbow joint. He also pointed out that in the prison environment, there would be no post-surgical care, and that an open bone would require dressing and medication daily.

I then laid down on the iron army cot and the Japs arranged themselves on chairs in a semi-circle around the cot to watch the show. Then, after injecting the Novocain and with Ramsey holding me down, Col. MacKenzie began to cut. The amount of Novocain was indeed inadequate for this type of surgery and I cried out in pain. This seemed to irritate the Jap Warrant Officer. He left his seat and approached me with his hand raised as if to strike me, but changed his mind and cussed me out instead. Col. MacKenzie continued with the amputation and I continued to holler with every incision, and eventually my arm was severed at the elbow and stitched. The show was over and as the Japs left, my cellmates, Joe Levine and Bill Walsh, were allowed to come and help me walk back up to our cell on the second floor. Two or three days later, the little Jap orderly came in and painted my stump with mercurochrome, but no clean bandage. I worried about infection, but in spite of the unsanitary conditions, my wound began to heal. Three or four weeks later all airmen were taken out of Solitary, #5 compound, and placed in #8 compound, which was a tremendous relief for us. It afforded me the opportunity to expose my arm to sunshine, and it healed nicely.

Three or four months after this, we were liberated by the British and taken to the Army General Hospital in Calcutta by a British Hospital Ship. We were rehabilitated and sent home to the States. Col. MacKenzie had done such a good job, that I never needed any further surgery.

Our lives are ours again. . . .

Richard Montmery married Margaret Bruder in July 1945. They had one son and three daughters. He was discharged in January 1946. He was permitted to re-enlist in November 1946 with a medical waiver and remained in the Air Force until retirement in June 1972. He served a total of 30 years and obtained the rank of Chief Master Sergeant. In retirement, he operated a one-man clock repair shop.

This narrative was obtained through "Circumstances of Capture and Liberation" report sent to Harry Chagnon, the 40th Bomb Group Historian by Richard Montgomery.

Richard Brooks "TRUNK"

Ted Freeman, Unit: 2nd Battalion The Kings Own Yorkshire Light Infantry

Served: Burma (captured) Rangoon Jail

Here is my story of the event just as it happened.

I mention the following because it is really the beginning; I was stationed in Maymyo, a Hill Station above Mandalay in peace-time Burma in March 1941 after being conscripted in 1940. Before being captured I had already travelled much of the country from Mandalay to Toungoo, Nyaunglebin, Pegu and also from Mandalay down the west road to Yenaungyyaung which is east and west of Pegu Yoma, a small mountain range. Naturally, I didn't think of the ominous consequence Yenaungyaung held for me. The reason I did so much travelling was because I was the driver for a Brigadier with his staff car and this was ultimately the reason for my capture. I used time to immobilize the car. The order had already been given unbeknown to me, for "every man for himself," but I was the last to be told, in fact, I was left waiting for the Staff Captain to return and collect money and documents from the car. I delayed a little- a little too long. Meanwhile, British and Indian troops crossed the YinChaung, a tributary that flows into the Irrawaddy. This was where the Japanese troops were waiting, on horseback in the water with their swords and rifles, for stragglers trying to cross the Chaung.

I had traveled in a truck with Rajputs for a while, solely on my own. During the retreat from Burma in April 1942, I along with 6 others were travelling in a truck towards Yenang-Yaung oil fields when we ran into a mortar attack and the truck stopped- it was the only one moving. There were many, many other trucks nose to tail caught up in this road block, under mortar attack. That is the way things happened in 1942. We scrambled off the truck and dived underneath it as mortars fell. Two men were seriously wounded. I suffered four shrapnel wounds. We scrambled over and under some barbed wire surrounding some fields but were eventually captured by the Japanese. We were locked up in an empty house along with some others, plus the wounded men, for two days without food or water. The seriously wounded men were a Signal

Sgt from the Glosters whom I knew well as he was attached to No 1 brigade HQ. The other was KOYLI. The two men were eventually shot, being unable to stand to face the march we all had to do. It could so easily have been me. Three others were unaccounted for and another Sergeant and myself were the only two survivors. I made signs to the Japanese that there was a wounded man by the roadside- could I bring him in- and he nodded and I managed to do this. We also met some other men, about 25 of them- Inniskillins and Cameronians who had also been captured and we were all kept in the empty house. After two days we were ordered to take off our boots- the laces being used to tie our hands.

There were only two battalions of British troops in Burma in the beginning and only four aircraft Gloster Gladiators- and they were at Magwe, so this gives an idea of the state of unpreparedness we were in. We marched off 4 abreast down a stony track to Yenang-Yaung village, hopping and scrambling in our bare feet, to another empty house where we were kept for another two days, still without food. There were also 2 more men in this house who were near to dying. Finally, we were taken to Rangoon jail after being locked up in Magwe jail overnight. In the jail, we met more men who had earlier been captured. They were from the West Yorkshire regiment. A number of them had been physically beaten into submission to conform to Japanese orders and so the remainder of us followed suit- we had to. The beatings and humiliation of us all continued for two years on and off, so you can imagine our state of mind after three years. We learned orders "parrot fashion" in Japanese, but the language was a great problem. There were notices placed around to the effect that anyone raising his hand, for whatever reason, against a Japanese soldier would be shot. There was a man with me in my little party who was crucified upside down before my eyes and left for several hours in the hot sun, simply because he did not bow to a patrolling guard, and there were two men shot in cold blood. Just two examples of the cruelty of the Japanese.

One month after being taken prisoner, whilst still in a fit condition, I was taken with 23 others to another part of the prison to become a guinea pig for Japanese doctors. We were subjected to 3 injections of

Dengue fever, blood tests and temperature checks. These experiments lasted for a period of 4 weeks. Two men died later but the cause was unknown. The men in the experiments were from West Yorkshires, the Inniskillins, Cameronians and the Glosters. I was the only KOYLI at that time in prison.

The food in prison consisted of rice and dahl (split peas), later to improve to rice and watery vegetable stew. This was our staple for three years and I worked it out at over 3,000 meals of rice for each man. Incidentally, the food we were given during our guinea pigs stage was rice and jagri lumps (a form of solidified sugar), but day in day out, year in and year out, the food was the same-streamed rice with a few vegetables. Hard labor, short on food, short on clothing, no material things such as string, paper, nails or even forks, simple basic things, anything at all- anything except what we were able to obtain ourselves, but gradually books began to appear due to our own efforts in stealing and thieving. Water we had to obtain from a well. Later due to bombing raids the electricity and water supply broke down so we carried on in pitch darkness after 9 p.m. for two and a half years.

After two and a half years, the Japanese decided to pay us for our labor. 1 rupee per month due to the "Spirit of Bushido" – a Japanese mythical spirit- a sentiment similar to our own self consciousness to do things right. This money all went into a main fund and we were able to buy cheroots and then share them-about one per week each. And we broke them into little pieces and packed them into bits of paper-any sort of paper, which we rolled into tubes and stuck down rice to make rough cigarettes.

We used to sleep on three planks of wood which were supported by two blocks of wood, but there was no bedding at all of any description until later when we were given washed hessian rice bags and a few blankets which were full of holes. Later on more KOYLIs arrived having been captured earlier at Moulmein, and I had to go with them. We slept on the wooden floor and that was how things remained until the very last; just sleep and work and be ready to jump if a Jap appeared.

The days didn't vary much. It was work all day, supper at 8 or 9 p.m. Food didn't vary either. It was always the same-sweepings up of rice with maggots and mouse droppings; rice for breakfast and dinner; and rice with watery vegetable stew for supper.

After six months in the prison, the officers who were captured in early 1942 were released from solitary confinement. There were about 16 of them, including three doctors, two of whom among other things, eventually successfully amputated a leg of each of two prisoners, without any anesthetic. They also attended to all kinds of other illnesses-jungle sores, cholera, dysentery, beriberi, etc. as best they could with no medicines of any sort. Lice infected everybody about this time, but we eventually overcame that problem.

Finally, after enduring the rigours of three years of Japanese prisoner of war life, the Commandant ordered 200 men, fit and not so fit, to get ready for a march on 29th April-that was the fateful date when the Japanese began to evacuate Rangoon, a process which was to continue for a week or more. I had just completed my third year as a prisoner of war and during the early part of my captivity I used to lie awake at night thinking of how I would try to escape if a certain situation arose. This situation did arise on 29th April-very similar to the one I had so often thought about.

Before commenting on events, just a few more words on life as a prisoner. Generally speaking it was very rough indeed-degradation, illness and death for some and not a scrap of any material thing whatsoever, the only thing we owned was our skin. We had tropical sun, flies and hard labor. Rice was our food, cooked the best way we knew how-which was a failure every time in the early weeks. Later on we became perfect-myself included-cooking rice for 200 men three times a day in near naked conditions. There were no such things as plates, we used corrugated iron cut and hammered into shape with a large stone, very primitive indeed, and my first meal in four days was a rice ball eaten off a banana leaf. We used tin cans for water etc but later on we were given mess tins.

Work was hard, mostly digging always with the sun beating down, but the main thing was to try and keep well. Where there is life there was hope, though faint, was still always there. For many choosing life with hope was a bet against sickness and death as their companions. It would have been better for some to have died quickly rather than suffer their illnesses.

Towards the end of 1944 prison life became easier (but up to then it was quite terrible), no doubt because of organization by the Japanese, British and ourselves. Even so, we had become well organized before then, under the circumstances, with bits of the basic material things of life taken from places where we worked. But 1942, 1943 and 1944 were grim years indeed.

The Japanese occupied all the land up to India and escape was totally impossible. During the latter part of 1944 we heard from local Burmese of the British advance into Burma, but we got very little news of any sort except Japanese propaganda. Not a word about Europe. The British attack in Burma was over some of the world's worst terrain- mountains and formidable rivers, jungle and swamp- all of which were 800 miles from us. Eventually, one million men and arms gained the upper hand against 11 Japanese Divisions and the tide was turned, which brought our men, after having made gigantic efforts, with substantial loss of life, towards the Plains of Burma, south from Mytchina and Mandalay.

Time and work went on unceasingly, until on 29th April we set off on this march, most of us unshod, some half-dressed in various rags of clothing. I wore a Dutch army jacket and Rangoon fire service denims which had been given me by a fireman at Rangoon Fire Station. I was well clothed in comparison to some of the others, but always you had to look after yourself. A motley crowd we looked to the local people who saw us go- 200 raggle taggle British flanked by Jap guards. Most of the men were barefoot but we had been so long like that it made little difference, I was lucky, I had boots which I treasured and they were given to me by someone who knew he would not have need of them where he was going. I could still nevertheless, like all the others, have managed without them.

Behind us was the prison with its ugly high walls and rows and rows of two-tiered long buildings which had been our place of incarceration for 3 years. I didn't look back. Incidentally, the place was hit eleven times by the RAF and American bombers, killing British and Japanese alike whilst we were there, and we had to rebuild the thick walls which were demolished in the raids. We only had a vague idea of our destination but my mind was made up. I was not going to be taken across the Sittang River if we were intended to go to another camp out of the bottleneck of Rangoon (The Sittang River was where a company of KOYLs were left on the wrong side of the river after an officer had ordered the bridge to be blown up and they ended up in the Rangoon jail with us).

The going wasn't hard and we took turns at hauling the handcarts loaded with Japanese belongings and any bits of our own piled on top. We were never told the reason for this march by our captors, and I assumed afterwards that we were to be used as hostages if things became too difficult for the Japanese in their retreat, bearing in mind the important thing that Rangoon is situated at the tip of a Peninsular, and to have hope of getting out they must travel 40 miles to the main north/south road to Pegu- an important junction. Also, I found out later, there were 30,000 Japanese troops north of Rangoon between Nyaunglebin and Toungoo trying to join the main body across the Sittang River.

We plodded on our way quite cheerfully in the hot sun enjoying the tropical scene -it was a welcome change from the harshness of the prison. The march began at 9 a.m. and was uneventful until late afternoon when we were spotted by an RAF reconnaissance plane- air activity had greatly increased- and sure enough RAF Strikers followed later with some light bombing- they obviously thought we were a Jap column of some sort. Orders came for everyone and everything to take cover in the ample foliage of the semi-jungle which came down the roadside. Guards and prisoners worked hard to get everything under cover. We certainly did not want to get shot up by the RAF now.

Further raids followed, but by now the day was wearing on. I decided to have a look around our immediate countryside to see what the chances might be, and at the right moment I slipped away. I travelled a short distance through the undergrowth, tingling with excitement. Then I saw one of our men lying in a hollow in the ground terrified of the air strikes, so I jumped in with him. He was calling out hysterically "I'm not staying here" and asked if I would "go with him." Another plane came and, although its bombs fell wide, upset this man even more. In a flash, I made up my mind.

It was dusk now and I made my way back to the column and told my immediate friends that I was going that night, before the march began again. So, in full view, I rifled the Japanese baggage for what I could lay my hands on and managed to get several packets of Japanese cigarettes. I didn't know for sure what they could be used for. Then I paused for awhile and looked at the faces of the men I had seen and slaved with for three years. They were looking at me probably working out what my chances would be. Some men said "good luck." They probably thought that there would be plenty of Japanese in the hinterland making their retreat- they were right too, we had passed several small groups on our march out. Then a voice called out "Can I come with you Ted?" It was a friend with whom I had worked a great deal. I was glad as I knew him to be reliable and one of the best- he was one of the original soldiers captured earlier at Moulmein in 1942. My original plan was to go alone.

I said "all right, but go and get some more cigarettes." Another pause whilst this took place- the guards could not see everybody- then we were ready to go. The men were looking all the time and wondering. Then two more men, very good men too, were prepared to take their chance in an escape bid and asked me if they could come as well. Once again the comedy of stealing cigarettes (but comedy it was not) was secretly carried out, though each man had to take the risk of getting them himself; it was not for me to be the only man to do it. In the prison camp, one gets to know who are reliable and who are not. These three men were reliable and that made three KOYLIs of which I was one, and one Cameronian.

It was quite dark now and we slid away separately into the undergrowth, to meet again further in as arranged, well away from our guards and fellow prisoners, picking up the man hiding in the hollow on the way. The men said later that they were surprised I took him. We lay low in the heavily wooded countryside within earshot of the column. Eventually we heard shouts and knew they were ready to continue, we just made it! The shouts could have been our names, we couldn't tell and no one came looking for us. Soon we were alone- but free. It was a good feeling, even if apprehensive.

The night was dark, but there was enough moonlight for us to be able to see and we had only gone a little way when we heard a whistle nearby. An RAF sergeant appeared. He too had been in the column but he had not long been a prisoner, nor browbeaten as we had been for three years; just a few weeks. Could he come with us he asked. That made six. I asked him if he could tell us which the North Star was, he did so and I decided we would go in the opposite direction back towards Rangoon, but not by the road that we had marched up 12 hours earlier. We gave the road a good look over from the trees and crossed over carefully and quietly and began our walk into- we did not know what. With three years of Japanese prisoner of war life behind (at least for us) we were very careful indeed. We didn't want to bungle things now. Despite our anxiety I was thrilled. Freedom of a fashion. But, had we jumped out of the frying pan into the fire?

We made our way through semi-jungle, and then we skirted a small plantation until we were brought to a halt by reaching a small river. We turned and followed the river, using a little track by the side. The night was very dark now. Soon we reached a village and dogs began barking so we stopped and looked carefully in that direction. We didn't know what to expect. After a little while, after looking carefully over the place, I suggested that the five of us who could speak some Japanese words would go boldly through talking loudly in Japanese, to give the impression to the villagers that we were Japanese soldiers passing through. This we did with grim humor, and we carried on. We were to learn later from the Headman of the village that we were taken for a Japanese patrol. Through the village and on. Very soon it would be daybreak and then we could look around, but Rangoon was our target and that was about twenty miles away.

As first light appeared we could see we were in flat country. One of our party decided to try to get himself a drink of water, so he climbed down the embankment to get one. He stepped into the river, right up to his thighs in mud. That was an anxious moment, but with help from his friend he managed to get back on firm ground. No water-but much wiser. During this episode a long canoe came into view with several villagers on it calling across in Burmese not to drink the water, so within a short while, people in front and behind us would know there were six nondescript Britishers in the vicinity. However, events were "so far so good."

Later, while we were resting by the river, a lone villager passed us without saying a word. None of us could speak Burmese, but he must have had the shock of his life. He must have reported our presence because later, another villager came out to us to go back with him to the village, the one we had passed through in the night. We did, and were told how very dangerous it was as Japanese groups were continually passing through. We were told this by the Headman who was called Ma-e-tin and his wife was called Ko-ni. Quick explanations followed and he said he would give us food and drink and shelter but it was very dangerous for us, and for him. We understood.

We were kept for nine days in this village in a Basha (a bamboo bungalow on stilts), which was a meeting room for the village and it is the same all over the country. Night approached and inside the room it was pitch, pitch dark, so dark we were unable to see each other, but there was a small window space cut out of the wall to let night air in. It was a vantage point for escape if necessary. During the night we could feel the silence, black and heavy.

We heard a Japanese patrol enter and leave the village. They were very near our hiding place-actually underneath it- we listened to their voices. We were very scared, it is no use denying it, but eventually they moved off and the same thing happened again the next night. We were all prepared to go through the opening in the wooden wall if we had to. This was simply a desperate thought in a desperate situation- the window was twelve feet above the ground but someone had found a rope.

In the inky blackness inside, each had his own thoughts and mine went to saying the Rosary. I had managed to get them while working in a building somewhere in Rangoon. Good fortune stayed with us again that night, and once more we thankfully listened to their departing footsteps. These troops were on the run and making their way in the same direction as we had been when we moved up the road, their intention apparently was to cross the Sittang and Salween Rivers and on to Malaya or Thailand.

We were still not out of the woods. Six more days and night we were to stay in the village and we were not allowed outside the building, so we were still not free. The days were hot and dry and the nights pitch black and there was very little we could do, and the little Burmese lady, Ko-ni kept bringing us rice and vegetables to eat. They were taking a risk by harboring us.

One morning, very early, we were roused and told to run to a chicken hut across the paddy fields. A young boy showed us the way and then left us. We ran across the dry soil and unto a hut, and that is where we stayed, with chickens, for several hours until mid-morning. I remember standing there on the floor in the gloom, when several of us shouted out in chorus. We were being bitten by huge red ants on our bare feet. We shook them off and tried sitting on shelves or chicken roosts or anything where our feet were off the floor and trying to be quiet at the same time. We held our breath and ticked off the minutes, waiting for the boy to return to tell us it was safe to return to the village. When we got back, we told our hosts that we wanted to go back to Rangoon, but we were still forced to remain there. Perhaps they were negotiating with a village further away in our direction to take us, and we found out afterwards that this is what they had been doing. These were dangerous times for anyone harboring Britishers.

Twice more the race to the chicken hut took place and twice more we spent the night there, until the boy came to tell us it was safe to return. There must have been lookouts. One time was a false alarm but three nights in the hut was something to experience.

We had been nine days in the village-its name was Thandin- and events were moving very fast although we knew nothing. We asked Headman to be allowed to go and he finally agreed-he was probably relieved to see us go. He asked us all to sign our names so he could give them to the Army when they came. We did this and made our grateful thanks and set off- this time with a guide.

Along the river bank we went, feeling good and in high spirits and crossed over to the other side via a foot bridge into another village where there were quite a number of Burmese villagers about, some with rifles, and it must have been a big surprise for them to see six ragged Britishers, the first that had seen for several years. They probably knew of our presence and the reason for being there as no doubt their neighbors in the other village would have told them, and also the ones in the canoe. We gave them the remainder of our cigarettes and it made our presence easier as we moved off they called something after us in Burmese, but we didn't answer them. We had previously given some of our cigarettes to the friends in the first village and we also gave some to our guide. So the cigarettes came in handy after all.

Soon after passing through the second village our guide said he would have to leave us. He pointed out to us the railway line which was a little further on and would take us back to Rangoon 20 miles away. We thanked him very much and continued on and then we walked toward the railway line, climbed the embankment and over the rails and down the other side. A wonderful feeling of exhilaration filled us. After three years we finally were on our last lap to freedom.

We walked fast, through the morning and into the afternoon. The hot sun blazed down on us and we talked occasionally and joked a little. We were very keen on getting back to Rangoon where we hoped to meet the 14th Army. We reasoned that all the Japanese would have left the city and as mentioned before, events were moving very fast, of which we didn't have any knowledge whatsoever. Back in the prison we had heard via local Burmese, whilst we were working outside that Mandalay had fallen to the British and Indian troops. Mandalay was 400 miles away and that was a long way indeed, but the Emperor's army was in retreat and the British and Indian soldiers moved very fast after Mandalay as we were soon to find out.

Towards mid-afternoon, still walking very quickly, we passed Indian soldiers dug in, in their forward positions. They must have had us in their sights for quite some time as we were the only moving objects for miles. They greeted us with welcome smiles, but what a sight we must have looked. We laughed and waved back and kept on walking until met by an astounded British officer who couldn't believe his eyes at seeing us. He took us to the Field Officer in charge who showed great surprise also. We were warmly welcomed and after telling our story rum was handed all around. They asked us if there were any Japanese around. We said no, not at least as far as the last two villages were concerned. The date was 8th May 1945, 10 days after we left Rangoon. The officer asked us if we knew the date. We replied "no" and they told us it was VE Day but we knew nothing of what had been happening in the world apart from bits we heard whilst working in the City.

We were later given clean field uniforms and then we burnt the clothes we had worn for so long. We were finally free and the war was over for us (but not in other parts of the Far East- there would be another three months of hostilities)-we were new men- and free.

Soon after, we went aboard transport planes in twos and we flew off from a makeshift air strip. I was the last to go- I was no longer in a hurry-and so our journey to India and England. Looking down from the plane I could see rich green of the Burmese jungle and the parched dry earth of the paddy fields. It was my last view of Burma where I had spent the last 4 years and 9 months. I couldn't help but think how my circumstances had changed.

I flew to Chittagong via Akyab then to Madras, Poona, and Karachi, then to somewhere in the Middle East- I could tell by the smell of camels- landing at night time and departing early in the morning. Then to Palestine, Cyprus and somewhere in France and then Sussex in England. We must have been given some preferential treatment because everything was done so quickly and efficiently. All the flying was done by transport planes.

I was indeed, finally free.

This narrative was obtained through www.pegasusarchive.org/pow/ted-freeman.htm

G. M. Etherington, (Bud), 1ˢᵗLieutenant, 20ᵗʰ Air Force/ Engineer, B-29, 20ᵗʰBomber Command, 40ᵗʰ Bomb Group, 45ᵗʰ Squadron.
Home City: Birmingham. Home State: Alabama.
Dates of Imprisonment: 12/07/44 thru 05/07/45.

On December 14, 1944, eleven planes from the 40ᵗʰ Bomb Group made two passes over the target in Bangkok but we were unable to get a visual sighting because of cloud cover. We then proceeded to Rangoon to bomb the rail yards. The weather cleared as we approached Rangoon. Apparently we had taken the Japanese by surprise as there was no defensive action. Seconds after bombs away there was a tremendous explosion, we were hit and hit bad.

Under protest we were carrying a mixed load of 1000 pound and 500 pound bombs. (Bombs from our formation, which we later learned damaged every plane in the formation.) Four planes were lost.

The exact events of the next several minutes are not clear in my mind. I guess all four engines had been hit. Two engines were on fire- #3 and one other. My first concern was to get these fires out which fortunately I was able to do. One of the other two was running so rough that we decided to feather it. The gunners reported there was a big hole in the right wing and the control surfaces were badly damaged. Bob and Fletch had a lot of trouble flying but managed to control it. There were several holes in the plane, but miraculously nobody was seriously hurt. I had a scratch on my left arm and Julian Cochran had a small piece of metal in the sole of his shoe and a small wound on his leg. His parachute had been shredded, and he went through the tunnel to get a spare chute which just happened to be in the back.

We were heading west, hoping to make the Burma coast. If we would be able to ditch in the Bay of Bengal, we stood a good chance of being picked up by air-sea rescue. We were losing altitude so we restarted the engine that had been so rough; #3 and #4 were still out. We began to throw out everything we could to lighten the plane. Benny caught his chest pack on something, and the pilot chute started to pop out. Somewhere in this time period I seem to remember that we all said the Lord's Prayer together over the intercom. We had to feather #1 again, leaving only #2 running.

We managed to fly 15 or 20 minutes after being hit and were somewhere over the delta of the Irrawaddy River at about 6,000 feet with a higher mountain range ahead of us when #2 engine started to burn. I don't remember who was the first one out of the front of the plane, but I knew I had to help Benny get out with his partially popped-open chute. I switched on the autopilot to give the pilots a better chance to get out and told Bob and Fletch to come right behind me. Then I jumped and pulled the rip-cord. There was quite a jolt as the chute opened- but it sure looked good to me. Several chutes were open in the direction we had come from. After what seemed like a long time, two more chutes opened. Soon the plane turned to the left and started toward me, with #2 engine now burning fiercely. It turned again to the left, losing altitude, and as it was flying away from me, crashed and burned.

Arnie Basche and I were probably less than fifty yards apart when we landed in a field near a small Burmese village. As we were descending in our parachutes, we heard a gong being rung in the village. The men from the village came streaming out armed with old rifles and long rice knives and had us practically surrounded by the time we hit the ground. We had a few pieces of personal papers which we managed to bury as the group closed the ring around us.

These people were not really hostile to us, and they took us into their village. The village consisted of a number of mud and thatch huts, for the most part surrounding a cleared central area. They put us into one of these huts. No one in this village spoke English, but within a couple of hours they had gotten someone from another village who spoke a bit of English and served as interpreter.

In the meantime they had brought us some food. The thing I remember was some huge eggs- perhaps goose eggs. I told Arnie that he better eat something because there was no telling when we might get to eat again. We were trying to negotiate for a boat; if we could get down the river and out to the coast, we might stand a pretty good chance of being picked up by air-sea rescue.

By mid-afternoon Hank was with us, and the village people had a boat lined up. They had taken our parachutes and a few pieces of debris from the plane and put them in the boat. We went from the center of the village a few hundred yards down a jungle path to their boat landing. The whole village went with us. We were anxious to get going but we were told that we must wait until dark and that we must now go back to the village. I sensed something wrong but had no idea what it was. Reluctantly we started back toward the village. I was leading the procession, beside the village head man and the interpreter, with the enlisted men right behind me. As we made a turn on the path to the central clearing of the village, the three of us- Basche, Pisterzi and I- were suddenly alone. Across the clearing we were facing a Burmese Warrant Officer and two soldiers with rifles leveled at us. We had been captured. The Warrant Officer (W/O), who had at one time been with the British army but had changed loyalty as the fortunes of war shifted, informed me, "This is your lucky day. For you the war is over." I had trouble believing that for some time.

We walked for two or three miles under the surveillance of the two guards and the W/O to another small village. On the way we went through some knee deep muddy water and the two packs of cigarettes in the shin pockets of my pants became casualties of war. From that village we were taken by motor launch to a larger village several miles away. The W/O was pleased as he took the shells from my GI .45 pistol, because he figured he would have some new ammo for his revolver. However, the cartridges fell right trough the cylinder and the barrel of his revolver. This dismayed him. I knew when I had been looking down the barrel of that revolver as we were captured, that it was the largest caliber pistol I had ever seen.

It was after dark when we arrived at a larger village. We docked at a restaurant/store/warehouse type of structure. Here the W/O ceremoniously turned us over to the Japanese. Lenz had joined us either at the previous village or this one; I don't remember which. We were taken again by boat to what seemed to be a small Japanese Army outpost and were put under guard, in an out-building where we spent the night.

The next day was the first of numerous interrogations. Sometime in the early afternoon a guard came and took me to another building. I was to stand at attention in front of a table where a Japanese Lieutenant was seated. Behind me was the guard with his bayonet touching my back. The lieutenant had on the table various items taken from us which he wanted me to identify. He had a Japanese-English dictionary and had to look up nearly every word, as he really spoke almost no English. One item he wanted to identify was the silk escape map that we carried. His small dictionary used the word "chart." In an effort to be as uncooperative as possible, I insisted that it was a map. He could not find the word "map" and was quite frustrated. I had a small wallet of pictures of my wife that I had always carried with me in a shirt packet. These had been taken from me, and he wanted to keep them. Thinking I didn't have much to lose, I raised a big fuss about this. To my surprise, he gave them back to me, keeping only one or two pictures. I managed to keep these through the rest of the internment and still have them today. I believe that one or two of the gunners were also interrogated, but I do not remember if they all were. That evening we went by boat to another village; I believe it was there we met Cocky and Nick and maybe other members of our crew. What I'll call a motorized rice barge took us somewhere else along the river. I remember being almost in the bilge and I thought I was going to be eaten alive by rice weevils.

By the third or fourth day, all of our crew were together again. Fletch had sprained his ankle when he landed and had trouble walking for a couple of days. At each place where we had a new set of captors we were interrogated again. It seemed that the closer we got to civilization, the better informed, and apparently more intelligent, the captors were. As a generality, you had to give some kind of answer to the questions or get punished, but the answer could often be the biggest lie you could fabricate. Once we were being questioned by a Japanese officer in something like a public square of some little village. Someone (maybe Ferrell Majors) was beaten because he didn't answer something quickly enough.

After some point, we stayed with the same group of three or four guards who took us from one place to another en route to Rangoon. We moved by various means of transportation—boat, train, truck, and walking. These guards treated us reasonably well and saw to it that we were fed every day. We usually traveled at night because we learned; there was much greater danger of being attacked by Allied aircraft during the day. We had not realized that the Japanese Air Force in Burma was, at this point, so weak, as to be almost non-existent. We later learned that the entire Japanese military effort in Burma was in serious trouble from lack of supplies, and their armies in the North had been ravaged by disease and malnutrition. It was said that everything that moved in Burma during the day got shot up, and I guess there was some truth to it.

I don't remember the exact sequence in which the next several things occurred, but I will remember each of them. One day we spent in a little village in a jungle or forest. There was a large pavilion-like structure with a large Buddha. This temple was our place of internment for the day. The village people prepared food for us during the day. Before we left, the village head man got permission from the guards to give us some cigars. I don't remember just how it was expressed, but we left that village knowing that those people would have liked to do more to help us but could not. The Japanese domination over Burma was very strong.

One day or longer we spent in a building like a chicken coop, made of Bamboo with a thatched roof. This seemed to be some kind of military headquarters area, and here we were given one of the more thorough interrogations. The interrogating officers spoke pretty fair English and had an intelligence book written in both Japanese and English which among other things, seemed to contain answers to all questions they asked about the 45th Bomb Squadron. They had identified us, probably by tail markings. As they asked questions, they had the book open, and I could read many correct answers. I remember seeing in the book that we were based in Chakulia and that Oscar Schaaf was our Squadron CO.

You could lie about some things though, for example, I had only been in India for a few days before the mission, or was this my first mission, or I've never been to China. I didn't mind giving them information I knew they already had, and it made life easier to be able to give them answers to some things without too much hemming and hawing. One night we were in a rather large house, and Cocky and I helped with the cooking chores that evening. Another night we were taken to a train station and waited several hours for a train. We slept for a while on the station platform before the train came. One of the guards was trying to make a phone call- we thought to his superiors. The communication system was so bad that he must have been on the phone for a couple of hours before he got his call through.

The train had some long baggage racks over the seats, and as I recall it, Benny and I slept up there for part of the night. It was a bright moonlight night, and at one point the train stopped for quite a while, probably because of Allied planes in the area. We were on a bridge that had been shot up and some of the smaller trusses appeared to be temporarily repaired with something like bailing wire. It was very uncomfortable being such a good target; on a train, on a bridge, in the bright moonlight. I didn't much care for that train ride.

The last stop before Rangoon was a place where we stayed in what we called a bear cage; one side had bars from floor to ceiling; the other sides were solid walls. We were there maybe a day and a half. One afternoon they has us all out working-cutting and hauling bamboo. We were always closely guarded. At this place a Japanese Captain and a Major, both of whom spoke rather good English, interrogated Benny and me together and they were after different information than we had been asked before. They asked how many B-29s were being made each month; of course, we didn't know and told them so. They said that was all right but we must guess. We hemmed and hawed for awhile and finally told them that the U.S. was probably making about 3,000 B-29s a month. We knew that this was preposterous, but it had the desired effect of really concerning them. Then they asked how many B-29s there were in the U.S. Again the same routine. We don't know, all right; you must guess. Having told one whopper, we figured we should be consistent, so be said probably about 30,000. Now we had them really upset, so they sent us back to our bear cage.

The next morning we were taken by truck to Rangoon. For a number of miles along the side of the road was a pipe several feet in diameter which was at least part of the water supply for the city of Rangoon. Part of it seemed to be constructed of wood, held together with steel bands. Periodically we would pass an area where the pipe had been strafed, and jets of water were spraying many feet into the air. In many place efforts had been made to patch the holes.

Our first destination in Rangoon was Judson College, which was serving as Headquarters of the Japanese Air Force in Burma. The Headquarters was adjacent to, or part of, a hospital area plainly marked with red crosses. Here we were interrogated by a Japanese officer who had a degree in aeronautical engineering from a West Coast college. He asked me about engine performance and some other questions that I didn't understand. He finally produced a copy of Air Force Magazine which was far newer than any we had seen. In this magazine was a write-up of the new development he had been asking us about of which we knew nothing. My recollection is that we were taken by truck to Rangoon Central Prison that evening. We arrived there on Christmas Day, 1944, and remained for several months.

OUR LIVES ARE OURS AGAIN . . . . .

Bud Etherington married Margo Beck from Normanna, Texas in 1944 in the Base Chapel. After discharge, he earned a Master's Degree in Metallurgy from Massachusetts Institute of Technology. He had one son, one daughter and three grandchildren. He worked primarily in the Foundry Industry particularly in the areas of research and management. He was the recipient of the American Foundrymen's Society Award of Scientific Merit 1976. He retired in January 1985 and resided in Birmingham, Alabama. He continued as a part time consultant within the industry.

This narrative was obtained through the "40ᵗʰ Bomb Group Association,"Memories" Issue #6 and the 40ᵗʰ Bombardment Group History /Turner Publishing Co.

Julian Cochran (Rank Not Available), 20ᵗʰ Air Force/Navigator, B-29, 20ᵗʰ Bomber Command, 40ᵗʰ Bomb Group, 25ᵗʰ Squadron.

Home City: Not Available. Home State: Not Available.

Dates of Imprisonment: 12/14/44 thru 05/04/45.

I have no memory of ack-ack on this mission. The explosion beneath us was of gigantic proportions. I immediately felt something hit my right ankle on the inside about one inch above the top of my GI shoes. My left shoe had a hunk of sole knocked out just in front of the arch. A small piece of metal, probably skin of the plane, was just under my skin. It bled a little and did not hurt. I picked up my chest chute from the floor and found it blossomed out in white. The whole bottom was shredded. I announced on the intercom that my chute was ruined, and Nick came on to say there was an extra chute in the radar room. I immediately flew thru the tunnel to get it, and when I got back up front, I was out of air and quickly hooked on the oxygen at the front of the tunnel. I was of course immediately aware that the plane was badly damaged but paid little attention to it until my personal problem was fixed. I am not sure what each engine was doing. I think that #3 was dead and #4 dead or mostly so; #2 was possibly the best. It seems to me there were one or two fires on the right side. Bob asked me for a heading, and I gave him one for the ditching island west of Rangoon. I remember grabbing the wrong map once.

Bob and Fletch couldn't hold the plane level. The right wing would fall; they would bring it back up, and then the left wing would fall. This happened two or three times. I knew if we fell off into a steep dive we'd never get out. While we were flying in this erratic condition, Nick crawled into the rear bomb bay and kicked out a hung-up 1000-pound bomb. I don't remember the order to bail out nor discussion as to who would go first. I know the nose wheel was lowered, and I immediately climbed down straddling the hole and standing on the handholds, pulled my legs together and dropped out. I thought I was first out, but two chutes were already open. Two of the guys in the back moved even faster than I did. I remember looking up toward the plane and pulling the cord as soon as I was clear. I never remember seeing the rip cord handle in my hand. I apparently simply pulled it and dropped it.

I landed in an irrigation ditch, in waist-deep water and up to my knees in mud. Mine was probably the softest landing of anyone. Then I observed the plane off to the west, probably at 1,000 to 2,000 feet turning slowly to the left and going down. I don't remember seeing any other chutes, but it never occurred to me that everyone might not get out. I started walking west. A large water buffalo stood up in front of me, causing me to reverse my direction. About that time several Burmese came toward me holding what appeared to be sticks about four feet long with a rather long knife affixed to the end—rice knives, I think. As I recall, they took my .45 but did not threaten me with it. (Probably they did not know what to do with it).

After dark we arrived at a shack on the river, where I met Nick and two others of the crew. I cannot remember who. Nick still had his first aid kit and put some sulfa powder on the small hole in my ankle. It never did get infected. Soon some Japs (2 or 3 of them) showed up in a motorboat and took everything personal from me. To get to Rangoon, we traveled by motorboat, large rice barge (rice bugs chewed on me), train and a truck. We also slept on a railway station platform waiting for a train. We spent a day or more in wooden cages called "bear cages." At some point we were interrogated several times by different officers. Some of the men were slapped from behind, across the side of the head when an answer was not what the officer wanted to hear.

We finally arrived at Judson Collage in Rangoon by truck. We were forced to stand up in a small building on a road leading to the college. Here we were joined by two officers of the British Army, an Aussie pilot of a Mosquito and his navigator, a New Zealander. Bill, the pilot, had a bad facial injury. They were buzzing a river when a prop hit the water.

Next day we were taken to the Rangoon city jail, which was used for POWs. We were placed in a two-story brick building, four to a cell. We found that other B-29 crew members were in the building. About half the space was taken by a wooden platform which we slept on. We had only a few pieces of burlap for so-called bedding. We stayed there for about a month; I do not remember any interrogations after arriving in Rangoon. While there, we were severely beaten by guards with a club nearly the size of a pickax handle. Two crewmen of other planes had gangrenous wounds, and one, Montgomery, had his arm amputated about four inches above the hand (it was to be amputated again at the elbow). All the B-29 crewman were moving to another building without cells: officers on the second floor, enlisted men on the first. There were about 105 men, all but one in the Air Corps.

We each had two hand-made dishes, about 6" by 8", soldered sheet metal, about 2" deep, one for tea, the other for food. Meals were wormy bran for breakfast, tea and rice for noon meal, tea and soup for evening. We had little meat, usually a small front quarter of water buffalo thrown over the wall into the dirt. A Capt. Hunt was in charge of the cook crew. At first we slept on a platform made of bamboo, full of bed bugs. Then we used that for firewood and slept on the floor. We never had enough firewood so we burned wood decorations from the long porch roof which was on one side of the building. Also a great number of heavy bracing timbers were removed from the attic area of the building. No one from our building was placed on work crews, as were other POWs from other buildings. They received extra food; they left the camp in the morning and returned each evening. We received no tobacco and had nothing at all to do except walk and talk. Once or twice, Indian POWs threw tobacco over the wall, wrapped in newspaper. We also had no toilet paper and used leaves from our one tree until they were gone.

Once a guard asked for a typist and I volunteered, hoping I'd get out to go to the office building (maybe to get something to eat). No luck- he brought the typewriter and a table and chair into the compound. I was given a stack of forms to enter POW names so each could sign saying he would not attempt to escape. I hurriedly tried to count the forms and thought there might be extra ones. I gave them to others to be used for cigarette paper. Before I finished the list of names, I ran out of forms. The guard was very very mad to say the least. I thought I was going to get the kicked out of me. He finally gave me more forms with no bodily harm.

All the time there, I had one bath at an open hydrant with a small piece of soap. About two months after we entered the camp, B-29s attacked Rangoon and severely damaged the water supply; thereafter, we had even less water, none to wash with. I grew a beard which was finally shaved off using a sharpened silver-plated table knife and a sharpened iron spike. No soap, only water.

Many had beriberi; everyone had malaria; everyone had lice to a degree. By wearing only a loin cloth, I gave them no place to hide. We all lost weight. Those weighing 180 pounds lost as much as 60. I lost only about 10, for I weighed only 128 when I went down. You were required to bow to the guards, and if you were caught not bowing, you were forced to stand at attention in the sun for hours. I think the New Zealander was caught once. There was one fighter pilot from Arkansas who had a mental problem and couldn't talk. Another POW who did not have a full deck took care of him.

We got the word that those who could walk would go by foot to another camp, we assumed to the east in Thailand or the Malay States. Those who could not walk or were too weak were left behind. We left in the afternoon carrying buckets of cooked rice, some pulling 2-wheeled carts loaded with the guard's belongings- food, cigarettes, quinine (more than we knew existed). About dark we stopped to eat, and by that time the rice had soured, but as I remember, we ate it anyway. We walked at night and slept by day, hiding from the British aircraft that shot at anything that moved. At one point I was near the end of the procession, or one segment of it, when a man fell over due to exhaustion. He was clubbed by a Jap guard. I removed myself from that area speedily and do not know if he was killed. I believed we walked 4 nights, a total of about 51 miles.

We were taken into the village of Pegu, and about dawn the guards abandoned us. A Union Jack (where it came from I have no idea) was displayed in an open field, and the letters POW were spelled out using white knee-length underpants that the Japs wore (where these came from I also have no idea). Shortly thereafter we were attacked by 3 to 5 Hurricane fighters with small bombs and machine guns. The only person killed was a British Brigadier General captured about 3 years earlier in Singapore. One or two other British soldiers were wounded. The rest of us were only scared nearly to death. That night we were led to another village where Burmese fed us the most we had eaten in over four months. Then we were led to the British lines and bedded down with the soldiers right at the front. They also fed us, including a ration of rum. There were a few American GIs manning anti-aircraft machine guns on a GI 6x6.

We were taken by a truck to a forward airfield from which Hurricane fighters were operating. While waiting for transport, we were again nearly killed when a Hurricane bellied in and the wooden prop splintered, flying too close for comfort. We spent one more night before some DC-3s arrived to take us to India.

OUR LIVES ARE OURS AGAIN.....

Julian Cochran married Leona Callahan in Little Rock, Arkansas. They had one daughter Judy and one granddaughter Katie. He was employed by the Corps of Engineers for 1½ years in Manila, Philippine Islands. As part of those duties, he was assigned to put together work parties that consisted of Japanese POWs. He was employed by Western Insurance Company, Ft. Scott Kansas for 34 years in their Claim Department as a supervisor of Illinois claims. He retired in 1982.

This narrative was obtained from the 40th Bomb Group Association "Memories" Issue #6 (1) and the 40th Bombardment Group History/ Turner Publishing Company.

Men with a home-made Union Jack, shortly after they were free
– Courtesy Pegasus Archives

**Dudley W. Hogan, Jr. /Rank N/A, 10th Air Force /Pilot, P-51,
311th Bomber Group, 307th Squadron.**

Home City: Augusta. Home State: Georgia.

Dates of Imprisonment: 11/27/43 thru 05/04/45

Five of us P-51 pilots were escorting two groups of heavy bombers when
we were jumped by 45 Jap fighters. I was hit and forced down on the
outskirts of Rangoon. There I made contact with an old Burmese and a
young boy. We stole a wooden dugout and paddled for three days in an
attempt to reach the less densely populated areas where capture would
be less likely. Our strength gave out and I was turned over to Japs by
natives.

The Nips took me to the Rangoon New Laws Courts where I was
thrown into a dungeon along with a motley crew of murderers and
thieves. You see the Japanese were being especially hard on captured
airmen and they did not consider me a prisoner of war but rather as
a war criminal. The conditions were horrible and everything you read
about Japanese cruelty is true. Some things they do are unprintable.

After spending eight months in the jail dungeon, the military prisoners
were moved to the Central Rangoon Prison where we were put into
solitary confinement which consisted of two floors of small cells. One of
the prisoners was being clobbered with a club wielded by a Nip guard.
This man was murdered because he picked a cigarette butt off the floor.
You see we were forbidden to have tobacco and the Japs had their own
way of enforcing this rule. It was bad. It was something a man must
erase from his mind. We were allowed no change of clothing and our
latrine facilities consisted of an empty ammunition box in the corner
of our cell.

I was truly a man raised from the dead. I was captured on November
27, 1943 and was listed as missing for the first 12 months of my capture.
The Japs didn't bother to notify the War Department of my capture.
At the end of one year, I was marked as "deceased." My insurance was
paid to by beneficiary.

When those prison gates were opened by the British it was like being reborn.

OUR LIVES ARE OURS AGAIN . . . . .

Dudley Hogan came home to practice Law.

This narration was obtained through "Circumstances of Capture and Liberation" report sent to Harry Chagnon, the 40ᵗʰ Bomb Group Historian by Dudley Hogan.

<u>**Richard Brooks "TRUNK"**</u>

Denis Gavin, Sargeant, Infantry.

Home: New Zealand.

Dates of Imprisonment: May 1942 thru May 1945

Captured at Moulmein in Southern Burma. Imprisoned in Rangoon for almost three years. Was on the march from Rangoon Prison to Pegu in the north. Left column and hid in jungle and finally contacted British troops approximately two weeks later. Then repatriated to United Kingdom via Chittagong and Segunderbad. Trip took almost three months.

This narrative was obtained through "Circumstances of Capture and Liberation" report sent to Harry Chagnon, the 40th Bomb Group Historian by Denis Gavin.

Douglas G. Gilbert, Colonel, 112 Infantry, Chinese Division.
Home City: Warrenton. Home State: Virginia.
Dates of Imprisonment: 11/23/43 thru 4/19/45

In late November 1943, I was assigned as liaison officer to the 112th Infantry Regiment of the Chinese Division, then operating against the Japanese in the Hongquong Valley…about sixty miles south of the American liaison headquarters under General Boatner at Ledo, Assam, India.

On November 22, I returned to the forward C.P. after two or three days at the supply headquarters seven miles to the rear, contacting General Boatner's headquarters. The moment I arrived at the C.P. heavy firing continued throughout the night, during which a soldier inside the dugout got excited by the firing and fired his rifle killing their guard at the entrance. I could not communicate with the Chinese and in the jungle anything that moves draws fire so I stayed put. At dawn we were made prisoners.

I was kept in the C.P. area for several days as the Chinese attempted to retake the area, during which time I had a physically rough interrogation and served as a trussed up parapet for a soldier's fox hole. Fortunately, we were in a depression so the bullets flew overhead. After a few days I was evacuated by train south to Maymo where I joined Jean Lutz, Chris Morgan, Bow Bowman, Bill Flynn, and Charlie Montagna. Chris was critically ill but after urging, the Japanese let us take him with us on a stretcher on our evacuation to Rangoon by truck.

On April 1945, the Japanese marched all of us who were fit enough, north for four nights before abandoning us as the British 14th Army drew close. That same day we were strafed by the Allied fighters but lost only Brigadier Hobson. That night, Jean Lutz made contact with the British and we were evacuated, half that night and the remainder the next day.

This narration was obtained through "Circumstances of Capture and Liberation" report sent to Harry Chagnon, the 40th Bomb Group Historian by Colonel Gilbert.

Richard Brooks "TRUNK"

Leslie Spoors, Rifleman, 1st Battalion, The Cameronians (Scottish Rifles),

17th Infantry Division, U.K.

It was in 1940- the 13th of June, a Thursday- when I received my call up papers. I got a 4-shilling postal order as well, with which I needed to buy certain odds and ends, such as shaving soap and boot polish, and a railway warrant. I had been conscripted to the 1st Battalion, Scottish Rifles- The Cameronians- and their barracks were at Hamilton Racecourse, about 180 miles away! My training lasted until 3rd January 1941 when I boarded the aptly named converted liner, the Empress of Japan, arriving in India 8 or 9 weeks later. India was to be my home until February 1942, when the troop ship Aurelia would take me to my place of "work" for the next three years and more-BURMA.

On the 21st of February 1942,we arrived at Rangoon River which was shrouded in a thick mist. They finally docked at Rangoon. Rangoon, a proud and rich city, was predictably deserted except for looters and pariah dogs. But there was no time to see it; the ship had to be unloaded. We learned we were to support the 17th Division of the Burma Army, who were fighting the Battle of Sittang River Line. So after only a couple of days in Burma, we were to see action.

The 17th Division had been withdrawing for 22 days and the tactics were to make it as difficult as possible for the Japanese to advance, by blowing up bridges and destroying oil fields and so on. Unfortunately, we couldn't cross the Sitting River before they destroyed the bridge, so this meant we were trapped on the east side of the river.

The next few days brought almost continuous fighting and moving. More men were killed and one of them was found beheaded. Orders for withdrawal were received, but we became surrounded by Japanese. Suddenly the firing stopped, and a voice shouted in broken English: "Come out, we're friends." Japanese surrounded us, and with few weapons between us, resistance was pointless. We walked out and were told to put our hands above our heads. Then we sat in a circle on the ground and were given a drink of water.

I was captured on the 19th April, having been wounded in the arm with shrapnel the day before. I was one of a group of 12 prisoners, and was the only Cameronian amongst them. We were all wounded the day before. We were all wounded-that's why we were taken so easily, and couldn't make a run for it. We were taken to a group of Burmese huts where our boots were removed and the laces used to tie our hands behind our backs. More and more men were brought in during the night until eventually we were cramped together on the floor. It was a Sunday when we were put into the huts and we were there for four days and nights. We had nothing at all to eat and nothing to drink, although we did make feeble attempts to drink our own urine. All our body wastes just collected beneath us in the huts. I thought we might never see the light of day again. But we did, after four days we were freed from the indescribable stench.

Captain Bradford-Martin had been brought into the hut during the first night, along with his Batman. On the third day, we heard rain on the roof- a Mango shower as we called it and Bradford-Martin decided to try and break through the thatched straw. Whether he intended to escape or just get a drink I never knew, but his Batman followed him. They had both got through the hole they had made when two shots were heard. The Batman fell back through the hole, Bradford-Martin was never seen or heard again. It wasn't long before the Japs came in and if the Batman wasn't already dead, they soon made sure that he was.

We were tied together and after four days were marched about five miles back down the road. Over 30 were killed on the way; mostly men dropped through exhaustion or lack of food or drink. They were just dragged to the side of the road where their backs were broken with a rifle butt. A bayonet was used to finish the job. When we eventually arrived at the banks of the Irrawaddy, we were allowed to sit and watch the water move irresistibly on towards open sea and freedom. We were all very thirsty, it being our 5th day without a drink. I remember seeing a bottle lying a few feet away on the bank. It had an English label on it-Apple and Honey Chutney, I think. I was determined to have it but with my hands tied behind my back it was going to be difficult. I thought that if I could get my mouth to the bottle, I could tip it over and lick the chutney out; there was no top on the bottle. So I had a go. One of the guards saw me and came over and started talking and it was obvious that he was asking me if I wanted a drink. He indicated that I should open my mouth, which I did without thinking. He lifted the bottle towards my face and then flicked a lighted cigarette right down my throat- that's what I got instead of a drink.

I was cut loose then and dragged to one side. A Japanese officer then started asking me questions in English, about the position and movement of British forces in Burma. Well I couldn't help him; I think he must have thought I was an officer myself. Anyway, he had a length of conduit in his hand it wasn't long before I found out what he wanted it for. He hit me from behind across the side of my face, bursting my ear open. I sat there dazed; the blood just flowed down the side of my neck until it caked.

They marched us down to the river, and we walked in it until the dirty, oily water flowed into our mouths. Two of the lads who had somehow got their hands free made an attempt to swim across to the other bank. They were allowed to get about half way, before the Japs shot them. We were taken from there to some Burmese houses- wooden huts with iron bars for windows. We were crowded in shoulder to shoulder on the floor, and the doors were locked. We were given some rice after about four days- our first food for nine days. Every morning when we woke up there were 1 or 2 dead amongst us. Every morning the Japs came in with hankies round their mouths because of the smell of excreta and urine, dried blood and sweat.

Then after about seven days, we were taken by truck to a burnt out gaol at Magwe- Magwe Gaol- about 30 or 40 miles away. They supplied us with rice again, all we had to do was cook it. What a laugh! We had raw rice, burnt rice, crisp rice, at least we had some variety. We got water for cooking and drinking from the Irrawaddy, in big petrol drums that we just rolled up the river. It didn't taste very nice, but you drink anything when you are thirsty. We drank Irrawaddy water for all of the three weeks or thereabouts that we were in Magwe.

After a couple of days we had some meat. In fact they gave us a cow; an old bony cow that looked on its last legs anyway. It looked as if it would fall over if you touched it. The only problem was how to kill it! All we had were pieces of broken slate, but we were a bit reluctant to start attacking the poor old thing with them. So we managed to persuade one of the Jap guards to shoot it for us. Then we attacked it like savages, ripping at the flesh with the slate. We cooked the meat, as best we could over a fire, but it was still pretty raw when we ate it-and I never liked my steak rare.

There was no toilet at the gaol except a water trough, which was never emptied. By the time we left Magwe it had been filled to overflowing-everyone of us had constant diarrhea.

From Magwe we were taken by truck to Rangoon, a distance of about 300 miles. Our home was to be Rangoon Gaol, a civilian prison that the Japs had commandeered for their own use. At our first roll call, we were lined up standing to attention, which we did as best we could. However, this was not good enough as the guards came round and rapped our knuckles with the sticks they were carrying. Eventually, we realized that it was the way we held our hands that was the problem. The Japanese Army stood to attention with fingers pointing down, not clenched as in our drill. None of the guards appeared to know any English, or if they did they were not letting on, and we had to make out their instructions as well as we were able. We were given sweet potatoes and rice, which we had to cook for ourselves and we were thankful for it.

We were segregated into compounds. Three compounds of mostly British troops, including Australians; one of Indians and Gurkhas; and another of Chinese and others. Our compound contained about 300 lads. We were kept in cells designed to hold about 20 men although there was at least double that number in ours.

With the exception of the cooks, none of us were allowed out of the compound for nearly six months-which was when we started work. In that time the daily routine was fairly monotonous. Locked in the cells at night, let out in the morning. Breakfast followed by roll call, Tenko, for which we had to learn our number in Japanese. We were soon quite proficient at Japanese numbering particularly 1-10.

The cooks were allowed to go out occasionally to pick up rations- under guard of course. I became a cook eventually, cooking rice, marrows and pumpkins, and occasionally-about once a week-meat. When the meat was shared out, it worked out a piece about the size of an Oxo cube for each chap.

It was not until we started work at the Docks, loading and unloading ships, that we were able to have our first smoke. That was because we started to get paid. Although we never in fact saw the wages, the equivalent of two pence ha'penny a day, as our Officers pooled the money to buy luxuries once a month. Hence we were able to buy either an egg, or one and a half cigars, which we could break up and make into cigarettes.

We used to get up at 6 o'clock in the morning, breakfast at half past, roll call at quarter to 7, and then out to work until 6 in the evening. When we got back we washed down without soap, we never had any soap. Then it was dinner time, well we used to call it dinner, rice with a little bit of soup made of marrows and pumpkins usually. Then at 7 o'clock the final roll call of the day. After that we were allowed to sit in the compound until 10 o'clock-bedtime. That was the routine every day, except one day a month, which was our rest day.

On our day off we were allowed to have a bit of a singsong. I remember one night during our first year in the gaol, they brought in a military band for us to hear, and we had to listen to it. After about half an hour of tunes that were as foreign to us as the bandsmen, we had to clap. The whole episode was filmed, no doubt to be used as propaganda back home to show how well we were treated.

We only had one chair in the compound, and that was used for minor operations. Colonel McKenzie was our medical officer, pulling out teeth was his particular speciality. Of course there was no anesthetic of any kind, he would simply put a piece of wood in the mouth to stop it closing during the pull. I sat in it once but not to get a tooth pulled. I had a big lump sticking out of the back of my head and I went to see Colonel McKenzie. He took a look at it and said "Spoors, I don't know what it is, a cyst, abscess or what, but I'll have to cut it out." So he cut it out with a lance, a razor blade stuck between two pieces of bamboo fasten together. After that I had to have it dressed every morning before I went to work. He'd fitted some kind of drainer in it to let out the accumulated pus every day.

I mentioned earlier that eventually I ended up in the cookhouse. As a matter of fact, I became the best rice cook in the compound if not the gaol. Strangely enough I became a cook because of my bricklaying skills. I must have been the only bricklayer in the prison because I was suddenly told to go to the Japanese barracks to build some vats or "set pots" for them to cook rice and other foods. While I was there I noticed how they cooked their rice, the amount of water, cooking time and so on. So when first I cooked some rice, everybody complimented me on it and I became a bit of a celebrity. So naturally I hung on to my new found status.

There were four cooks in the compound, and working in pairs we cooked on alternate days. That meant getting up at 5 o'clock so as to get the rice ready for breakfast at 6:30. It was all go, cooking for the 300 men in our compound. We would sweat so hard; it was just like working in a Turkish bath. The officers got exactly the same food as the rest of us. Although we were cooking for about 300 originally, the numbers gradually reduced over the months, perhaps one a week would die, not through our rice I hasten to add.

We would see a new face occasionally, a new prisoner, perhaps an airman who had been shot down. They would be put in solitary confinement for 2 or 3weeks and interrogated and then put in our compound. There was one day a truck came in with a group of airmen from some Flying

Fortresses that had been shot down and caught fire. They were all badly burnt but were still put into solitary confinement where three died the next day. Our medical officer Colonel McKenzie saw the Commandant, and got three transferred to our compound and three to another. Only one of them survived, a young lad of about 19 years whose face was burnt, and hands twisted with burns, but he lived and stayed until the end of the internment. One of the chaps who died in our compound had no eyes at all. His face had been badly burned in the fire, and when he was put into solitary, he'd lain unconscious on the earthen floor and his eyes became badly infested with maggots, which just ate his eyeballs away.

We had a hospital of sorts in our compound, a cell that had been "converted" for the purpose. Very few of those who went in there came out alive. Beriberi was the biggest killer, a disease that caused swelling that started in your feet and traveled up your legs to your stomach and eventually your heart. The swelling was due to water that just built up on you. Once the swelling reached your stomach you were put into the "hospital." You died when it reached your heart. I had beriberi but it only got as far as the tops of my legs, and stopped there for a few months. I was very lucky. It was strange walking around on fat legs and feet, and they felt so heavy, just like the feeling you get when you come out of the water after having been swimming some time. But in about six months, it left me. For some reason I was one of the lucky ones.

Those unfit for heavy work were put in what was called the "Candle Factory" inside the gaol. You used to sit there all day long making candles. You had to fold this thick paper on a stick, turn it round, stick it down then put a little bit of sawdust in the cylinder you made, and then fill it up with tallow. The money "paid" to those who worked had to be split amongst the sick who couldn't do any work at all. But even the sick were supposed to be active, they had to catch flies. Two small bottles were left by the Japs every morning and the sick left behind in the cell had to catch flies and fill the bottles. Most of them found it very difficult to do, so every night when we got back from work, we would go around collecting flies to fill the bottles.

There were also those who became mentally ill during our stay. I clearly remember a chap called Gilroy from the Inniskillings who had lost one brother in the fighting and another had died of a jungle sore the size of a tea plate on his thigh. He cracked up eventually and every morning he would stand by the fence, stick two fingers in his mouth and whistle as loud as he could. He got on our nerves, but it must have been worse for the Japs. Eventually they could take it no longer and he was put into solitary confinement where he stayed until our release nearly three years later. By this time he had the appearance of a real wild man, unkempt long hair and beard and staring eyes. When we eventually were released he was kept on board the hospital ship in a cage like a zoo animal.

Punishment: If you failed to bow to a Jap you got your ears boxed. I had mine boxed a few times. When I was working in the cookhouse I had to walk past a water tower that was patrolled by a Jap sentry. If I failed to see him and bow, he would come right into the compound, stand me to attention and hit me round the ears a few times. Some of the other Japs would kick you for showing disrespect. There was one who would never actually hit you, he would stand you to attention and flick the end of your nose with his finger until it felt as if it were swelling up like Snozzle's. I've got a big nose to start with. Even the Brigadier had to bow to the sentry. Brigadier Hobson took the responsibility for everything, for he was in charge of the compound. He was a very nervous man by the time he got out of the gaol. He was one of the 400 or so fit blokes marched away by the Japs when they began to desert the gaol towards the end of April 1945. Unfortunately they were caught in an attack by some of our own planes and he was killed. 167 men left behind-I was one of them-with a couple of Jap guards. A few days later, the guards left also. It was night when the guards left. One of the lads had gone to the "toilet" which was an old ammunition tin, where he found a piece of paper pushed through the railings, a very rare and precious material in that area, on which was a message written in English. He could see the message clearly in the moonlight, which was extremely bright in Burma.

The message read in English:

"To the whole captured persons of Rangoon Jail. According to the Nippon Military Order, we hereby give you liberty to leave this place at your will. Regarding other materials kept in the compound, we give you permission to consume them as far as necessity is concerned. We hope that we shall have the opportunity to meet you again on the battlefield somewhere. We shall continue our war effort in order to get emancipation of all Asiatic races."

We took the message to Colonel Powell and from him it passed around the rest of us. We were so excited that we stayed up all night. We went down to the guard house-it was deserted. In the morning we found a couple of pigs that the Japs had left behind. We slaughtered them and had a good feed.

However, we still had problems. In fact we were in more danger than we had been in for some time, as the Allied planes were dropping bombs all around. We thought they might not know there were still British prisoners in Rangoon. So we decided to get up on the roof and paint a message to show our presence. The first message "Japs Gone, British here" seemed to have no effect whatsoever. Perhaps the R.A.F. thought it was a ruse on the part of the Japanese to protect themselves. One of our R.A.F. lads suggested using "Extract Digit" which was an air force expression for "get your finger out and get things moving." This did the trick and a couple of officers, Wing-Commander Saunders and Flight-Lieutenant Stevens, landed at Mingladon in a Mosquito on 29th April. Unfortunately they crippled the plane on landing, hitting one of the many bomb craters in the runway. When they arrived at the gaol we told them the Japs had gone, and how we had lived for three years. They took photographs, which I have tried to find unsuccessfully. They told us they would have to leave so they could tell the navy not to shell Rangoon- this had been planned for the next day. So off they went to the docks from where they took a boat to the mouth of the river. The next day instead of bombs, a plane came over and dropped Red Cross parcels and K rations, which consisted of cigarettes, chocolate, biscuits and chewing gum. They dropped them right into the compound; one even went through the cookhouse roof. What a day we had-it was a very happy time for all of us. Fresh bandages for our sores instead of old bits of rags and paper to keep flies off. Sweets to eat, cigarettes to smoke.

When the relief force arrived more photographs were taken. I have been unable to trace those photos with me on them. However, the photographs show some of my mates, and scenes from the prison. We were taken down to the docks and put on to minesweepers that took us right to the mouth of the river. There we boarded a hospital boat- The Karapara. On board we took off our old rags and threw them over the side-old shorts and raggy vests. After a nice hot bath, our first for all those years, we put on fresh clean underwear, shirts and shorts. It was marvelous. We embarked for India and landed in Calcutta. There we went into a hospital for a couple of weeks and then to a rest camp for rehabilitation. It was wonderful feeling to be **FREE.**

We were asked how we wanted to go home, by air or sea. I said immediately "The quickest way." It took 36 hours with about six stops on the way, before we landed at Merryfield, which was somewhere in the South of England. We gave our names to the Officer in Charge, with details of our regiment, last address and so on. We were allowed to go out that night for a drink. Next morning we had to report back to the Officer in Charge. We went in one at a time to find out family news and where we were to go. His very words were "Father dead, Sister Evelyn, 16 Stanley Terrace." That's all! Marched out, and given railway warrants and a small amount of money.

When I arrived at Newcastle Central, all the family was there. I never found out how they knew which train I was getting. We went home by taxi, and at Shiney, the whole Quarry Head had turned out, and it was nearly an hour before I got in the house because everyone was kissing and cuddling me. They had written on the outside wall "Welcome Home Leslie" in great big writing. It was a good feeling and I was very proud. I was very sad because my Dad wasn't there to meet me, as he had died in 1942 from the shock of hearing that I was missing, presumed dead. I was very upset. They had a good meal on for me, and I really felt as if I was back home. I don't think I stopped talking and it was the early hours of the morning before I got to bed, and then I couldn't sleep for the excitement.

I only had two "souvenirs" of my time in prison; a silver spoon that my Dad had given me when I joined the army. I kept it with me through everything. I was so worried that it might get stolen in the prison, that I warmed it over the rice stove, and twisted the shaft so I would know it anywhere. The second was the tin badge with our name and number on, in Japanese, that we had to hang on a string around our necks at all times.

This narration was obtained from Gerry Spoors, daughter of Leslie Spoors who was, rightly so, proud of her Dad and submitted to "The Wartime Memories Project-Rangoon Jail-POW Camp."

Jean Newland

K.P. MacKenzie, Colonel, Royal Army Medical Corp., Senior Medical Officer, Rangoon Jail.

Home City: Aberdeen. Home Country: Scotland.

Dates of Imprisonment: 02/22/42 thru 05/04/45.

Dr. MacKenzie's history and narrative are from his account that is detailed in his amazing book: "Operation Rangoon Jail" printed in 1954 in Great Britain by Page Bros. Ltd (Norwich) for Christopher Johnson, Publishers Ltd.

Exact numbers of men who were captured and died at the hands of the Japanese will never be known. Unlike the German Army, who kept meticulous records, the Japanese did not. For Dr. MacKenzie, a man who was trained and dedicated to saving lives, his imprisonment was especially cruel. He watched men die and suffer, unable to help many and unable to obtain even the most basic medical supplies. He attended the wounded as best he could and watched as men also suffered from various diseases. He was faced with broken bones and lacerations from daily beatings, terrible infections, dysentery, boils, jungle sores, beriberi, malaria, diarrhea, diphtheria, dengue fever, lice, bed bugs and smallpox. Cholera was a constant threat. To have access to his account is invaluable.

Colonel MacKenzie received his Medical Degree in Aberdeen Scotland, March 1914. He served as a medical officer in France and Greece. In 1919 he was in North Russia when he made the decision to remain in the Army. He was then posted to Jhansi and Jubbulpore India from 1939 to 1941. Up to that time, England was at war with Germany. The events at Pearl Harbor on December 7th 1941 suddenly changed everything. England then entered the war against Japan. They had been trained and were equipped for Desert Warfare; they were not prepared for the sudden jungle role that was thrust upon them. The British were totally unprepared for the speed in which the Japanese moved through South East Asia.

Dr. MacKenzie's narrative follows:

We arrived on 6th January 1942 to a scene of desolation that had been the Rangoon Docks, before the Japanese air raids had started. We proceeded across Moulmein Bay to Moulmein, where we were to remain until the end of January. We evacuated to Mokpalin where I passed into captivity on February 22, 1942.

On the 25th of June, a day of drenching rain, we were ordered into lorries and were taken to the jetties at Moulmein to embark on a three thousand ton cargo boat. It was a horrible nightmare. We were all crammed into the after-hold. There was little ventilation and quite apart from the dirt, the smells of saturated sticky bags, human sweat and excrement as many of the men were very ill and suffering from continual diarrhea and having no control of their movements due to beriberi, exhaustion and dysentery. The next day we pulled into Rangoon Docks at a berth near the Sheve Dagon Pagoda. We disembarked and marched through the city, as best we could, pursued by millions of flies, attracted by our sticky, dirty clothing to the Rangoon Jail. I had reached the place where I was to spend the remainder of my imprisonment. I was 51 years old.

One hundred years ago, Rangoon was a small fishing village but by the time of the Japanese occupation on February 20th, 1942, it had grown into a city of half a million people. The city was dominated by the great Schwedagon Pagoda. It is higher than the dome of St. Peters and the gleam of its beautiful gilt exterior in the harsh Burma sunlight can be seen for miles around.

The great importance of Rangoon is as a port. It is by far the biggest port in Burma. Here also on Commissioners Road is Rangoon Jail, a stark ugly collection of buildings which comprise one of the largest jails in the British Empire. In normal times it could accommodate 3,000 prisoners.

I was brought before the Commandant (Captain Coshima) and asked if I was a doctor. I replied yes and he informed me that my services as a doctor would not be required; he said "we have plenty of good doctors." Obviously, his "good doctors" were not at Rangoon Jail, as we were to discover. His decision to talk to me was to get me to sign a document that was a manifesto he had written as Japan's right to wage war. He hoped to use the prisoner's signatures as a propaganda document. He stated that the war would last 50 to 100 years. When I refused to cooperate, I was sent back to my cell. On August 17th we were paraded from the Punishment Cells (solitary). We marched into the Execution Yard, a fact that did not make us feel any more cheerful. The yard was a mass of uncleared wreckage, a relic of the heavy bombing of the City when the Japanese captured Rangoon. Captain Coshima, the Commandant, appeared carrying a steel golf club shaft in hand and we were told to come to attention. "You have refused to cooperate; therefore I am going to punish you." He pointed to Power, telling him to step out.

Some Burmese prisoners were promised their freedom if they would beat the British officers. I counted the blows, 22 or 23 hit Power before he swayed and fell to the ground. He pluckily got to his feet again but was obviously very groggy. No mercy was shown. It took 8 or 10 further blows to knock him out finally. He just stood there, receiving them, with his face bruised and swollen, his lips and tongue cut, swollen and bleeding. When he finally fell, the Japs just let him lay, a prostrate figure amongst the dust and wreckage of the yard.

Immediately, Loring was called out to take Powers place. He stood up to 30 blows and never turned a hair. There he stood, without flinching, like the Rock of Gibraltar.

What was so terrifying was the systematic way in which the Japanese brought into play every device physical and mental to break the spirits of their captives and to make life an absolute misery.

One of the sadistic ways in which the Japanese treated some of our Officers was the case of a tall young Sapper Lieutenant who was wounded in the chest in North Burma and then taken prisoner. This poor fellow was brought into jail after marching part of the way and then transported by lorry. He was suffering from a bad attack of his beriberi and his feet and legs, thighs and other parts were very swollen. When I saw him he had a bad buckle bruise imprinted on his forehead. He had received this earlier in the day when he failed to rise to his feet when a Japanese sentry entered his cell. It was quite impossible for him to rise without assistance, but the sentry had taken the buckle end of his leather waist-belt and smashed it into the officer's face. The officer had then managed to rise to his feet with the aid of the wall and had received a lashing with his belt. I managed to have him moved to the prison hospital, but, although he put up a brave fight, he became generally oedematous and died.

The only difference between our hospital and the other rooms in the block was that the patients we had there did not have to go out on working parties. The squalor, stink and misery of such conditions were depressing and humiliating, it took a heavy toll and the plight of the sick and suffering cannot be adequately described by any words that are at my command.

The blocks were of uniform construction. Each had a ground floor of cement and an upper floor of wood, which was reached by cement steps at both ends. On each floor were five rooms with five long, barred windows on each side. These windows had no glass and did permit a certain amount of breeze and fresh air to enter the rooms day and night. The maximum authorized capacity of each room, during the days of British rule, was twenty-eight in each block, two of the upstairs room were allotted to officers, who slept twenty-six in a room. The other rooms were occupied by other ranks, who lived, in the first tier or so, forty-four to a room. The end room downstairs was used as a hospital and four orderlies slept in a bunk that was at the end of the verandah that ran around the block.

Conditions were worst during the monsoons. The surface of the compounds were muddy and drainage was nonexistent. We walked out in bare feet through squelching, sticky mud, water and latrine washings to perform our natural functions, both by day and by night.

Then we had to return to our quarters, and get back into bed. The bed coverings became masses of the infectious germs of intestinal diseases. During our imprisonment we also faced an epidemic of cholera and smallpox. Through great ingenuity we were able to contain them. Our great scourge however was beriberi, and thirty three percent of the men lost were lost to beriberi.

There were a number of other doctors in the jail in addition to myself and Major McLeod, who was from Ontario Canada. We did not have poor Dr. Kilgour with us for long; he died while we were in "solitary." I did what I could to organize a prison Medical Service, as was my duty as the Senior Medical Officer in Rangoon Jail.

At first, I had no instruments at all. Then Gavin, one of our nursing orderlies, had a bright idea for making me a scalpel out of a much used safety-razor blade. He fixed it into a short piece of wood about five inches long and with it I was able to make small superficial incisions into boils and abscesses.

My first pair of forceps was made from a piece of hammered-out zinc sheet but was not a success. The blade gave if much pressure was exercised. Some men in the working parties managed to "win" a pair of artery forceps for me when they were out.

I shall always remember the pitiful sights I witnessed day after day, as prisoner after prisoner slipped out of life through beriberi. It was devastating for a doctor to know that he could have saved a life so easily and be denied the means of doing so.

One morning a young soldier, a fine boy, said to me, as I was touring the hospital: "Oh sir, I can see two of you." I forced a smile and replied: "That's a pity; surely one of me is bad enough." I made the joke with difficulty for I knew that the lad was suffering from double vision, the beginning of his final coma. Yet he smiled to me, after my remark and then settled down into his long, last sleep.

Early one afternoon, we had seen from the windows of Brigadier Hobson's room, an old captured five ton lorry arrive outside the Solitary Block. Out of this, a number of heavily bandaged human beings were decanted and then helped and carried into the block by one another. That evening, the "bush telegraph" buzzed with the information that we had amongst us, the crew of an American aircraft, that had been engaged upon a bombing mission and had been hit and forced to make a "crash" landing" outside Rangoon.

At a later date, I discovered that Major Werhner, who was Captain of the bomber, had on landing, rushed to the exit door and dragged his crew of six from the blazing wreck. They were all severely burnt about the face, head, neck, arms and legs, their clothing having been practically burnt off. Major Werhner himself escaped with a slight concussion. After his allotted time in "solitary" he was put into No. 3 cellblock in Brigadier Hobson's room, and thus became one of us.

His companions were less fortunate than he. It was natural that the type of treatment they received in "solitary" did nothing to improve the serious condition they were in on arrival. Throughout the night, we could hear these poor fellows moaning in their agony, and we knew that, as they lay there, they had not even the sparse comforts of proper beds and blankets.

It was however, the fifth day of their presence in camp before I was told by the Jap medical orderly, whom we called "the paper boy," to follow him. He led me the short distance across to the Solitary Block.

When I arrived there, I saw a sight that I shall never forget as long as I live. This block like the others, had along one side of it a verandah, the usual flimsy structure with concrete floors with sloping wooden slats to form a roof. Five of the unfortunate Americans had been dragged out of the cells and laid on the verandah, for me to see them there. Two of them were lying quietly on the floor, with only strips of rush mating between them and the concrete. The other three, however, had their heads completely swathed in bandages so there were only openings left for the mouth and nose. They could not see and were crawling about on the dusty floor blindly, like badly-bitten animals. The burns on their necks, heads and faces had been dressed with Vaseline, on top of which sheets of grease proof paper and layers of gauze had been placed. The grease-proof paper had been most ineffective and the Vaseline had soaked right through the bandages, with the result that a horrible clotted mass of sand and dirt from the ground and grease from the dressings covered the entire necks and heads of the airmen. They had been crawling around their cells for four days in this condition, supporting themselves on their knees and elbows. They were unable to see, unable to use their hands and unable to feed themselves and were still dressed in the same burnt clothing that they had been wearing when captured.

In the meantime, however, I was in the Solitary Block and the rules of the prison prevailed. I was allowed to examine the patients, but not to speak to them. The first airmen I looked at was in a profound state of collapse from the spread of general infection throughout his body. Clearly, he had not long to live. I realized that the greatest kindness I could render was not to disturb him further.

I turned my attention to the others, before long, I was convinced that this was not a one-man job and I took my stand. I insisted that "the Paper Boy" should get Major Ramsey along to help me. This was done fortunately without undue delay, and after we had each examined these unfortunate fellows in turn we held a consultation.

We formed the same opinion about what should be done and it was the opinion that any doctor in his senses would have formed. We realized that all these men were in a deplorable and dangerous state and I sent a message, through the interpreter, O'Hari San, to the Camp Commandant. I announced that, if any of the men were to have a chance of life, it was essential that they be transferred without delay to a Japanese hospital in Rangoon and that they needed proper attention there. O'Hari San came back with a point blank refusal. In the next hour, we did our best to try to clean up their wounds. What a shock it was to me to find that all the burnt areas, as well as cuts and abrasions, on the scalp, ears, eyes and noses of our patients were crawling with maggots. There were maggots in nostrils, maggots in the cheek wounds and maggots between the fingers as well. Ramsey and I picked out these horrible larvae one by one with the aid of an old pair of Japanese dissecting forceps. When we cleaned them up a bit, I put forward the suggestion that, if the Commandant would permit it, I would take 3 of the men into number 3 Block Hospital while Ramsey would take the other two into number 6 Block Hospital.

O'Hari San went away again. He returned in a half hour. This time his answer was more favorable. We would take them into our hospitals on the usual conditions for prisoners in "solitary." The other prisoners were not to speak to them, so there could be no risk of information passing one way or another.

We readily agreed to this. It was a relief to me to get the three patients under my care and I was able to arrange, by taking from other men, that they got fresh clothing, blankets and mosquito nets for the night. I also saw that they were fed in a proper manner with such meager rations as we could provide. I was particularly fortunate in that I had, in reserve, two ampoules of morphine solution for injections. These had been salvaged several months before from some fresh arrivals, all of whom made it a custom loyally to hand over to me any medical supplies that they happened to bring with them.

This precious pain-killing drug has seldom, if ever been put to better use. I injected the two worse cases, bringing them to peace of mind and release from suffering that they deserved and craved. It was, however, too late for me to do more than this. One of my charges died during the night.

The second lingered for forty-eight hours. He was a brave man, sane and courageous to the end despite his desperate plight. How he maintained his reason, I just do not know, for both his eyes had been destroyed, eaten away by maggots, which, when we first saw him, filled the whole of his orbital cavities.

The third patient, Sergeant Daley, an unusually burly type American, provided a more cheerful story. Amazingly enough, he recovered completely, after a grueling ordeal of many weeks.

The two airmen, under Ramsey's care in No.6 Block hospital died. The miracle was that we were able to save the life of one.

Another American airman was the recipient of my surgical attention in a different fashion, some two or three months later. I was sent for one day by the Jap medical lieutenant from Rangoon, who visited the jail occasionally.

I was conducted into his august presence by the small, bespectacled, chattering, puffy-faced O'Hari San. I disliked this medical officer intensely. He wanted me to assist him in an operation. I noticed, on my entry, that he was studying a Japanese text book on surgery, in a somewhat perplexed fashion. He asked if I would assist him. I offered to do the surgery and he seemed greatly relieved when the interpreter translated my offer. He said he would permit me to do that. I asked if I could be allowed to have Major Ramsey assist me. He agreed to that also. I asked to see the patient before the operation but was refused.

I was curtly dismissed with the unhappy thought that I had committed myself to operate on some unfortunate being, which I had never seen and of whom I knew nothing. I was sent for an hour later and escorted to the very primitive and highly extemporized operating theater at the old Water Tower. There was just room in its precincts for the iron hospital bed which was to act as an operating table and for another table on which to place necessary instruments and dressings. It was to be alfresco surgery, for the alcove, of course, lay open not only to stifling air of early afternoon, but also to all dust of the compound with its accompanying germs and risks of infection.

I concealed my anxiety and dismay about these conditions, however, as I saw being conducted towards me a dark-haired man of medium height, whom I could easily discern, from his tattered uniform, as being an American airman. He came from No.8 Block, where they were imprisoned entirely separated from the British. I was given the strictest instructions that I must only talk to him within our limits as could be easily be understood by the interpreter and that I must confine my conversation absolutely to such necessary interchange of words, as we were permitted by the interpreter for me to diagnose his condition. It was only therefore,at a much later date, that I found out my patient was Air Force Sergeant Richard Montgomery.

Montgomery had been hit in the wrist by a splinter of ack-ack shell when his plane had been brought down a week or two previously. The Japs in the front line had amputated his forearm, just above the wrist. The result had not been happy. When I saw the amputated stump was filthy and septic, infected ends of bones were protruding from it and Montgomery was suffering from severe nerve pains, going right up his arm.

I had two choices. One was to amputate higher up the forearm; the other was to disarticulate at the elbow-joint and remove the whole forearm. The second choice involved, of course, a more drastic and crippling operation. My decision rested on two points. The first came out in my preliminary talk with the Japanese lieutenant, when I explained the alternatives to him. "The lieutenant says," interpreted O'Hari San, "that, if you amputate again the forearm, and that wound goes septic, then there are no more dressings left for you, when you have to remove the elbow." That sounded decisive but, had I still had any doubts, they would have been settled when I saw the instruments at my disposal. These were a small collection, taken from a captured British Army Field Surgical Pannier, consisting of four bluntish-looking scalpels, four small artery forceps, two tiny needle holders, two "rat toothed" dissecting forceps, a few rusty looking, half curved, non cutting surgical needles, some strands of fine horsehair, a quantity of surgical silk in ampoules with a hank of fishing gut in a tube, two hypodermic syringes and a medium sized bottle of methylated spirits. In addition to these, there was a saw, just an ordinary butcher's saw, such as used for cutting meat. If I amputated through the forearm, I would of course have had to saw through the two bones of this part. If on the other hand, I disarticulated at the elbow, I would not need to use a saw. I resolved to disarticulate at the elbow. I am very glad I did not have to employ that saw.

I was allowed to say sufficient to the patient to inform him that I was carrying out the operation with the greatest possible reluctance and with misgiving because of the miserable facilities at my disposal. I spared him the details of the reasons for my decision. I merely told him what was quite true, that I was operating in an attempt to save his life and that I would be as gentle as possible.

The patient lay down on the iron bedstead, still wearing his dusty boots. The Japs found me, thank heaven, two ampoules of two percent Novocain, under normal conditions used as a dental anesthetic, but now a Godsend to me as I could use it for local anesthesia, in the absence of a general anesthetic. I considered myself fortunate at that moment that, in my younger days, when I was House Surgeon to the great Sir Henry Gray, at the Aberdeen Royal Infirmary, I had a chief who specialized in this particular form of anesthesia and I had acquired considerable experience in it, myself, under his tuition.

Working under these conditions, we started. I cut slowly away and infiltrated with fresh injections of the anesthetic as I cut, while the Jap medical orderly, Yamamoto, applied the tourniquet, applied it very efficiently, I have to admit, and Major Ramsay helped me. The lieutenant stood by in helpless and bewildered fashion. The operation took an hour and a half, by the end of which time I had removed the forearm and provided a good flap of skin to fold over the lower end of the humerus bone. The stump was bandaged, the tourniquet removed and my patient was conducted back to his block. There were of course, no such refinements as operating trolleys. The poor chap had to stagger back, assisted by two comrades. I returned, unthanked by the Japs, to No.3 Block.

This was the first and last time I saw Sergeant Richard Montgomery. Although I asked to see him the next day, I was refused. I was unable to obtain any information about my patient and I kept watching the

American Block for the familiar signs of a funeral procession. I heard nothing directly but, through diverse channels in the next few months, the news came that Montgomery's arm had recovered completely and it was a source of comfort and joy to me to receive grateful messages and thanks from him the same way.

Several years later, when I was a free man again, I picked up the Daily Telegraph and read the following extract in Peterborough's column:

"PROSTHETIC LIMBS"

"An indication of the remarkable efficiency of artificial limbs in America is the fact that disabled ex-Servicemen, equipped with these limbs, are being drafted back into the Forces.

"This is the case, for instance, of Master-Sergeant Richard Montgomery. He lost his left arm and has rejoined the Army Air Force as a radio operator. His "prosthetic" arm performs nearly all the functions of a natural one.

"Montgomery bailed out of his plane over Burma, and in doing so lost his left hand. Owning to neglect in a Japanese prison camp in Rangoon, gangrene set in.

"His only hope was to have the whole arm amputated. There were no medical facilities in the prison camp. A British officer, Colonel K.P. MacKenzie, offered to perform the operation. He did so, without anesthetics, and saved Sergeant Montgomery's life. The Sergeant has never seen Colonial MacKenzie since Rangoon was taken from the Japanese in May, 1945. He speaks of him with the highest admiration and affection, however, and would like to get in touch with him. Perhaps Colonel MacKenzie is a Peterborough reader, or is known to one.

"Dr. McLeod also performed some remarkably difficult operations in Rangoon Jail. I was not present at any of these but saw some results he obtained, when amputating without anesthetics. One case in which he achieved a wonderful result was when he removed the leg of a sturdy little Welshman, Corporal J. Usher from Wrexham, just below the thigh. Thank to the skill of McLeod, Usher made an excellent recovery and was amongst the party liberated, when the British eventually re-entered Rangoon."

The Japs tried to bluff us into believing that all was well but, in spite of the absence of authentic news of what was happening on the battle fronts, some sixth sense told us that we were on the eve of a great crisis. We felt the end was very near.

It was an exciting time but, in some ways, it was a terrifying time too. We could not be sure that the Japs would not panic and perhaps carry through a massacre. Many of the Japanese with whom we came into contact were hardly sane by European standards and it was impossible to predict what they wound do under the strain of a dire emergency.

On April 21, 1945, our prisoners, working in the Quartermaster's Store, were ordered to make up rations for five days for 200 men. They were told to divide these rations into four consignments, each for fifty men. For this purpose they were permitted to draw on Japanese field rations. At the same time, all British and American prisoners were told that they would be put into one of two categories. They were either "fit to march" or "unfit to march." This classification was left to the senior officers amongst the prisoners. We tried to muster as many as possible in the "fit" category, for the men were anxious to stick together and nobody who could move wished to face the unknown in a deserted Rangoon Jail. The "unfit to march" consequently consisted of hospital cases and hopeless cripples, through sores and wounds. We gave the most careful consideration to these lists and it was therefore, mortifying, when they were submitted to the Japanese, to have them returned immediately for alteration. There appeared to be no reason for this, except for pig-headedness. We asked what to do about medical officers and received the reply that this matter would be arranged for us. Eventually, Major McLeod was detailed to stay with the sick, and Ramsay and I were told that we were to remain on the marching party.

We saw that the Japanese medical staff were burning the medical records in the M.I. hut. Clearly they did not want to leave any evidence of their conduct in matters medical.

We realized that, whatever might befall us, we were about to leave Rangoon Jail. Our destination was shrouded in mystery. It was many weeks later I learnt that the Japs in desperation had decided to make us march, through Siam, into Japan.

I was a sick man (suffering from Beriberi amongst other things) and I was not used to walking much. In fact, I do not think that I had walked more than a quarter of a mile at one stretch the whole time I was in Rangoon Jail. Neither was I used to footwear, for this was the first time that I had had stockings or shoes on my feet for a period of nearly a thousand days. Upon leaving the Jail we were all issued a soft cap, a pair of long white pants, some rubber shoes and a pair of khaki shorts. It would have been difficult for Allied planes to distinguish us from our Japanese guards. Lt. Gover and I carried a shared bamboo pole on which we carried our pathetic little stores of belongings. We marched grimly on through the night. As day broke, we were called to a halt at the side of the road and allowed to rest. We hid in the jungle scrub to avoid attracting attention of Allied aircraft. I was unable to think of anything else except the need to put one foot in front of the other. Every part of my body seemed to be aching and the weight of the pole on my shoulder was almost more than I could bear. I must have looked in bad shape, for a Japanese guard came up to me and took away my bundle and placed it in a handcart. I do not know the man, or at least in my condition, I could not recognize him, but he did me a good turn indeed that afternoon, Later, I made out the familiar features of O'Hari San, when he came down with a message that the Commandant had given permission for the baggage of Hobson and myself to stay on the handcarts throughout the march.

The second day I was like a man in a fog. All the time I kept repeating top myself: "I must keep going, I must keep going." That second day I was also helped by a stick that Sergeant Farrar gave me. But even then, before a halt was ordered, I had come to the end of my tether; I had to resort to the device of holding on to one of the handcarts, to enable me to keep moving. Then a surprising thing happened, along came one of the most objectionable and bumptious of our guards, whom we had nicknames "Pompous Percy" and he ordered that I should be lifted on to one of the handcarts. I finished the day being pulled along still in a daze.

I have little recollection of the third day as we were now being harassed by Allied planes; however, the convoy had to take cover on several occasions. Light bombs dropped all around, but no one was injured. There is nothing remarkable in the fact that our pilots thought we were Japanese soldiers; it has to be remembered that we were all dressed like our captors.

I who had seen so much beriberi should fall victim to the results of this disease at the last lap of our adventure was an irony of fate. I had lost all sensation in my feet, I kept knocking my toes against stonesand against the railroad sleepers and I found it increasingly impossible to lift my knees in a last effort to maintain my position with my comrades. When we halted, I knew it was all up. I sank to the ground and sent a message up to Hobson telling him that I was unable to walk a step further, that my legs and feet had given way completely. I told him I should have to be left behind. Nothing more was said until the end of the halt. I rather expected some of my friends to come and say goodbye but nobody did so. When the order came to move again, I just lay still, relieved to think that now it was all over and that I should not need to renew the struggle. But it was not to work out that way. Just as the convoy was moving off, Squadron-Leader Duckenfield and Captain Brown of the K.O.Y.L.I came up to me silently, placed my arms around their shoulders and struggled forward, bearing my inert body between them. Brown tried to get me across his back after a time, but this proved too much for him on the rough ground and in his weakened condition. They were not able to help me for long, when they faltered; their places were taken by other men. We stopped every hour and at the end of each resting period, there were always two men beside me to drag me along and speak a few words of comfort and good cheer. For the last two hours, the burden was borne by Sgts. Handsell and Martin. They did more for me, as did the others, than any man had a reasonable right to expect. Most of the time I was in a state of coma and delirium. On 29th of April I asked O'Hari San if I could have an interview with the Commandant for I had come to a decision. He asked why I wanted to see the Commandant. I told him it was a personal matter. "Please O'Hari San, get the Commandant. I am finished. I cannot march any further. My legs and feet are useless and I am impeding the progress of my friends. I have disposed of my kit and, before we leave here tonight, I want the Commandant to do me a personal favor. I want him to put a bullet through my heart. I will mark the place on my shirt with a piece of paper or mark my chest with a colored pencil, so that there will be no mistake. I cannot face being left behind to be murdered. The sooner the better, Mr. O'Hari, please, so that I may be buried before the column moves off again."

O'Hari appeared stunned and called around him a group of Japanese N.C.Os. They jabbered amongst themselves excitedly but nobody made a move to fetch the Commandant. The next thing I knew was that Brigadier Hobson was called to speak with the Commandant. When he went, I lay under a banyan tree, not caring much what happened now. Within half an hour Brigadier Hobson called out to our bewildered assembly of nearly 400 Allied prisoners:

"We are free, we are free!" I lay there unable to take in the news and was almost surrounded by thirty or forty N.C.Os and men shouting: "You made it," "Congratulations, Sir," or "Well done, Colonel, well done."

I could not speak but I held my hand feebly out and one by one my companions ran up and shook it. It was perhaps the proudest moment of my life. It made me realize that what little I had been able to do for these splendid fellows in the way of doctoring and by being, as far as I could, their guide, philosopher and friend was deeply appreciated. What better tribute could any man wish from his companions in adversity?

That day was spent in obtaining food from the Burmese villages in the neighborhood and it was supplied against promises that we would pay for it when we reached our own lines. The members of the R.A.F., under Duckenfield, employed themselves in making a huge Union Jack from pieces of cloth that the Burmese gave them and from the long white pants which had been issued to us by the Japanese.

I was rushed to a hut as the Allied aircraft came overhead and began to drop bombs. Hobson lifted me to the floor and lay down beside me as a forty-three pound bomb exploded just behind the hut. "My God, that was a near one," I heard Hobson say. "I don't think it's all over yet," was my reply. Then the aircraft began to machine-gun us. The first bullet from the left hand gun hit Hobson, squarely in the right kidney region and inflicted a deep wound about two inches long. I felt the concussion as it communicated to me through his hand and forearm. Blood was pouring from the wound and Brigadier Hobson was dead. Poor Hobson! Could anything be more poignant? He was destroyed by our own side after the years he had suffered at the hands of the enemy. Yet, I am sure that if he had to go, he would have not wished it any other way. He died in a moment of triumph for surely it was his finest hour, shortly before, when he stood in front of us, waving a piece of paper and announcing: "We are free."

I straightened his body out as best I could and called to two men sheltering below, to give me a hand and to find Captain Harvey, who had succeeded Colgan as our adjutant. When Harvey came in, I told him what had happened and suggested that we had better leave Hobson where he was, until we could have to opportunity of burying him, when the danger of the raids were over.

If those aircraft had come over a few minutes later, we might have been spared the final disaster of Hobson's death, for Duckenfield and his men had ready their Union Jack and had prepared from white pieces of cloth a massive notice: *FOUR HUNDRED BRITISH PRISONERS HERE NO FOOD S.O.S.* Our message was picked up by a Spitfire pilot, who pinpointed our position on his map and informed the nearest Brigade headquarters by wireless.

During the whole time I was in captivity, my wife received no communication from me. She heard nothing from me in my own handwriting from my capture on the 22ⁿᵈ February, 1942 until I walked into her Kensington flat after breakfast, on June 7ᵗʰ, 1945. She received one telegram darted March 28ᵗʰ 1942 and read: Regret to inform you of notification from India that Colonel K.P. Mackenzie, M.B., R.A.M.C. was reported missing on February 22ⁿᵈ, 1942 letter follows, signed Under Secretary of War. The second dated May17th, 1945 had the message: Pleased to state that Colonel K.P. Mackenzie, M.B. recovered from Japanese hands present address BHM Delhi letter follows, signed Under Secretary of State for War. Here I shall comment, without prejudice, on the experiences of my wife and children, while I was prisoner. The telegram informing my wife I was missing was placed in the letter box of her home with a bundle of other letters and as soon as I was posted "missing" all pay and allowances to my family ceased. As I was not proved dead, she was not eligible for any benefits and would not be allowed to draw on my account. It all seems to have been an unnecessary muddle and a cruel muddle at that, for the result of red tape and procrastination was that my family had to give up their house and become homeless for the rest of the war.

OUR LIVES ARE OURS AGAIN . . . .

In 1954, Dr. MacKenzie wrote his book "Operation Rangoon Jail." His story is honest and insightful. He became a Town Councilor of the Royal Burgh of Inverness. I do not know if he ever continued his practice of medicine on his return.

Majon McLeod (left) examines Corporal Usher's leg, which he cleanly
amputated without the aid of anaesthetics – Courtesy Pegasus Archives

British compound and hospital. Courtesy US Signal Corps

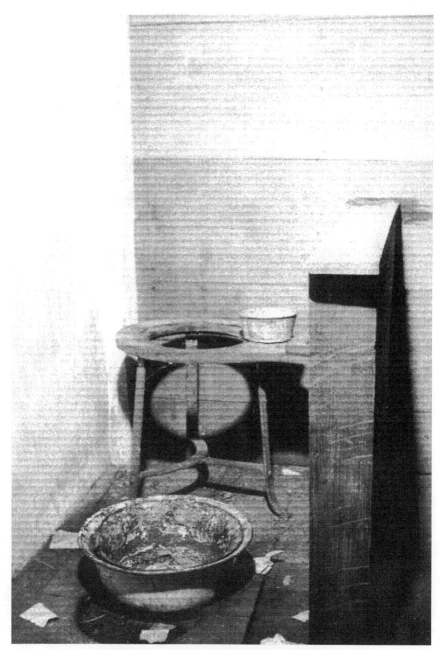

British soldiers' toilet. Courtesy US Signal Corps

Cook House. Courtesy US Signal Corps

British sleeping area. Courtesy US Signal Corps.

Lional F. Coffin, Lieutenant Colonel, 20th Air Force/Co-Pilot, B-29, 58th Bomb Wing,

40th Bomber Group, 25[th]Squadron.

Home City: Duluth. Home State: Minnesota.

Dates of Imprisonment: 12/14/44 thru 05/04/45.

After the bomb drop and the resultant explosion just under A/C formation, we found our A/C with a fire in the bomb bay. #3 engine had dropped off, the controls were useless, and the A/C was in a 20 degree bank to the left with airspeed of 140 mph. Our radio operator had a partially severed hand, so we attempted to evacuate the pilot compartment as rapidly as possible. Bud Meyer and I were able to keep A/C flying for several minutes, and then we both bailed out at about 12,000 feet.

Upon landing, I was taken to a Burmese hut and shortly afterwards was reunited with Bud Meyer. We thought we had a chance to escape as the Burmese paddled us downstream in a dugout canoe, but after some 30 min. of travel, the canoe was beached near a small town. There we found ourselves looking at a squad of Japanese soldiers with rifles pointed at us. The night was spent in a Burmese jail with a Christian Burmese jailer and his family.

The next day, MPs from Rangoon arrived by river boat and we were transported to Rangoon. We spent the night under the floor of an MP headquarters building and taken to the New Laws Court city jail the next morning. I was put in a cell with Richard Brooks and was happy to see that other survivors of our crew were there. Late that afternoon we were marched into a small open courtyard. They told us to kneel in a row....I thought we were going to be beheaded, but we were soon loaded into a truck and transported to the Rangoon Central Prison.

I was first to be interrogated, and was roughed up when I refused to sign a paper promising not to attempt escape. Because of this I did not receive the ½ gunny sack (blanket), and no tin food tray. I was then marched to a solitary cell on the second floor of cell bloc #5 and remained alone there for the next several weeks. After the first 4 days without food (no tin trays), one of the guards persuaded the interpreter to come back with the paper I had not signed. I signed and got some rice and cold tea. Monty was in the cell next to me and often asked for prayer to ease the pain of his severed hand. Finally, the Japanese had a POW (British doctor) amputate Mont's arm at the elbow without benefit of any anesthetics. After the first week in solitary confinement, it became a practice to offer evening prayer for the well being of those in the prison, and specifically to have the Japs move us into a compound that would enable us to take care of our sick people. I remember us losing several POWs each week, because we could not help them.

The Japs finally did move us to a vacant compound (cell block #8), and there were only three deaths in the next four months before freedom. In our new compound, I worked in the sickroom with Paul Almand, whose only request was to be home and put his head in his mother's lap. Paul was the first to die after moving to our new compound. Nutritional ulcers developed on my legs, 37 on my left one, and I wondered if I would ever be normal again.

When the Japs marched off and left us, a flight of B-24s dropped medical supplies, and by a miracle, the sores were healed by the time we were transported to the hospital ship (H.M.S Karapara) that brought us back to Calcutta, India and the 142nd General Hospital.

My telegram to my wife and mother, that I was OK and coming home, arrived on Mother's Day.

Praise the Lord!

OUR LIVES ARE OURS AGAIN . . . .

Lional F. Coffin returned to the U.S.A. for Pilot Instructor Duty at Denver, Colorado. Separated from Service in February 1946, he served with the 9703rd Troop Carrier until retirement as Lt. Col in August 1979. His civilian occupations include furniture business, School Teacher and University Professor with retirement in 1984. Education: B. S. Business Education, B.S in Industrial Education and Master's Degree in Education. He married and had five children.

This narrative was obtained through "Circumstances of Capture and Liberation" report sent to Harry Chagnon, the 40th Bomb Group Historian by Lionel Coffin.

<u>**Richard Brooks "TRUNK"**</u>

Hubert Ross Garrett, 1ˢᵗLieutenant, 10ᵗʰ Air Force/Bombardier, B-24 CBI Command,

7ᵗʰ Bomber Group, 492 Squadron.

Home City: Madisonville. Home State: Texas.

Dates of Imprisonment: 05/08/43 thru 05/04/45.

I was a Bombardier on Robert L. Kavanagh's crew. We were on our 17ᵗʰ combat mission out of India on Sunday morning May 1, 1943. The target was to bomb cargo ships in the harbor at Rangoon, Burma.

Immediately after the release of bombs, we were hit by fighter planes. The first attack knocked out #2 and #3 engines. Injured were Edward E.Bodell, Norman P. Dohn, Joseph Kellner and John E. Lavery. We fell out of formation and numerous fighter planes continued the attacks. Our pilot then went into a cloud bank with only one engine remaining at full power. The only fire power left were the nose guns as the others were not operating due to loss of power and injuries of the crew. Approximately one hour later, we crash landed in a rice paddy close to the jungle, North West of Bassein, Burma. We were shot at continuously by fighters. Sometime during the attack, Norman P.Dohn bailed out. We were told later he died of his injuries. Joseph P. Kellner, waist gunner and John Lavery, tail gunner, were dead when we landed.

The remaining crew started walking in the jungle "Hoping for India." The crew was ambushed by a Jap patrol when Jack Redmon was killed. We continued to move north until we hit the coast about three days later. We were ambushed two more times by a Jap patrol that was not in uniform. On May 8ᵗʰ, on our third ambush, John Kavanagh was injured and we were captured. We were carried to Bassein, then to Rangoon City Jail, solitary confinement, then finally to Cell Block #6 at the Rangoon Central Prison. The crew members that died in prison were Robert Kavanagh, the pilot and Edward Bodell, engineer.

Kenneth Moxley, navigator and Waldo E. Cotton, co-pilot were part of a large group of prisoners that the Japanese took with them when they left the prison in the latter part of May 1945. I was left behind with the others to fend for ourselves. The British came a few days later and we were finally liberated on May 4, 1945.

This narrative was obtained through "Circumstances of Capture and Liberation" report sent to Harry Chagnon, the 40th Bomb Group Historian by Hubert Ross Garrett.

Richard Brooks "TRUNK"

S.R. Lissenburg (Lisay)/Rank N/A, British Ground Forces / Ordinance Man

Home City: Donvale. Home Country: Victoria, Australia

Dates of Imprisonment: 06/42 thru 05/04/45.

When the Japanese attacked Malaya, we were driven back to Singapore. On the fall of Singapore, two other ordinance guys and I, along with a few others, left Singapore docks in a life boat. This was in the early hours of March 16, 1942; unfortunately the boat was fired upon and badly damaged. However, we managed to get into a small island before the boat sank. Most of the others managed to get into other boats, while three of us were stranded on the island. The village chief had us ferried over to another island a few miles away in a small dugout canoe. We found a hut with an Australian in charge, which we discovered was part of the escape route. The three of us had to split up as the boats arriving with supplies were rather small. I was picked up by a sampan, which arrived with only three on board, so they had room for one more. We island hopped and managed to get to Sumatra in seven days, where I met up with one of the other ordinance guys. A few of us decided that the "Organization" was too slow, so we took off and walked about 20 miles, got a lift by car, then a bus, and finally a train to Panang on the west coast. We missed the last boat out, and when the Japanese took Sumatra, eleven of us took off in a small river sailing boat. We spent over two months at sea, and covered approximately two thousand miles before we were driven ashore south of Moulmein. This is where we were eventually captured. We lost one crew member who died of malaria and another who washed overboard during one of the many storms we encountered at sea. We spent six weeks in Moulmein and then shipped to Rangoon. Four of us were put into solitary confinement. The Japanese wouldn't believe that we had traveled two thousand miles in a small sailing boat, and said we were spies. However, after seventy-seven days of bashings, starving, etc., we were released to join the other prisoners on Block 3, where I spent three years before being freed by the 14th Army.

"Mentioned in Dispatches" for "Gallant and meritorious conduct whilst Prisoners of War in Japanese Hands."

This narrative was obtained from "Circumstance of Capture and Liberation" report sent to Harry Chagnon, 40th Bomb Group Historian by S.R.Lissenburg.

RICHARD BROOKS "TRUNK"

Owen J. Baggett, 2nd Lieutenant, 10th Air Force/Co-Pilot, B-24D, 7th Bomber Group,

9th Squadron.

Home City: San Antonio. Home State: Texas.

Dates of Imprisonment: 03/31/43 thru 09/07/45

Shot down while flying formation (unescorted) of four air craft near Magwe, Burma. We were attacked by an estimated 40 Zeros. Other air craft, though shot up, were able to make it back to India. Four of my crew members survived: Lt. Lloyd Jensen-pilot, myself, S/Sgt. Bud Costic- top turret, and S/Sgt. T. (Red) Higgenbothem-tail turret. Five of my crew member who didn't make it were: 2nd Lt. Max Davis-Navigator, 2nd Lt. Bert Smith-Bombardier, S/Sgts Kenneth Sleicker, Stephen Burke and Joseph Mercier. Some of those who jumped were killed by strafing Zeros, and I believe one or two were killed when a 20mm shell exploded in the waist section. Those of us who survived were all strafed in our chutes while descending.

After three months in solitary in the Rangoon Central Jail, Jensen and I were flown to Singapore, (Hq. all POW camps in Southeast Asia).

Since we were the first B-24 pilots captured, we were being sent to Tokyo. Something happened, and after 5 months in isolation and an interview with Commander of the Southeast Asia POW camps, M/Gen. Arimura, we were put in Changi Camp.

We were liberated on September 7, 1945 by members of the OSS who parachuted into camp, secured that airfield, and brought in a C-54. The plane was large enough to take all the American POWs to India. We only had 8 officers and 29 enlisted men in the camp at the time.

M.Gen.Arimura, the POW commander (Rangoon was one of his responsibilities), was hanged by the neck after the war as a war criminal!!!!!!!!!!!

This narrative was obtained through "Circumstances of Capture and Liberation" report sent to Harry Chagnon, 40th Bomb Group Historian by Owen Baggett.

RICHARD BROOKS "TRUNK'

John W. Boyd, Technical Sergeant, 10th Air Force/Radio Operator, B-25, 341 (M)

Bomber Group, 22nd Squadron.

Home City: Mayfield. Home State: Kentucky.

Dates of Imprisonment: 08/03/43 thru 05/03/45.

In an experimental skip bombing mission on August 3, 1943, our B-25 bomber was the last of three to go in on the target at tree top level. With heavy ground fire an explosive shell started a fire in the Bombay. Lt. McCook then pulled to about 1000 ft. The heat was so great Sgt. Leisure with chute on, released the emergency hatch and motioned he was going out. All chutes were seat type.

I motioned Sgt. Burk out of the turret and helped him with his chute. By this time the plane was below 800 ft. and in a landing approach angle. The tree tops were very close as I put my arms through the straps, with hand on the rip cord and standing over the hatch, I closed my legs and went through the bottom hatch standing straight up without the chute being strapped on. I pulled the cord as my head cleared the door. The chute opened, my head flew back and my feet hit the ground at the same time. The plane hit in the same field and blew up. Killing the four remaining crew members. I was paralyzed from the fall, immediately captured and beaten. I was a prisoner in Rangoon Prison Camp, Rangoon, Burma for 23 months.

John W. Boyd was Liberated by the British 8th Army, May 3, 1945.

This narrative obtained through "Circumstances of Capture and Liberation" report sent to Harry Chagnon, 40th Bomb Group Historian by John W.Boyd.

RICHARD BROOKS "TRUNK"

Clifford Emeny, Flight Officer, Mosquito-Fighter Bomber/RAF.
Home City: New Plymouth. Home Country: New Zealand.
Dates of Imprisonment: 11/11/44 thru 05/04/45.

I led a flight of six Mosquito fighter-bombers from Silchom, Assam, in a "just after" dawn raid on Meiktila Airfield in a low level attack on September 11, 1944. My plane was badly hit by heavy ground fire on my run in. Lost one engine and the other was damaged. Attacked by Oscars who shot out my remaining engine. Made successful crash landing in jungle. I along with my Navigator, Johnny Yanoto, of Blairesmore, Alberta, Canada survived the crash. Captured by Japanese patrol the next day. We were taken to Rangoon and severely interrogated. After several months in solitary (compound # 5) we were moved into compound # 8. Out of solitary and with more freedom to move around, I was active in leadership, assisted sick and wounded. Stayed behind when many prisoners were marched out in later part of April 1945. Assisted in takeover of prison when Japs left.

Took part in sortie to Mingladon Airfield where we participated in repairing runways in the preparations for the arrival of Allied forces. Flown to Calcutta on May 5, 1945. Returned to New Zealand in late July 1945.

OUR LIVES ARE OURS AGAIN ....

Cliff Emeny went home to New Zealand to become a Nutritionist and Iridiology Specialist.

This narration was obtained through "Circumstances of Capture and Liberation" report sent to Harry Chagnon, historian for the 40th Bomb Group by Cliff Emeny.

Richard Brooks "TRUNK"

William Matthews (Bill), Sergeant, Infantry, 2ⁿᵈ Battalion Duke of Wellington Regiment, 1933-1951.

Home City: Ipswich. Home Country: Suffolk, England.

Dates of Imprisonment: ? thru 04/28/45

I was a regular soldier in action on N.W. Frontier in India against tribesman raiding India from swat and mountains. Months of hard foot-slogging had toughened us up. With the Japanese threat to East Asia in 1941-42, we were shipped to Rangoon Burma. Rode in lorries to Sitting, Moulmien and south to three Pagoda areas.

Fighting from Tavoy (aerodrome) with our Indian troops, we were desperately taxed by eight divisions of Japs fresh from Singapore conquests. 10-12 to our 1....impossible odds. Bitter hand to hand fighting, as they still came on against 15 machine guns and mortars. We kept retreating for 13 days to Sittang River Bridge, heat, dust, no food or water but we kept on to the Bridge to enable us to set up defenses there. The Japs, lightly clad, were aided by Burmese traitors who showed them the jungle paths to encircle us. Bridge blown up as well as our vehicles. So two regiments, the 2ⁿᵈ Duke of Wellington and the K.O.Y.L.I., stayed on this side and were killed off in three days wounding only three of my Platoon. I was stabbed and bludgeoned from behind as I fought a Jap officer who lost his sword that I had swept aside. I was knocked down and roughly grabbed and tied up with hands behind me. Quickly hustled away with my two survivors. In late afternoon, I was interrogated at a hastily set up Jap HQ at Chaito, not too far from the Sittang River....all was lost! Refusing to cooperate, I deliberately mimicked a Scotch accent whereupon the Jap officer got angry and said I must speak in slow grammatical English. Just then mortar fire was heard nearby, and I was hustled into a hut that was guarded by a sentry. Nearly dusk, I told the other two that I had a razor blade up my sleeve. They were tied back to back, so we got the blade from my wrist and cut me free. I quickly cut them free and we sat there with our hands behind us as if we were still tied. The interpreter soon came back still raging and livid...I'd fooled him and he had lost face. He ranted "You English and Americans live too soft..." I swung a right cross to his chin

(I was a lightweight class boxer at Regiment). He dropped and I took his pistol, then jumped the sentry…it was dark and confusion reigned! We headed among rubber trees to the river layback. I stopped as I heard cries of Japs offering rewards to Burmese. One took me on with a Dah, nasty weapon, got me right in my shoulder as I shot him at the same time. Wounded badly, I headed for the river…and fell in and swept away. Good swimmer as I was (water polo player at Regiment), I was helpless and I was swept away for 5 or 6 miles in the dark. I crawled out on muddy bank and fell, dizzy and hardly aware of being near death. Crawled into jungle and pulled out dressing to my bleeding shoulder wound. Exhausted I fell asleep and awoke next morning at sunrise.

An Indian Tamil boy approaching, unaware of me hiding near his village. I called him to come! He was frightened and indicated and said "Japany looking! Stay there till dark…I come!" That night he came as promised with headman of the village who had me taken to a hut and his doctor dressed the wounds on my back, shoulder and chest. Then they hid me in an ox-cart and took me to a cave in the hills. I rested there for three days, and then moved further up hills to Red Kareni tribesman who were friendly to the British and disliked Japanese. Rested there a week, then on to Toungoo further north. Joined retreating troops that were meeting up with Chinese Sun Yat Sen's fighters who greeted my escape with relish. I was bitter and fought the Japs with no quarter. Took on Jap HQ one night with Kareni irregulars (guides) and used grenades at HQ but…SURPRISE! One of my group dropped a grenade short in doorway where I was shooting away. I got it in my right leg and down I went. I crumbled and hopped when this Jap officer with teeth missing and head cut, pasted me and kicked at my leg wound. He was furious…I was, he thought…a British Paras. "Where from, tie him up." They tied me to a tree at night.. I was barely conscious, more in a coma.…I thought *was* flying…weird. A Burmese girl unseen by the Japanese threw water in my face. (There were some brave pro-Brits). Next day at the interrogation, two Ghurkhas were brought in. They also were wounded. We were all loaded into a lorry that was to take us to the Rangoon Central Prison. The ride was uncomfortable with my wounded leg propped onto the lorry's spare tire.

Finally arriving at Rangoon Prison, we were interrogated again, and I stated that I was a straggler from fighting in Pegu where the British were. I was put in with the Brits #3 compound and had to rest and take care of the sick and wounded. Later, I was moved to #6 compound where I attended many Chindit survivors and American airmen, who were also wounded and burnt. Some died in agony, maggots in eyes…sheer neglect by the Japs… Sadistic and deliberate hate for U.S.A. flyers.

WE SURVIVED!

Years after the war, we were united in the U.S.A as the Rangoon Ramblers. Many of them knew me at first reunion… and we still meet every two years. How much we Brits owe the courageous flyers who kept our moral up at the cost of torture and beheadings by this cruel race.!

OUR LIVES ARE OURS AGAIN . . . .

From 1945 to 2000, **William Matthews** was a Farmer, Marketing Director, and Natural Healthcare Practitoner. He and his wife were trained in Herbology and Iridology. They strongly believed in teaching the health and goodness of natural resources for health instead of drugs. He entered politics and became Chairman of the New Zealand voter, and was a Voice of Federation for Independence from Social system in New Zealand. In the final analysis, he was a dedicated defender of responsible human freedom and dignity.

This narrative was obtained through "Circumstanced of Capture and Liberation" report sent to Harry Chagnon, Historian of the 40ᵗʰ Bomb Group by Bill Matthews.

<u>Richard Brooks "TRUNK"</u>

Richard D. Moore, Captain, 10th Air Force/Pilot, P-38.

Attached to British 3rd Tactical A.F. 459th Squadron.

Home City: Waco. Home State: Texas.

Dates of Imprisonment: 09/08/44 thru 05/06/45.

Mission on September 8, 1944 was by 16 P-38s with one belly tank and one 1000 pound RDX bomb. Target were the jetty's in the river at Monywa, Burma.

We arrived on target approximately 8:30 a.m. Flak was very heavy 40mm about 3500 ft. and 90mm at our altitude of 9000 ft. Plan was to peel off in a steep dive and release bomb at 3000. I began my pull out on schedule but then sustained direct hit on top of the leading edge of the right wing between the engine and pilot's nacelle. Aircraft was difficult to control due to violent turbulence caused by a large hole. Regained control at about 200 ft. Fuel tank in right wing was ruptured and engine quit. Attempted to maintain altitude on single engine but failed. Crash landed with only scratches to show.

I found I was on the edge of a small village. Hid under a bush until 11:00 am. Discovered by a small boy who could see under the bush (long time before I liked children again). He shouted and my bush was immediately surrounded by Burmese and Japanese. Beaten, kicked and tied up with a stick thrust through my elbows in back and my hands tied in front. Tossed in the back of an ox cart and taken to Monywa.

Next month was spent being interrogated in Monywa, Shwebo, Meiktilla and Mandalay. Learned to speak some Japanese and some Burmese talking to the guards. Found after many beatings for refusing to speak or lying that they had all the scoop on the Squadron anyway. Including almost a complete roster of personnel.

Finally reached Rangoon and my story becomes a carbon copy of everyone else's.

Reached home, I thought. After two weeks became partially paralyzed due to malnutrition and spent the next four months in and out of hospitals. Other than bad teeth, high blood pressure, loss of hair, wasn't hurt a bit.

This narrative was obtained through "Circumstances of Capture and Liberation" report sent to Harry Chagnon, the Historian for the 40ᵗʰ Bomb Group by Richard Moore.

<u>Richard Brooks "TRUNK"</u>

William C. Schrader, 2nd Lieutenant, 10th Air Force/Co-Pilot, B-24, USAAFCBI,

7th Bomber Group, 493 Squadron.

Home City: El Paso. Home State: Texas.

Dates of Imprisonment: 10/14/43 thru 05/09/45.

We went on a bombing raid to Rangoon. The target was a boundary on an island just south of Rangoon. Fighters were around us during the bomb drop, shortly after that they made a couple of head passes at us, but a twin engine I-45 came in under our right wing and hit us in the bomb bay tank setting it on fire. We tried to get out of formation and finally got it in a shallow right diving turn, the controls had almost been completely burned out. Sawyer got out the right waist window, but got pretty badly burned, as flames were pouring out of it.

After we got home, the navigator in the plane behind us said that was the last he saw of us, as the fighters were all over them. I don't know how long it was before the tail, and the right wing and nacelle came apart. Goad and I were thrown out through the cockpit canopy, safety belt and all. King and Gefert got out through the nose wheel door, and the last I saw of the top turret gunner, he was trying to get out of the turret. I don't think he made it before we came apart. I passed out when I was thrown out. When I came to I could see parts of the plane all around me, but some distance away. Delayed opening parachute, but not long enough. A twin engine fighter strafed me a couple of times before I got on the ground. Sprained both ankles when I hit, and was picked up by Burmese about 15 minutes later. That evening the Japanese arrived and things got rough. The next day they took me to the tail section but the Burmese has already buried them. There was a big bulge in the end of the tail near the turret, I guess they were all in a bunch when it hit. We were taken to Rangoon City Jail for 2 days, and then transferred us to Central Jail.

A British invasion force liberated us on 05-09-45. Put on a hospital ship taken to Calcutta.

This narrative was obtained through "Circumstances of Capture and Liberation" report sent to Harry Chagnon, the 40th Bomb Group Historian by William Schrader.

Richard Brooks "TRUNK"

**Christopher W. Morgan,311 Fighter Group, 529ᵗʰ Squadron, P-51
Home City: Yonkers. Home State: New York.**

**This narrative was obtained from NWF daily news.com News and
Information for the Emerald Coast. Chris Morgan's rank and dates
of imprisonment are unavailable but his squadron's job was to
relieve the Flying Tigers, the 1ˢᵗ American volunteer group.**

Like most people alive in 1941, he remembered exactly where he was
when Pearl Harbor was bombed by the Japanese on December 7ᵗʰ.
"I was standing in front of an ice cream shop with my buddies," says
Morgan, who was a high school senior in Yonkers, New York. "We
wanted to sign up right then. We all wanted to go to pilot training."
Two years later, he was the only one of his friends who had earned his
wings.

After training in Montgomery, Alabama and in Northwest Florida, he
was assigned to fly the P-51 fighter. "I was 19 and flying one of those
things," he recalls with a laugh. "That's better than a Corvette."

In the summer of 1943, he boarded a troop ship in San Francisco bound
for Bombay. The journey lasted nearly 50 days, and the only pastime
was gambling. "I lost all my money in the first couple of days, so I spent
most of my time up on deck watching the flying fish."

In October, he finally arrived at his base in Dinjan, India in the war's
China-Burma-India theater. His squadron's job was to relieve the Flying
Tigers, the 1ˢᵗ American Volunteer Group.

"My first mission was October 16, 1943, and that was the day I went
down. I had been flying over the jungles of Burma. My flight leader got
disoriented; the sad part of it was I knew where I was the whole time. I
told him I could get him home, but he just pointed to his collar and told
me to get back into formation. Being a good solder, I did. I eventually
ran out of fuel and had to land in a rice field.

"I evaded for three days. I hooked up with some Burmese natives who led me into an ambush. Barely 20 years old, I found myself in the hands of Japanese soldiers. I wasn't afraid of the Japanese, I was afraid of the unknown.

"After surviving interrogation, the enemy set off with me toward Rangoon Jail. We walked, rode camels, and rode railroads. It was a 1,000-mile trip. All the illnesses you pick up in that section of the world, I had them.

"I arrived at the Rangoon Jail on a stretcher, but that didn't stop the Japanese soldiers from putting me in solitary confinement for three months. Their psychology was that it was supposed to break our spirit."

It didn't work and eventually his captors let him stay among the other prisoners. It was mostly British and there were Chinese and Indians in the camp. It was a place of starvation and constant sickness, where prisoners survived on a pittance of rice, clear soup and pumpkins. "We had very little to eat, the biggest killer in the camp was beriberi." Beriberi is like drowning from within. Cholera struck the prison camp in June 1944. It killed with swiftness that amazed him. It was a most dreaded disease. You're violently sick at 5 a.m. and then dead by 5 p.m. Morgan and one of his friends, a Canadian flight officer named Jim Drake, volunteered to sit with the dying men. "There was nothing we could do for them. The fixation we talked about was getting out, going home." Morgan remembers that Drake was worried they would all be dead by Christmas 1944 if they weren't rescued soon. His friend he says lost his hope. "Drake died from beriberi on Christmas Day. That scared the daylights out of me," adding that his friend's death motivated him to stay mentally and physically tough. To stay alert, he and other inmates would do calisthenics and quiz each other on the 48 states and their capitals. To this day he does a crossword puzzle daily.

As their captivity lasted into the next year, Morgan and other inmates began thinking about breaking out. "We had plans of our own; we were going to take them over." They never got the chance because on April 29ᵗʰ, 1945, the Japanese separated the men into two groups- those who could walk and those who couldn't. The sick were left behind at Rangoon Jail and the rest were marched north about 50 miles. Among those prisoners was a British General. "The Japanese told us to give their men 10 minutes and then you are free. And that's what happened. They left us in a rice field.

"But nearby British forces began strafing the field and inadvertently killed the British General. The prisoners scattered in fear. I jumped in a well and jumped on top of five other guys and about 10 more jumped in on top of me."

After surviving the rescue, Morgan, who was 21 by then, was shipped back to the states to recuperate in Atlantic City, New Jersey. When he was able, he made his way back to Yonkers.

"The most emotional moment I had throughout everything that happened was coming home. My parents collapsed in my arms."

This is the same Chris Morgan who wrote for the 40th Bomb Group "Memories" and was the special lead in the beginning of these narratives that was so poignant.

Alexander McKay Gibson, Lieutenant

Unit: 8th Gurkha Rifles.

Served in Burma

This narrative was obtained through the courtesy of Steve Fogden who wrote the Introduction and was obtained through www.pegasusarchive.org

Alec Gibson was one of the three young 8th Gurkha Rifles officers who, in January 1943, were sent to join Wingate's first Chindit operation just days before it ventured into Burma. He found himself a member of column three, consisting mainly of Gurkha troops and commanded by the famous Mike Calvert.

What follows is his own account of his time in captivity and his memories of Rangoon Jail.

He told me that he was captured near a village called Taugaung situated on the Eastern banks of the Irrawaddy River. He was taken to the railway town of Wuntho, from which he was transported to the transitory POW camp at Maymyo. Here is his story:

"Missing from April 4th- last seen swimming the Irrawaddy." That was the news given to my parents in July 1943 by Lt. McKenzie of the 3/2 Gurkha Rifles, who managed to return to India from the first Chindit operation. My parents had no further news of me until I was reported "recovered from the enemy on April 30th 1945."

Following Wingate's dispersal order, we were trapped on the east side of the Irrawaddy, my party was unable to find boats, so swimming was the only alternative. After two abortive attempts, I found myself alone with one Gurkha when we were jumped by eight Burmese Independent Army soldiers who tied us up and dragged us to the nearest Jap outpost some 5 miles away.

When initially interrogated by a Japanese Captain who spoke a little English, I refused to answer and had a sword stuck at my throat! I thought that was to be my end, but managed to survive the ordeal with very evasive or completely inaccurate answers. Later, I was taken by train, with many others prisoners, to Maymyo near Mandalay. Our hands were tied and 26 men were crammed into a railway wagon meant to accommodate only four cattle. At Maymyo camp we had to learn Japanese drill: commands were shouted to us in Japanese and we were expected to understand them. If we got the drill wrong then we were knocked down with rifle butts, pick handles or bamboo canes. We managed to learn it in about two days! I was again interrogated and beaten if my answers were unsatisfactory. Both officers and men were up at dawn and made to work on various jobs till dusk. We all had to go and collect our food, two meals a day of rice and vegetable stew.

As a deliberate policy of humiliation we were lined up at least once per day and subjected to considerable face slapping by the Jap guards. Every now and again a prisoner would be called out for interrogation and you knew that you would undergo considerable punishment before you got back again. At night and during air-raids we were locked up, four to a wooden hut about the size of a bathing hut back home. There was a small oil drum inside to use as a latrine, this had to be emptied by one of the four each morning.

At this camp I met one of the Gurkha Subadars wearing the armband with the Jap Rising Sun the sign of the Indian National Army! I asked him how he could do this and he relied "Don't worry Sahib- I have plans to get out of here." I heard later that after training with the Japs he and the rest of the Gurkhas were given arms and sent to the front, here they promptly killed the Japs with them and went straight across to the Allied troops

After several weeks at Maymyo we were transported by train to Rangoon, once again tied up and in cattle trucks. On arrival we were marched to what was previously Rangoon Central Jail, and placed into the solitary confinement block. These cells were about 9 feet square with one small window, dark and gloomy, with only the stone floor to sleep on. We were given one blanket each. The guards patrolled the block and we were not supposed to talk to each other, any breach being punished by a beating. Food was brought to us in the morning and evening, by one of the British POWs in the jail. We were only taken out for interrogation. By this time we had all agreed to give various pieces of misleading information, this we hoped would save us from further torture and punishment. The difficulty was remembering what one had said previously and I nearly got caught on two occasions. I was in solitary for only a few weeks but some prisoners spent months there.

Then the day came when I was transferred to one of the open blocks. Rangoon Jail, built during the colonial times, resembled a large wheel with a well and water tower as the hub and the main blocks radiating out from there like the spokes of a wheel. The blocks were contained in compounds made of seven-foot high brick walls and high iron barred fences at the centre and outer perimeter. The guards patrolling the centre and the hub could see the whole compound. Whenever a guard appeared the nearest person had to call the whole group to attention and all had to bow to the guard. Failure to do so incurred an immediate beating. The blocks were two-storied buildings, each floor containing five rooms with long barred windows down to floor level on one side, and floor to ceiling bars on the whole other side, which opened onto a corridor running the length of the block. Stone steps at both ends led to the upper corridor.

In the compound was a long concrete trough containing water and a basha containing lots of ammunition boxes used as latrines. These had to be emptied every day by the Sanitary Squad. Apart from the solitary confinement block and the punishment block, two of the other blocks were occupied by British and American prisoners, two more by Indians, one by Chinese and one by American Airmen in long-term solitary confinement.

In number 3 block where I spent most of my time, the officers were in two rooms on the upper floor, about 26 of us in each room. The other ranks occupied the other rooms with between 30 and 40 POWs in each. There was no glass in any window so the Monsoon rains just poured in, but at least this did cool things down. We all had to sleep on the floor with just our blanket and using what you could for a pillow. The Japanese had taken all we possessed; leaving us with tattered clothes we stood up in. No more clothing was issued; we had to patch whatever we had with materials stolen while out on working parties. Most of the time we wore only a fandoshi or loincloth made from a rectangle of cloth and a piece of string. As our boots fell apart we went barefoot, our feet soon got pretty tough.

Things settled down into a regular routine, up at dawn for roll call, numbering in Japanese, a brief cup of tea (so called), then detailed off for working parties as notified from the previous day. Every fit person including officers had to work. Working parties consisted of one officer in charge, 15 to 20 men, two or three Jap guards; there were sometimes work parties made up entirely of officers. We marched out of the jail taking with us rice and vegetable for our midday meal, plus all tools needed for the job we were on. One man would cook the meal while the rest of us were employed as slave labor.

We worked on the railway, unloaded rice and stores at the docks, helped to build underground headquarters for the Japs, repaired roads and bridges, dug up unexploded bombs and cleared up after air-raid damage. Sometimes we had to work further away such as Mingladon airfield. On these days we were transported in trucks. If anything went wrong, the man concerned and the officer in charge were both beaten up. At dusk we returned to the jail where our cooks would have a meal ready for us. Then after another roll call we were shut up for the night, there were no lights in the blocks.

On Sundays we were usually allowed a rest day, when there were no outside working parties. Sometimes we played football or netball, always being careful not to injure ourselves. On the odd occasion we were allowed to have a concert party, at which I used to sing some popular songs, accompanied by a band consisting of one mouth organ, two men on paper combs and another emulating a trumpet. The Japs used to come along to watch as well. We had no cigarettes but used to make some from Burmese cheroots, rolled in newspaper and stuck down with rice. No Red Cross parcels were ever received and only twice did we get any mail, most of us had never been notified as POWs anyway. No attempts to escape were made, although it would have been easy enough to get away. Apart from being unfit for such efforts; the chances of travelling hundreds of miles trying to look Burmese Indian or Burmese were pretty slim.

For those not fit to work outside, there were inside working parties for sanitary duties, sick bay orderlies, gardening parties to grow vegetables, cleaning the cell blocks and collecting and delivering food and firewood. All this was interspersed with the need to stop and come to attention and bow every time a guard came near. Some men were permanently on cooking duties and did their best with the rations we were given. This was basically rice and vegetables with occasional meat scrounged from outside, or maybe a pigeon caught on the inside! Sometimes we had a sort of porridge made from ground up husks of rice. It tasted horrible but contained vitamin B1 and was a great help against beriberi. We also had tea, or rather hot water with a few leaves thrown in, no milk and no sugar.

The odd thing about working parties was that the men were paid, albeit only 10 cents (about 2 pence) per day. Officers were paid a salary once a month, for my rank this amounted to 160 rupees about 12 pounds. However, deductions were made for board and lodging, contribution to Japanese Defense Bonds and various items. I actually signed for a received 10 rupees each month, half of which went to fund extra food for sick bay.

We were able to buy small quantities of sugar, eggs, and sometimes meat, and Burmese cheroots through the Jap Quartermaster. These items became scarcer and more expensive as time went by. On outside work parties we had become accomplished thieves and stole anything we could lay our hands on. In spite of a search at the guard room when we returned, we used to smuggle in meat, eggs, dried fish, sugar, books and English language newspapers. Sometime we were caught and severely punished, often beaten or made to stand at attention in the hot sun for hours, but it was worth it.

The things that kept us going was the conviction that we would win the war, a great sense of humor and a determination to outwit the Jap at every opportunity. The last was particularly difficult path to tread. Any deliberate wrong doing incurred immediate and severe punishment, so everything had to look like an accident or show the British as being incompetent idiots. The following stories indicate some of the plots in which I was involved, each needing careful coordination between officer and the men. We were unloading rice from barges at Rangoon Docks, carrying it in large jute sacks. Holes were made in the bottom of these sacks so that we staggered to the warehouse we left a trail of rice along the dockside. Before Japs could intervene, I complained to them that all the sacks were no good. When unloading 40 gallon drums of petrol we made sure that each drum was dumped heavily on to one of the sharp stones we had placed on the dockside- the whole place reeked of fuel. On another occasion a crate of vital fuses for the Japanese shells fell overboard from the ship in spite of our valiant efforts to save it!! All successful attempts were of course a great boost to morale.

The one thing that really worried us was being injured or becoming ill as medical treatment was non-existent. We had several medical officers with us as prisoners but they had virtually nothing in the way of medicines or equipment. Jungle sores or ulcers were treated with copper sulphate crystals, dysentery with charcoal tablets, and beriberi with grain husks. Incredibly, two successful amputations were carried out with the crudest of instruments and no anesthetics. Most of us suffered from ulcers, dysentery, beriberi, or dengue fever at sometime, but if it became serious it was usually terminal. Two thirds of the complement of the camp died, and of the 210 captured Chindits from both expeditions 168 died of their wounds, disease or malnutrition. Fourteen POWs died when a Stick of bombs from a crippled American bomber fell right across the jail.

One point I must mention is that, whilst we were treated as dirt as POWs, the Japanese respected our dead. When a prisoner died, he was taken to a burial ground outside the jail by a funeral party consisting of, a British Officer, six other ranks and two guards. His body was carried on a small and cart covered in a very tattered Union Jack. We dug a grave, buried the man, held a brief funeral service and put up a wooden cross. The position of each grave was plotted on a map by our senior officer. Once I was scheduled to take out a funeral party for one man on the following day, by the time I went there were five bodies to be buried. The burial ground is now an official War Cemetery (Rangoon War Cemetery) beautifully laid out, and on the Far East Pilgrimage 40 years later I was able to assure some of the War widows that at least their husbands had been given a proper burial.

Eventually in April 1945, the Japs decided to move as many POWs as possible back to Japan via Thailand. Some 400 of us were classified as fit to march and on the 24th of April we marched out of the jail for the last time, leaving behind another 400 sick and crippled. After five grueling days and having covered about 55 miles, we were North of Pegu and nearing the Sittang Bridge when we ran into the 14th Army. The Jap Commandant left us in a village, told us we were free and disappeared with the rest of the guards. We were in no-man's land with firing coming from all sides. That night we managed to contact our own troops, the West Yorkshires, and we were released.

The following story, "Rangoon Rescue" was written by Bill Rooney in 1945 after he interviewed rescued 40th Group crew members in the hospital in Calcutta. It was submitted to AIR FORCE MAGAZINE but was never published. Because this mission was one of the significant episodes in the history of the 40th Group, we thought it might be appropriate to distribute this story at our Second Reunion, Arlington, TX, October 1981.

Air Force Magazine sure gets around. Even the Japs read it. But that isn't all that twenty-nine B-29 combat crewmen had to tell about their four months as prisoners of the Japanese.

Resting in the American General Hospital in Calcutta after being freed from the prison in which the Japanese held them for four months along with hundreds of other Allied prisoners, the B-29 crewmen looked back on their experiences pretty much as one of those bad dreams. The idea of seeing friendly faces once again, of sleeping on real beds with clean sheets and having clean clothes and real American food—with ice cream too—was almost too much after living for what seemed endless time in the filth and misery of a Rangoon jail.

On December 14, 1944, a B-29 task force struck at Rama VI Bridge, Thailand and the Central Railway Station, Rangoon, Burma. It was in the latter striking force that after bombs away a terrific explosion occurred just beneath the planes. Grave damage was sustained by several aircraft and crew members were forced to bail out behind enemy lines. Ordnance Officers have since determined that the explosion was caused by colliding bombs.

Completely cowed by the Japanese, the Burmese people gave only passive assistance to the downed men and with one exception, the men were all taken prisoner within 24 hours after their bail-out. T/Sgt E. F. Trinkner, tail gunner on one of the planes, managed to evade capture for six days before being turned over to the Japs by the Burmese. The plane from which Sgt. Trinkner parachuted, incidentally, crashed only 500 yards from the prison in which he was afterward held.

From the instant of their capture there began an almost endless routine of beatings and interrogations—until final imprisonment at Rangoon jail where interrogations stopped but the beatings continued.

Capt. Robert Shanks, Jr. and 1st Lt. Harold E. Fletcher, pilot and co-pilot, respectively, were fired upon by Japanese and puppet soldiers while Lt. Fletcher lay in a small hut, unable to move because of a sprained ankle. After Capt. Shanks held up his hands in surrender, the Jap soldiers in a maniacal display of temper flogged and beat the two men. Forced to their knees they expected to be executed. Instead the Japs made them walk barefoot for about five miles to a camp. Later they were taken by boat for some distance and then marched to the Jap area headquarters where they met other members of their crew. S/

Sgt. W.R. Lentz, right gunner on their airplane, was similarly treated by the Japs when he refused to answer questions in interrogation. Beat to his knees by an officer using a sword and scabbard, Lentz expected beheading then and there but the officer thrust the sword point in the sergeant's back and screamed at him that he would thereafter answer the questions he asked.

Mixed with the beatings and interrogations were a number of curious incidents which in small measure relieved the misery of their life in the hands of the Japanese. In one instance, a Burmese guard watching Lts. C.R. Benedict, J.C. Cochran, G.M. Etherington and a number of the men shortly after their capture, told the prisoners not to feel too bad. It wouldn't be too long until they would be free, he said. They asked him what he meant. Were the Japs going to be defeated? The guard said, perhaps not, but in four months Burma will be out of the war. Four months exactly from the day they were admitted to Rangoon jail these men were free and safely behind the British 14th Army lines.

On another occasion T/Sgt. Enrico E. Pisterzi, tail gunner, was being questioned by a Japanese interrogator. Suddenly, in a very hushed and secretive tones, after looking over both shoulders to see that no one was listening the interrogator asked, "What do you think of the B-29?" Sgt. Pisterzi carried on the act and answered, "I think it's a pretty good airplane." The Jap again cautiously looked over both shoulders and then in great confidence murmured for only Pisterzi to hear, "So do I."

Another time, 1st Lt. Galpin M. Etherington, flight engineer, was questioned about flight characteristics of the B-29. "How does the plane fly under the most favorable weather conditions?" asked the Jap captain. Lt. Etherington replied that he could not answer that. "Well then, how does it fly under the worst weather conditions?" queried the Nip. To this Etherington replied, "Under those conditions, it won't fly at all." At this the Jap nearly had a red-out mostly because of the face he had lost for asking such a foolish question which was so skillfully thrown back at him by his prisoner.

Ultimately all the survivors of the crashed aircraft were taken to Judson College in Rangoon which they surmised was the Jap Air Force headquarters in Burma. There they were interrogated by what Japs considered their interrogation experts. And it was at this point that the men were given an idea of the Japanese espionage activities. The interrogators told the men the numbers and locations of each squadron and group in the Twentieth Bomber Command and the names of the organization commanders. And it was here that the Japanese interrogator- who said he had studied at Washington State- pulled out a copy of the November issue of Air Force Magazine to assist him in the interrogation. (Like most GIs, the men said, he didn't pass his copy around and this angered some of the crewman because they hadn't seen that issue.)

Generally the interrogator's questions were taken from the magazine and curiously most of the questions asked were already answered in the magazine but this didn't deter the Japs from asking endless numbers of questions, mostly, of course, about the B-29. Many of the queries such as those about cruise control, landing speeds, load, bomb bay tanks, crew stations, duties of each crew member, etc., were off the classified list for some time. One question asked most frequently and this by nearly every Japanese who could speak English—was the age of each crew member. No matter what the answer was, young or old, it never ceased to amaze them.

In addition to queries about the aircraft and each crewman's duties, there were vast number of questions asked ranging from home life and conditions in the States, through life at the base including how many men in the organization wore glasses, to questions about the C-109 and P-51. Questions about radar and radio equipment were, for the most part, inexpertly asked indicating the Jap's lack of knowledge of these subjects.

Life in the prison to which they were sent after interrogation was one of misery, filth and starvation. The Japs were terrified beyond measure of Allied bombing and strafing attacks. The men learned this when they were brought from their bail-out areas to Rangoon. The Japs would never travel in the day time for fear of air attack. Because of this fear of Allied airplanes the Japanese vented their anger on the crewmen by giving them half the ration of the ground troops held in the prison, confining them to the limits of their compound area, refusing to permit them to go out on work details and administering beatings and punishment at any provocation, however slight. It was on New Year's day that the B-29 men were singled out from the rest of the prisoners and beaten in the Japanese's own special manner- bone breaking beatings on wrists, elbows, ankles and other joints with teakwood clubs. It was assumed by the prisoners afterward that the reason for this beating was more than just the results of hangovers after pay day night celebration but was probably because the Japs had heard of the 27th December raid on Tokyo by B-29s of the XX1 Bomber Command.

To relieve the monotony of prison and to keep their minds busy, the men participated with other British and American Air Force prisoners in classes ranging from religion to hand-crafts that were organized by the prisoners in the compound. Some of their comrades from the 10th Air Force, Air Commando outfits and other American air units had been in prison many months longer than they. Some had died there, too. One survivor, however was rescued with them was from the first American airplane lost over Burma; a B-17 that had gone down on a mission nearly three years before.

One of the prisoners drew from memory a map of Burma on the prison wall. Occasionally members from other compounds in the prison who had been out on work details would bring back news of British army advances on northern Burma. Each time after such news was signaled to them, the prisoners would go into the prison cell and look at the map. This they did until one day a Jap guard inspected their cell and after carefully studying the map to obtain information from it for himself, he raged at the men to wash it off. After this, it was mostly just listening and waiting. Two or three times they saw in the sky B-29s in big formations flying overhead. Once they saw the sky filed with Allied aircraft: B-24s, P-47s and P-38s as well as B-29s. This was March 22, the day Jap supply dumps and storage areas in Rangoon took a terrific pasting. The men cheered when they heard the bombs hit. Each day after one of these missions they would see a B-29 photo plane streak across the sky, snap his pictures, and head for home.

Soon there were signs of uneasiness among the Japanese. With this came better treatment too. Obviously the Nips were getting ready for something and then one day every man able to walk was told to get his effects together. These bare belongings together with all the supplies the Japs could locate were loaded on bullock carts. Eighteen B-29 crewmen who were able to walk together with nearly 400 other prisoners were made to haul the carts out of the city and up the railroad in the direction of Pegu. The Japs were trying to withdraw to Moulmein before the British 14th Army trapped them in Rangoon. Marching only at night and then for 11 to 16 hours the men dragged the carts along the railroad bed to Pegu and to a village a short distance beyond. There the Japanese saw they could go no farther with their prisoners and they called the ranking officer among the prisoners a British Brigadier. They told the Brigadier that he and the other prisoners were now free and then the Japs took off double timing it.

This left the newly liberated prisoners in the delicate position of being behind the retreating Japanese troops facing the powerful British army and virtually under the guns of these friendly forces. Already strafed a number of times by Allied planes during their march, the freed men were now strafed and bombed again and tragically one of the shells from a strafer killed the Brigadier, the only man lost to Allied air attack. Somehow one of the prisoners sneaked through to the advancing 14th Army lines and a rescue party cut back through the Jap lines and brought the prisoners to safety.

Meanwhile, back in the prison the men too sick to march noted a decided lack of activity on the part of the Japanese and investigation disclosed that the fleeing Nips had left several notes around the prison telling the men they were free. Not knowing how they would be treated outside the prison the men elected to act cautiously and stay inside the prison walls until they could find out more of what was going on outside.

"The first friendly men I saw were four British Marines who came into the prison after airborne and amphibious assaults had secured the city," said Capt. Shanks. "When the rejoicing was over we waited in the prison until they took us out to a hospital ship and evacuated us here.

"When it looked like we were going to bail out I called Col. Coronet (Lt. Col. James Ira Coronet) on command and told him not to send my stuff back home that I would be back, and here I am," Shanks concluded as he stretched out on his sack in the hospital in Calcutta.

All the men were full of questions about what had been going on in the four months they had been away. But the question on the lips of every one of them was, "How did the Japs get that November Air Force?"

**Roy A. Wentz , Lieutenant, 10ᵗʰ Air Force /Navigator, B-24,
CBI Bomber Command, 7ᵗʰ Group, 9ᵗʰ Squadron.
Home City: Wilmington. Home State: Delaware.**

Led two groups of B-24s to bomb Rangoon December 1, 1943. Attacked by fighter, lost two engines, parachuted near Bassein. Taken by boat to Rangoon and imprisoned at New Law Courts Building. Moved to Rangoon Central Jail about July 27, 1944 where we were kept isolated in cells until January 27, 1945. We were then moved into an open compound. We were liberated by the British on May 2, 1945 and taken to Calcutta by boat.

NOTE: Lt. Wentz had a more detailed account of his imprisonment in a diary style he offered to make available but unfortunately was unavailable after all this time.

Our Lives Are Ours Again . . . .

Lt. Wentz became a Captain before his discharge. He obtained a Law Degree in 1948. He was employed in the Office of Chief Counsel with the IRS in Washington. He then joined the DuPont Company in Wilmington, Delaware in their legal department and then back to the office of Chief Tax Counsel from 1963 to 1985. He was an early advisor and financial supporter of Senator Joseph Biden. He died on November 16, 2003 in Wilmington, Delaware.

Lionel Hudson, Wing Commander, Mosquito VI Fighter/ Bomber,

No 82 RAF, Mosquito Squadron.

Home: Australia

This narrative is entirely from Commander Hudson's astonishing book "The Rats of Rangoon." He wrote this book 40 years after his imprisonment after reading for the first time a dairy that he secretly kept while in Rangoon Prison. He was able to acquire a small amount of paper and an indelible pencil while there. These notes were so small that he had difficulty himself in deciphering them. He tells in great detail his experiences and it is a most worthwhile book. The events I relate here are but a small portion of his experiences.

Our release from Rangoon Prison was enacted in a week when there were some major developments occurring in the world, so the eyes of the world were focused elsewhere other than Rangoon.

1. Almost a million Germans surrendered in Europe and became POWs.

2. The war in Italy ended as the bodies of Mussolini and his mistress were strung up head downwards on meat hooks at a petrol station in Milan.

3. Adolph Hitler and Eva Braun committed suicide in a Berlin bunker.

4. The battle for Okinawa was at its height and the British fleet joined the fray and were savagely attacked by self-sacrificing kamikaze pilots

My flight to Assam that day was not really necessary. Group operations had no special target to offer but I wanted to test fire my cannon.

My navigator, Jack had given me a course to Mandalay. As I looked down and saw the Irrawaddy River below us I swished down and skimmed it. There was a jolting crash sound and a jarring note. I was still airborne and climbing but my Mosquito began to vibrate madly. Jack told me that the port engine was on fire. We began falling out of the sky like a leaf falling from a tree.

I blacked out and when I came to I was standing there in deep mud in a tangle of control wires with Jack slumped a little alongside me. There was a burning smell but I had no idea of what had happened to the rest of the plane. It seemed to have vanished.

There were Japanese soldiers there and they tied our hands behind our backs and loaded us into a truck. We didn't know it then but we were on our way to Rangoon. At one point we came upon a small, unkempt Buddhist Temple. A bulldog of a sergeant shouted an order in Japanese and pointed to a spot near the Temple wall. I approached it and knelt. It seemed like the thing to do. My hands were still tied behind my back. I looked up but his hand pushed my chin into my chest. There was a swish and I felt a rush of wind on the back of my neck. Shit...this was it was my sudden thought. Of course, I was in the classic beheading position. Another swish, this time my right cheek felt the breeze. My eyes were pressed tight but I knew it was his sword slicing through the air. Accompanying each stroke was a belly grunt and something that sounded like an oath. I froze with fear. The hairs on the back of my neck tingled. The swishing stopped and after a pause my executioner exploded into laughter and slapped my backside with the flat of his sword. He helped me to my feet and took me back to the truck. And Jack and I were back on the way to Rangoon.

Jack and I decided on a story that we would tell. If the Japanese were to find out who I really was and what I could tell them I would sure to be whisked off to Saigon or Tokyo. I had been involved in some of the invasion planning and as a Wing Commander was knowledgeable about a great many things. The story that Jack and I would tell would be that we had just arrived in India to form a new squadron that didn't even have a number yet.

When we arrived in Rangoon we were taken to the Japanese Headquarters (which we later found to be a University). They of course separated Jack and me for questioning. We both knew that we would have to endure some torture to make our story believable. After intense interrogation we were sent to the gaol (Rangoon Jail).

The British, Indian and Chinese were confined in separate compounds inside the prison walls and were free to move around in the yards. Within those prisoners were a few captured doctors. The men took care of themselves as best they could. They cooked and the fit men were able to work for small amounts of money outside the jail in working parties. This would enable them to sometimes purchase small amounts of food on the outside. They worked mainly on the docks for the Japanese loading and unloading the boats that came in.

The airmen were locked away in separate cells day and night and some in solitary, never to leave the cell except when it was their turn in their cell to empty the "binjo" boxes. These were old metal ammunition cases that were used for human waste. On very rare occasions they were allowed to visit the well and douse themselves with a bucket of water.

An edict had been issued from the top in Tokyo that all captured airmen were to be treated as criminals not prisoners of war.

We air crews were the pariahs of the prison. Other inmates went out on working parties, but we were not allowed to.

Before being sent to the "gaol" (Jail), airmen were held at the New Laws Courts cell block, it was a place of horror. Captured fliers were flung into dark cells with murderers, spies and lepers. From 5 to 9 people were crowded into each cell measuring 9' x 12'. They saw no sun and despite sweltering heat, they were given barely enough liquid to keep them alive. The food was scanty and medical treatment practically non-existent. Of 57 airmen incarcerated at the Rangoon Ritz (as it was called), 23 died from disease and bashings.

On March 28ᵗʰ we noted some fresh Jap guards. "Big Ti" (as we called the camp commander) was beginning to look stressed. We then spied several machine guns sitting on the veranda of the main gate building covered with blankets. This was an elevated position and looked down on the prisoners. They seemed to be manned by the new troops. We could see Allied bombing was increasing steadily but we saw very little ack ack from the ground and no Jap planes in the air challenging the B-29s or Liberators. We knew the Allies were close but did not know what the Japs meant to do with us. They were now scattered all around the prison. We knew that they were afraid that we might try to escape and they were making sure that we would not. We could only speculate as to their intentions.

The brutality practiced by the Japanese is unimaginable. One guard we called the "Cisco Kid" would order prisoners to stand at attention close to the bars of the cell while he pushed a rubber tube up their nostrils until it came out their mouths and laugh hysterically. He considered it a great joke. Many prisoners had black and blue fingernails from being hit by a club after being ordered to spread their fingers over a ledge. Then nails were pulled out with pliers sometimes over a period of months. The repeated beatings took their toll and many would die from them.

The men from the Indian compound managed to toss over the fence some extra food to us at great peril to themselves. They were loyal and noble men who did without themselves to help us.

On April 25ᵗʰ we noted that Japanese were scurrying from building to building, burning records and putting on new clothing and discarding old. Making piles of clothes. We were still unable to determine what was happening. Early that evening we saw them milling around like people all ready to go somewhere but where? We knew the Japanese did not quit. They stay and fight to death. We were still at a loss to understand what was going on. They had already told us to identify which prisoners were fit to walk and which were too ill. We saw some of the prisoners were being given Jap clothing. What their intentions were for the men left behind were still unknown. The machine guns still looked down on us.

Seeing our boys dressed in Jap uniforms and the odd lot of clothing worn by the Japanese confirmed that they were indeed getting ready to leave.

It was now April 26th and we were told that the prisoners who were able to go would leave at 4 PM. In my cell 52 men were going and 49 staying. We knew as these fellows marched out it would be hard for any pilot on strafing runs to know that these were Allied prisoners or even to distinguish them as Caucasians.

We had sad hearts when they marched out, surprisingly cheery and facing the unknown like that takes guts. They were gallant men. There had been a final prayer meeting upstairs unknown to the Japs.

As they left, first an advance party of Japs, then a large British Army Group led by Colonel Hobson. He marched erect and brisk ahead of his company. He and most of his men had been in captivity for more than 3 years. Each group was followed by heaped high hand carts pulled and pushed by 6 to 8 men. Retreat from Rangoon... a handful of Jap with 400 British and American hostages on foot. What chance did they have of avoiding the war machine that was the British 14th Army?

April29th we realized that the compound had an extraordinarily strange stillness. We began to cautiously explore our surroundings. We found 2 notes, one at the main gate saying that we were free. The Emperor was giving us our freedom.

The count in the gaol of men left behind was 668 officers and men. 474 Indians and Gurkhas, 123 British, 54 Chinese, 39 Americans, 3 Anglo-Burmese, 2 New Zealanders, 1 East African, 1 Canadian and 1 Australian. 400 men were marched away four days before.

The British were unaware that the Japs had evacuated from Rangoon or that a prison camp was there. We waited for the British to arrive. We had written with rice paste on the top of two gaol buildings in the largest possible letters "JAPS GONE" "BRITISH HERE".

On May 2nd at 9:30 AM an RAF Mosquito skip bombed the gaol, while no one was hurt the men were incensed and decided that the RAF did not believe what we had written and had decided it was a Jap trick. We were beginning to despair as to how to signal to the Allies. One of the men said "how are we going to get them to pull their finger out of their ass?" That's it I said. Paint a message on another roof, just say: EXTRACT DIDGET. That should stop the bastards. Tension built during the afternoon.

There was a scatter when 4 RAF Thunderbolts and a Mosquito fighter-bomber came over at low level. No bombs this time. Clearly their mission was to check out the writing on the roofs. As they flew away they waggled their wings acknowledging our message was understood. The time: 1535 hours May 2, 1945.

Our lives are ours again. . . .

Bill, an inveterate storyteller, joined the Sun Newspaper as a copy boy in 1930. Copy boys were paid a pound a week to race back to the Sun Building on Elizabeth Street with news written in long hand. He became a cadet journalist but entered the Air Force when war broke out in 1939. He joined the Empire Training Scheme, spent time in Ceylon and was a Royal Australian Air Force (RAAF) pilot, flying in South East Asia. Priding himself on being an individualist, he nevertheless made his way through the ranks in 1944 as Wing Commander. He was sent to command No.82 Squadron RAF flying Mosquito fighter bombers.

Unfortunately he crashed behind enemy lines in Burma, and spent 5 months as a POW in Rangoon. After returning from Rangoon Prison Camp, he worked with AAP Reuters and won a Nieman Fellowship to Harvard to study ancient Chinese history. He became Editor of AAP-Reuters in New York. He returned to Australia in 1956 to work with ABC supervisor of TV news. He made wildlife documentaries, sold them worldwide, made films in New York, Guinea and Antarctica. He was proud to be the 3rd Australian to reach the South Pole.

Message written with wheat paste on roofs after Japanese left. British pilots thought "Japs Gone" was a trick to stop bombing until British POW pilots wrote "Extract didget" which was recognized immediately as a phrase commonly used by British pilots as "Get your finger out of your ass."

Additional POWs made available through "Circumstances of Capture and Liberation"

These reports were sent to Harry Chagnon, the 40th Bomb Group Historian by each of these men.

Stanton L. Dow, staff Sergeant 40th Bomber Group, 25th Squadron, B-29.
Home City: Aurora. Home State: Colorado.
Imprisoned: 12/14/44 thru 05/04/45.

Mel Bowman, Fighter Pilot, 311 Fighter Group, 529 Squadron, P-51
Home City: Belvedere. Home State: California
Imprisoned: 10/16/43 thru 05/01/45.

M.B. Bukde, 1st Lt., 40th Bomber Group, 25th Squadron, B-29.
Home City: San Antonio. Home State: Texas.
Imprisoned: 12/14/44 thru 05/04/45.

Robert Bicknell, Jr. (Tex) Technical Sergeant, 1st Air Command/ Troop Carrier, CG-4A GLIDER.
Home City: Alexandria. Home State: Louisiana.
Imprisoned: 03/10/44 thru 04/30/45.

On Sunday night, March 1944, we left our base in India for Burma. We had two CC-4A gliders behind a C-47. Somewhere behind Japanese lines, our tow rope released itself from the C-47- reason unknown. We crashed in the jungle. My pilot Lt. Charles Liston was seriously injured and died enroute to Rangoon. Ted Yackie and "Pappy" Hart were with him when he died. I visited his family in Adel, Iowa after I was discharged in November, 1945 in North Carolina. I met his mother, sister and a sister-in-law. He had a wonderful family. I was with three English soldiers and we were captured the night of March 10, 1944. The three Englishmen were shot and one died in Rangoon from his wounds. When several men were marched out of Rangoon I was one of them. We were liberated April 29, 1945 after serving about 14 months (or 419 days)

FREEDOM AT LAST!

Richard Corbett, Pilot (Dick), Royal Canadian Air Force, 11RAF,Hurricane.
Home City: Don Mills. Home Country: Ontario, Canada.
Imprisoned ?/02/44 thru 05/04/45.

Shot down by Zeros.

Samuel Crostic (Bud), Staff Sergeant, 7th Bomb Group, 9th Bomber Squad, B-24
Home City: New Smyrna Beach. Home State: Florida.
Imprisoned March 1943 thru May 1945.

I was shot down over Pymaunna Junction. Four of us bailed out. The rest of the crew was killed. I was captured approximately four days later by natives who turned me over to the Japanese. I traveled by truck and train to Rangoon. Train bombed enroute by B-25s. Arrived at Rangoon to find rest of my crew Higgenbottow, Jensen, and Baggett already there. Jensen and Baggett were sent to Singapore. Higgenbottow and I remained in Rangoon until the Japanese attempted to move us May 1945 and consequently, we were released.

Leon Frank,Infantry in Kings Liverpool Regiment,13ᵗʰ Battallion,
77ᵗʰ Infantry Brigade under General Wingate (Chandits).
Home City: Higams Park, London. Home Country: England.
Imprisoned: 02/21/43 thru 05/04/45.

I was captured by the Japanese in North East Burma on my 23ʳᵈ Birthday. After initial captivity at the Memyo camp, I was sent to Rangoon. We were held in the Rangoon Central Prison on Commissioner Road in Rangoon. Around April 28, 1945, I was one of the 400 or so called fit prisoners, which included British, American and Commonwealth personnel who were to be marched into Thailand. After five days of marching, we were intercepted and soon liberated by the 14ᵗʰ Army. Many of my friends were American. They were mostly, if not all, air crew members. I remember Sgt. John Boyd and a man who was actually with me when we liberated whose name was Frankie Hubbard. There was an Australian Flight Sgt. Harvey Besley whom I remember also.

Looking back over the years, I often wonder where all those marvelous and brave men are. I think it is appropriate to say, old soldiers never die. Those who survive, carry on!

Bill Flynn, C.P.L., ATC/India-China Wing, C-46.
Home City: Falls Church. Home State: Virginia.
Imprisoned: 09/?/43 thru 05/04/45.

November 7, 1943 departed Sookerating, Assam Valley for Kunming, China. On return flight, encountered bad weather and radio problems. Flew far south of normal route to find better flight rather than ditch airplane. Crew split up. Hooked up with Charlie Montagna and headed west. "Befriended" by Burmese, and betrayed to Japanese search party. Taken through Mandalay to Maymyo, for approximately two months. We were joined by Col. Gilbert, Jean Lutz, Chris Morgan and "Bo" Bowman. Transferred to Rangoon early January 1944.

Grady M. Farley, Technical Sergeant., 7ᵗʰ Bomber Group, 493ʳᵈ Squadron, B-24.
Home City: Russellville. Home State: Alabama.
Imprisoned: 11/14/43 thru 05/04/45.

We were shot down November 14, 1943 over North Burma. E.S. Quick and I were the only ones that got out of the plane. Quick was captured that day and I roamed around 14 days before natives captured me and turned me over to the Japanese. I was carried to Rangoon and held in the Rangoon M.P. Headquarters for 13 months, and then we were moved into a compound. I guess this was Block 8; it was mostly Air Force personnel in the compound.

Daren Engel, Staff Sergeant, 12ᵗʰ Bomber Group, 83ʳᵈ Squadron, B-25.
Home City: Yuma. Home State: Arizona.
Imprisoned: 10/13/44 thru 05/04/45.

I was shot down near Mykteta, Burma on October 8. 1944 and arrived at Rangoon Prison 5 or 6 days after- along with John Russell, the only other survivor of my crew and Richard Moore a P-38 Pilot.

I spent the next 90 days in solitary confinement spending my birthday, Thanksgiving, Christmas and New Years in that Cell Block. I was then transferred to Cell Block 8 for the remainder of my confinement. I especially remember Johnny Hurt our Block 8 "Mess Sergeant," Wing Commander Hill, our appointed C.O. for Block 8, Cliff Emery, who took the major responsibility of caring for the sick and injured in Block 8 and of course, Dick Moore and John Russell.

After we were liberated by the English ground forces, I returned to the Military Hospital in Calcutta via an English Ship and eventually was returned to the States and discharged from the Army Air Force.

Francis R. Edwards (Bud), Sergeant, 40th Bomber Group, 25th Squadron, B-29.

Home City: Punta Gorda. Home State: Florida.

Imprisoned: 12/14/44 thru 05/04/045.

I was top gunner on Capt. C.C. Meyers B-29 crew. Our plane was disabled over Rangoon, Burma on December 14, 1944 in what is now known as the Rangoon Disaster.

The plane was burning and all communication systems were out. When I jumped I believe only Harlen Green was behind me in the aft compartment. My chute had taken quite a bit of damage so my descent was rather rapid. I landed on the bank of a river and was immediately surrounded by some Burmese civilians. They put me in a small boat and I thought I was being hidden from the Japs. However, at the first sight of a Japanese patrol, they started yelling and turned me over to the Japs.

I was then taken to a camp and interrogated, kicked and slapped me around for what seemed to me to be hours. Later I was taken to the Rangoon Central Jail and placed in cell block # 5. After about a month or so we were transported to another compound where we could move a bit more freely.

My recollection of my thoughts in prison was worrying about my family more than myself.....for I knew I was alive.

While in the larger compound I was appointed cook along with a couple of others. This helped make the time pass more quickly...not that there was much noted many times over.

When the Japs decided to leave by taking all the able bodied men as hostages on a march, I was left behind. Ulcers were festering on my legs. However we were eventually released and taken to the 142nd General Hospital in Calcutta.

NOTE: When the Army Air Force finally decided to notify my parents of my release, I was sitting at the dining room table and answered the phone from Western Union.

Joe Levine, 1ˢᵗ Lieutenant, 40ᵗʰ Bomber Group, 25ᵗʰ Squadron, B-29. Home City: Farmington Hills. Home State: Michigan. Imprisoned: 12/14/44 thru 05/05/45.

Target: Rangoon R.R. Marshalling Yards.

During bombing run, just after "bombs away," the aircraft was hit. Three engines were out, one on fire. The wing and bomb bay were on fire also. All 12 of us were able to bail out. The engine nacelle and right wing fell away before the plane hit the ground. Burke, Montgomery, and I all got to a small Burmese Village. Montgomery's hand was hanging by a thread; I gave him morphine and sulfa powder in the wound and applied a tourniquet to his upper arm. Monty deemed to be in shock. About 2 hours after the Burmese promised to help us escape (at night); a Japanese Lieutenant with a squad of about 8 men approached the village. I surrendered for the three of us.

The Japanese took us by boat to a small police (?) station where the rest of the crew were being held. All of us were made to stand with our hands tied behind our backs. It was now dark and about 6 hours after bailing out. I had been attending Monty's tourniquet for the first 3-4 hours, but now he lay in a heap with no attention. Both Walsh (our engineer) and I kept complaining about Monty and both of us got a few whacks on the head for our trouble. Finally, about 7-9 hours after bailout, a Japanese doctor severed Monty's hand, tied the blood vessels, and bandaged the stump. About that time, we were told to lie down on some beds.

At dawn we were awakened and marched outside, our hands still tied. I thought for sure we were going to be beheaded or shot. (I was hoping for the latter). Instead we were loaded on a truck and brought to the POW camp. We joined crew members of the other four planes in a large yard. There were newsreel cameras recording the capture of B-29 crews. It seems as if we hadn't any food or drink since we were taken prisoners. Monty was not with us but we found him later in the cell with us.I was with the group that marched out of Rangoon and then liberated by the British 5 days later.

B.A. Lukas (Ben), Staff Sergeant, 7th Bomber Group, 493rd Squadron, B-24.
Home City: Bluewater Bay Niceville. Home State: Florida.
Imprisoned: 10/18/43 thru 04/30/45.

October 18, 1943 –TARGET- TONGOO RAIL YARDS. South of Maymo attacked by Japanese fighters. Ascending, hit Bombay and plane caught fire. Crew evacuated with plane on fire and shortly thereafter exploded. Severely wounded with head wounds. I was picked up by Burmese natives who wrapped me up in my parachute and took me to a civilian police station in the proximity of Maymo. Because of my name, rank, and serial number were entered on a police blotter when the Japanese came into the village they had no alternative but to take me to Japanese intelligence in Maymo and subsequently to the Rangoon Jail.

Allen B. DuBose, Captain /Pilot, 530th Fighter Squadron, P-51.
Home City: Rockport. Home State: Texas.
Imprisoned: 12/01/43 thru 05/04/4.5

On December 1, 1943 I was shot down by a Jap Zero and parachuted off the Burmese coast into the water. I was later turned over to the Japanese by the Burmese.

Taken to Bassein, I was interrogated and taken to Rangoon New Laws Courts where I was kept for approximately nine months in a cell holding four to nineteen men. Later transported to the Rangoon Central Jail and put into solitary. After about three months we were shifted over to compound # 8. This compound gave us more room and we could walk around our small restricted area. Only airmen from solitary were in this compound. About a month or two later the Japs took all those who could walk and put them into a forced march towards Pegu. During the third or fourth night the Japanese departed leaving the prisoners to fend for themselves. The next day the British 14th Army rescued us and transported all the men to Calcutta.

Walter Lentz, Staff Sergeant, 40th Bomber Group, 45th Squadron, B-29.
Home City: Hudson. Home State: North Carolina.
Imprisoned: 12/14/44 thru 05/04/45.

I was on Robert Shanks crew- we were on the disasterous mission on the railroad yards of Rangoon, Burma- December 14, 1944. We bailed out about 100 miles west of target- we were picked up instantly by the natives who turned us over to the Japanese. It took them 10 days to get us back to the prison (December 25th, what a Christmas).

As liberation neared, the Japanese blew up ammo dumps around the prison. One morning, they were gone taking all prisoners that were able to walk and leaving a note on the prison gate as follows: "We have guarded you according to Japanese knighthood and hope to meet you on another battlefield."

Clarence A. King (Clancy), Captain, 7th Bomb Group, 493rd Bomb Squadron, B-24.
Home City: Eugene. Home State: Oregon.
Imprisoned: 10/14/44 thru 4/29/45.

Captured near Maubin, Burma, after bailing out of a burning plane. Other survivors: Harold Goad, Bill Schrader, Gene Sawyer and Russ Gebert.

Liberated by the British near Pegu after forced march from Rangoon. Japanese Guards fled during the night of heavy strafing by British and American fighter planes. British Brigadier, who had been the ranking officer in the P.O.W. camp at Rangoon was killed during this strafing.

Flown by C-47 to Calcutta and spent approximately 3 weeks in the 142nd General Hospital there. Flown by C-54 to La Guardia Airport with brief stops at Karachi, Abadan, Cairo and Casablanca en route.

Arrived at home in Great Falls, Montana in early June to find out that I had been declared M.I.A. when shot down; and officially dead one year later by the War Department. Memorial services were held in the spring of 1945 at the church where I attended Sunday school as a boy.

For me George Burns said it best: "If I had known I was going to live this long, I'd have taken better care of myself."

Donald M. Humphrey, Lieutenant, Pilot, Ninth Photo Recon., F-4.

Home City: St. Louis. Home State: Missouri.

Imprisoned: 05/05/43 thru 05/01/45.

Hit over Rangoon by ack-ack, one engine out, pursued and shot down by fighters.

30 days- City Jail- Rangoon Burma, 40 days- Solitary- #5 compound- Rangoon Prison.

Balance Compound # 6.

Recaptured above Pegu by Slim's 14th British Army on march out of Burma.

Fred K, Schwall, 2ndLieutenant, 308th Bomber Group, 324th Squadron, B-24.

Home City: Key West. Home State: Florida.

Imprisoned: 11/26/43 thru 04/30/45.

Went down about 100 to 250 miles Northeast of Mandalay. Crossed front lines about April 29, 1945 while being moved towards Thailand from Rangoon.

Ernest W. Trigwell,Pilot, RAAF 224th Grp, 27 RAF Squadron, Bristol Beaufighter.

Home City: Donnybrook. Home Country: Western Australia.

Imprisoned: 11/16/44 thru 04/30/45.

On November 16, 1944, flying a Bristol Beaufighter off the coast of Burma, I was shot down by mistake by a P-38 fighter bomber. Captured by the Japanese and put into Rangoon Central Prison until we went on a forced march by the Japanese in Late April. After a few days they left us near Pegu and we were soon liberated on April 30, 1945.

J.I. Thomson, Hurricane.

Home Country: Coffee Res. Station, Moshi, Tanganyika Territory.

Imprisoned dates?

Beating up sampans near the mouth of Mayo River. Noticed high red temperatures and headed for home informing my number 1 over R.T. (radio) Engine rapidly lost power and I had to land. Set fire to aircraft and made for the hills. Was at large for ten days using emergency rations and food from villages. Was caught by I.N.A. while trying to cross lines with the help of some Burmese. Was taken to Japanese, then to I.N.A. camp north of Akyab where I was kept for about nine weeks. Brought to Rangoon just before monsoon.

J.L. Russell, Captain, B-25.
Home City: Dedham. Home State: Massachusetts.
Imprisoned: 10/06/44 thru 05/04/45.

Our B-25 was attacked by 4 Zeros and set on fire. Hit by a bullet in the left leg and bailed out. The plane crashed while still on fire. 4 killed, two escaped; myself, and the radio operator and the tail gunner. Captured by Burmese. Shot down October 6, 1944, entered Rangoon Prison October 14, 1944.

Raymond A. Malony(Murph), 1ˢᵗLieutenant, 7ᵗʰ Bomb Grp, 9ᵗʰ Squadron, B-24.
Home City: Hemet. Home State: California.
Imprisoned: 12/01/43 thru 05/02/45.

I was the lead bombardier for two bomb groups on a mission to Rangoon on December 1, 1943. Lost two engines when attacked by a fighter. Finally forced to abandon ship over Bassein. Captured early next morning when betrayed by Burmese villagers. Taken by boat to Rangoon and imprisoned in New Laws Courts building. Later around July or August 1944, we were moved to the Rangoon Central Prison where we were kept in solitary until early 1945 when we were transferred to compound # 8. Liberated by the British May 2ⁿᵈ or 3ʳᵈ 1945 and taken to Calcutta by hospital ship.

Ferrell T. Majors, Master Sergeant, 40ᵗʰ Bomb Group, 45ᵗʰ Squadron, B-29.
Home City: Fullerton. Home State: California.
Imprisoned: 12/14/44 thru 04/28/45.

December 14, 1944- we were hit by explosion of our own bombs upon release over secondary target- Rangoon, Burma. (Bob Shanks crew) Flying on one engine, we were able to go about 100 miles from target before bailing out. All crew members were ok except Co-Pilot Fletcher sprained both ankles upon landing. We were turned over to the Japanese the same day by Burmese people. They were friendly, but feared Japanese reprisals. The Japanese took everything except coveralls and shoes. I received a beating for not having a revolver in my holster. I had no clips so I did not carry a gun.

We were turned over to Japanese guards who took us back to Rangoon eleven days later, after many interrogations and several beatings. After spending four and one half months in captivity, in late April, I was taken from prison and marched to Pegu 4 days later. The guards then left us on the run to escape British Army. That night I was picked up by the British and flown back to a hospital in Calcutta, where I gained 40 pounds in one month. I was then flown home, given a 60 day furlough and reassigned to Supply in Santa Monica. I was released from the service October, 1945. No problems from Malaria or Dysentery again.

Joseph C. McClung, Sergeant, B-24.
Home City: Redding. Home State: California.
Imprisonment:11/27/43 thru 04/29/45.

I got shot down November 27, 1943 while bombing Rangoon, Burma. We were bombing the railroad shops, they worked on all engines there.

We were flying from India, which was a 14 hour round trip flight. There were 53 Bombers on this mission. My plane lost two engines; therefore we couldn't keep up with the other planes. The Japanese fighters got us. I jumped at 12,000 feet.

I was first put into Rangoon Federal Laws Courts in the basement. I was in a 9 x 12 room where I stayed for 8 months. One of my crew died there. Then we were moved to Section 8 where I spent 5 months after which I went to the compound.

I was on the force march up the Burma Road with the other boys, but I never knew many of them.

I went on a kidney machine on December 23, 1979.

James M. McKernan, B-24.
Home City: Burt. Home State: New York.
Imprisoned: 04/44 thru 05/05/45.

I was in the Burma National Prison from April 1944 through May 5, 1945. We were then liberated and taken to Calcutta by hospital ship. I was an Engineer on a B-29 flying out of Ondal, India. The only other prisoner I kept in touch with was from North Tonawanda, N.Y. and he died a few years ago.

Bob Shanks, Captain/Pilot, 40ᵗʰ Bomber Group, 45ᵗʰ Bomb Squadron, B-29.

Home City: Grand Prairie. Home State: Texas.

Imprisoned: 12/14/44 thru 05/04/45.

This is the way I remember December 14, 1944 after 47 years.

It was 12:00 noon Rangoon time. We had just let our bombs go over the target when our aircraft was hit. We were at 20,000 feet and started losing altitude heading toward the west for about 30 minutes to 3,500 feet. It was time to bail out.

After all crew members jumped, I was last to leave the aircraft. I jumped at about 3,000 feet. While floating down, looking around I saw that our B-29 had done a 380 degree turn and was heading directly toward me. Just before it got to me it stalled and crashed.

Co-Pilot Harold Fletcher and I joined up and the Burmese gave us some food. About one hour later two Japanese soldiers showed up to take control of us. The two Jap soldiers sat Fletcher and me down and held a rifle to the backs of our heads. At that time I was not afraid, because I thought they were going to kill us. When they didn't shoot us, it scared me to death. It took about three days before all our crew were captured and brought together. We spent the next seven days travelling by Cart, boat, train and foot. Christmas Eve we arrived at Justin College, located in Rangoon. We were to stand all that night. About 5 o'clock Christmas Day we arrived at Rangoon Central Jail and were put into block # 5. After a month or so, we were transferred with all the others in block #5 to block #8 which was to be our home until we were liberated.

Liberation.....on or about April 28, 1945, the Japanese were getting ready for the march away from Rangoon Prison. All the prisoners who could walk were forced to go on the march (as hostages I suppose) while the others were left behind in prison with just a few guards. In a few days the remaining guards left and we were on our own until the British came a few days later and evacuated us to a hospital ship (H.M.S.

Karapara) that took us to Calcutta. There we were met at the docks by trucks and ambulances and a few nurses from our base to take us to the 142nd General Hospital for rehabilitation. Before the month passed we were on our way home.

Curtis F. Pritchard, Corporal, 1st Transport Grp., 6th Trans Squadron, C-46 Cargo.
Home City: Springfield. Home State: Missouri.
Imprisoned: 02/02/44 thru 04/30/45.

January 30, 1944, while on a mission, flying the Hump from Kunming, China to Chabria, India, we ran into a storm, got lost and ran out of gas. Then we had to leap out by parachute into North Burma. I landed in the Irrawaddy River, was captured by Burmese Army and turned over to the Japanese. I was taken to Mandalay, then to Maymyo, Burma, for about two or three weeks and then back to Mandalay for one day. I was picked up at midnight, with five Chinese and five Japanese, taken to Rangoon for a year until April 30, 1945. Then the Japanese took several men including myself. While on a march we were captured by the British Army and taken to Calcutta, India hospital for two weeks, until I gained 30 pounds, then to America.

Gus Johnson, 2ndLieutenant, 7th Bomb Group, 436 Bomb Squadron, B-24.
Home City: Stuart. Home State: Florida.
Imprisoned: 10/26/43 thru 05/?/45.

Hit by the Japanese "ToJo" fighters over Rangoon, lost at least one engine, then a running gunfight for 50 minutes at which time the Japanese fighters started using two fighters each pass, instead of one. Using two was a new tactic for them, they misjudged a pass from 7 o'clock low, with one fighter flying through the waist windows. Our B-24 broke in half, the front portion ending up in a GLIDE INVERTED, with no tail section. The navigator (Waller) exited through the Astrodome and I followed, very close to the jungle near G.W.A. Bay. After finding my way out of the jungle was picked up by a native Burmese and turned over to the Japanese army. Held captive in New Laws Court (Solitary) and became number one. K.P. Roy Wentz and Joe Wells arrived about Thanksgiving or Christmas and have been friends ever since. We all returned from Rangoon on H.M.S. "Karapara" (hospital ship) to the 142nd General Hospital and here we are!

Nicholas P. Oglesby, Staff Sergeant, 40th Bomber Group, 45th Squadron, B-29.

Home City: Greensboro. Home State: North Carolina.

Imprisoned: 12/14/44 thru 05/04/45.

The plane assigned to our crew for the mission on December 14, 1944 had some mechanical problems which seemed likely to prevent our participation. I am not sure what engine problems there were but, in addition, the compressed air charger for my machine gun was not working properly. The pressure switch would not cut off. My ground crew and I worked for quite a while and finally developed a system of manually controlling the switch, charging the system that way.

As a result of the various problems with the plane, it was fairly late on the night of December 13th when the check flight was finally set. My ground crew asked if they could hitch a ride so I asked them to check out parachutes. When we got back, it was well after midnight and a bit late for them to get up around 4:30 am to fly with us. I told them not to worry about the chutes as they could turn them in after we came back from our mission the next afternoon............. How fortunate they were.

So when Lt. Cochran exclaimed that his chute was ripped open by the explosion, I became an instant "hero" at least in his eye, when I handed him the extra chute my ground crew left in the plane.

Fred M. Pugh, 1ˢᵗ Air Command CBI Theater, Glider.
Home City: Athens. Home State: Texas.
Imprisoned: 03/05/44 thru 05/04/45.

On the night of March 5, 1944, more than 100 gliders became airborne headed for an obstacle ridden jungle clearing called "Broadway" in Burma. Within a few hours, some of them had landed safely, but some smashed into trees or hurtled over ditches. Seventeen had snapped loose from their tow lines while in the air and nine had crashed in Japanese territory. My glider was one of them. We were flying 1,000 feet above the 8,000 ft. Himalayas. I was separated from my crew when we were ambushed by the Japanese. I was in the jungle seven days before the Japs captured me and took me to a prison camp at Indow, seven miles away. I was at Indow 30 to 40 days and was interrogated and beaten 10-12 hours a day. They transferred me to a prison camp at Mandalay and finally to Rangoon.

I was liberated in the Spring (May) of 1945, we marched 65 miles to a pagoda village where the British 14ᵗʰ Army picked us up in trucks. Later, planes transported most of us to Calcutta where I was hospitalized at the 142ⁿᵈ General Hospital for 30 days and then flown home.

Charles Montagna, Co-Pilot, 29ᵗʰ Transport Grp., 99ᵗʰ Trans Squadron, C-46.
Home City: Mission Viejo. Home State: California.
Imprisoned: 11/07/43 thru 04/31/45.

We were flying aviation gasoline from India to China over "the Hump" for General Chennomb's 14th Air Force. We left Kunming, China at one o'clock in the morning on November 7, 1943 for our return flight to India. Through a series of unfortunate and unexplainable circumstances, our flight lasted through the night. As the first signs of daylight appeared in the east, our fuel was exhausted. Our pilot F/O Parris gave us the option of either bailing out or attempting a crash landing. It was decided that a crash landing would be impossible to survive in view of the jungle terrain. Consequently, the entire crew bailed out and into the jungle below. I was reunited with my radio operator Billy Flynn. For a short time, we attempted to locate and join up with the rest of our crew, but to no avail. Billy and I spent two days in the jungle trying to find somebody or someplace to help us out of our dilemma. What we ran into was a group of native Burmese who marched us through the jungle into a Japanese camp.

Henry E. Pisterzi, Technical Sergeant, 40th Bomber Group, 45th Squadron, B-29.

Home City: Arvada. Home State: Colorado.

Imprisoned: 12/14/44 thru 05/04/45.

December 14, 1944 we were on a mission to Bankok. Heavy cloud cover forced us to go to our secondary target, Rangoon, Burma. The moment we dropped our bombs a tremendous explosion beneath the formation damaged our plane badly. We were able to fly for another ten to fifteen minutes. Orders were given to bail out. Soon after reaching the ground, Burmese took us over and handed us to the Japs. They took us by sampan, truck and we walked till we arrived at the Rangoon Central Jail on Christmas Eve 1944.

After nearly six months of imprisonment the Japs ordered those able to march to get ready to leave Rangoon. We marched three or four nights (too risky to march in daylight and have Allied planes strafing us). At the outset of the march we headed North. We thought there might be a deal to exchange prisoners. But then we headed East and our thoughts also changed. Now we figured that they were taking us to another prison camp. On the third or fourth day at about noon, the Jap commander told us "You are free men," Hooray for us... Here we are in no man's land between the Japs and our Allied troops. We fashioned a sign made of white clothes etc. that read "400 Ex-Rangoon Prisoners... Send Help!"

A Piper Cub was flying over us so someone thought to flash a signal with a piece of mirror. The Piper Cub thought it was small arms fire and summoned help. Three Spitfires responded each with two 100 lb bombs on their wings which they released. Then they strafed us until their guns were empty. We were in an area not over 400 sq ft in size. We later learned that this area was due to be pattern bombed by a B-25 unit. Word must have gotten back to them that we were there....no bombing took place.

Somewhere near there was a makeshift landing field from where we would be flown to Calcutta. Because of the weather we had to wait until the following day. The planes came and took us to Calcutta and on to the 142nd General Hospital where we rehabilitated and three to four weeks later we were flown home.

John H. McClosky, Jr (Jack), Captain,Co-pilot, 12th Bomber Grp., 434 Sqd. B25-J.
Home City: Oakdale. Home State: Pennsylvania.
Imprisoned: 05/20/44 thru 04/29/45.

May 20, 1944, 7:20 A.M. Shot down on low level bombing mission seeking to put a single track railroad out of operation. We were hit with ground fire, and set afire in the bomb bay area, probably burning fuel. All we had time to do was to climb to 1,000 feet and bail out.

Our crew consisted of Tom Snee, Co-Pilot (I understand his body was found with chute unopened); Lofty Westberg, Navigator Bombardier and also squadron navigator; Norman Snyder, radio man; Ed Nyland, Engineer; and Leland Waltrip, Tail Gunner; all five of us were captured individually and sent to a Jap outpost where we stayed for about 5 days. Our next move was a railroad car trip south through Mandalay and down to Rangoon. We were put in the city jail under the command of the Jap military police, where we remained until sometime in August, at which time we were moved out to the main prison and put in a cell block.

We moved from cell block into one of the big compounds, and if I recall correctly, that was the sometime after the 1st of the year 1945. We remained there until April 25, when we were marched out on the infamous 4 day march before being abandoned in the middle of Burma. The rest is well known. The British troops came and took us out of there and back to civilization. Thank God!

William H. Thomas, Sergeant, 308 Bomb Group, 324 Squadron, B-24.

Home City: Cummings. Home State: Kansas.

Imprisoned: 11/43 thru 05/45.

Our B-24 was forced down in Northern Burma (Akyab) November 27, 1943. The pilot's chute opened in the plane so we decided to go down together rather than parachute out when the fuel was exhausted as originally planned.

No one was injured in the landing but the bombardier was shot in the back during gunfire exchange when Japanese captured us the next morning (November 28, 1943).

We marched and carried the bombardier for about a week. When we reached Mandalay, the Japanese furnished a truck for transportation to the Rangoon Prison. After about 45 days in solitary, we were transferred to Cell Block 5.

Out treatment was as all the airmen; beatings, starvation diet, etc.

About April 24, 1945, I was with the POWs who were marched North toward Pegu. After three nights of marching the Japanese guards left us in a wooded area. The POWs attracted the attention of an observation plane and shortly after we were bombed and strafed by four Allied (British) planes.

The next morning, we were picked by Gurka soldiers of the British 14th Army. After spending the night with the British we were flown to an Army Hospital in Calcutta.

Crew Members:

2[nd]Lieutenant N.G. Kellam, Pilot

2[nd]Lieutenant Fred K. Schwall, Co-Pilot

2nd Lieutenant John D. Marcello, Navigator

2[nd]Lieutenant George E. Harmon, Bombodier

Staff Sergeant Perry Marshall, Flight Engineer

Staff Sergeant Thomas E. Seneff, Radio Man

Sergeant Charles W. Perry, Ass't Engineer-Gunner

Sergeant William H. Thomas, Armorer Gunner

Sergeant Don Z. Davis, Armorer Gunner

Sergeant Norman E. Albinson, Armorer Gunner (Died in prison camp)

Francis E. Sawyer (Gene), Staff Sergeant, 7th Bomb Group, 493rd Squadron, B-24D.
Home City: La Crosse. Home State: Wisconsin.
Imprisoned: 10/14/43 thru 04/29/45.

The day was October 14, 1943; the target was Pazandaung Boat Works at Rangoon, Burma. We were to fly with the 9th Squadron that day. Little did I realize that would be the last mission I would ever fly. We dropped our bombs at Rangoon around noon; anti-aircraft was heavy. After we left the city, Jap fighter planes jumped us. The plane on which I was a gunner was hit in the bomb bay fuel tank. The mid-section of the plane was set ablaze. All men made ready to leave. I bailed out. Seconds later, the plane exploded and broke in half. Five of the ten aboard the plane survived.

We were approximately 45 miles west of Rangoon. After landing, I was picked up by Burmese villagers, who turned me over to the Police. They took me to Pantanau and there I met the four officers of my crew. We were questioned and slapped around. The next stop on our boat trip back to Rangoon was Maubin. After two nights there, we arrived in Rangoon.

On the eve of Thanksgiving Day 1943, while I was in solitary, the RAF accidently bombed the prison, followed by the 7th Bomb Group. Both raids killed a few men and damaged buildings. In December of 1943, we were finally put into a compound with other prisoners. Disease was all over the prison. We were given shots for typhoid, tetanus, bubonic plague, and small pox. More for the Jap's self-preservation and to keep their slates clean. Should we be liberated.

On October 30, 1944, I was officially dead by War Dept. Records and next of kin were notified. We were given orders by the Japs on April 25, 1945 to go on a march. Early in the morning on the 29th, those of us who could walk were stopped in a woods about 61 miles north of Rangoon. We were near Pegu, Burma. The Japanese leader gave us a note telling us we were free by order of the Imperial Emperor; then he and his men took off in full retreat. We were 5 to 7 miles from British front lines. Confusion reigned at this point, but later that evening, an American officer stole into the British perimeter and made our true identity known. We were picked up by the British 14th Army, spent two comforting nights with them, and then flown to Calcutta. The Americans went to the 142nd General Hospital.

I arose from the "dead" on April 30th or May 1st, 1945. After spending a week in Karachi, we started for New York City, and I landed at LaGuardia Airport the evening of May 28, 1945. **WE WERE HOME!!** For us the fighting was over. I had only 35 missions, but I was satisfied.

K.F. Horner (Jack), 1st Lieutenant, 7th Bomber Group, Recon. Squad, B-17.
Home City: Tampa. Home State: Florida.
Imprisoned: 06/04/42 thru 04/29/45.

On June 3, 1942, three B-17 fortresses flew from Hyderabad,India, an advance base in Calcutta. On the morning of the 4th, one of the planes was not capable of completing the mission so two planes headed for Rangoon to bomb shipping in the Irrawaddy River. During the course of the bombing, we were attacked by a squadron of Zeros and other unidentified aircraft. When we reached cloud cover, about 15 or 20 minutes later, we had shot down, by my count, over seven planes although officially we were given credit for only four. After entering the cloud cover, Sgt. Malok, the crew chief, entered the bomb bay to fight a fire. Some moments thereafter the bombardier, George Wilson and I either misinterpreted the order to bail out or were given the signal to bail out. Our electrical system was down and I was communicating with the pilot, Doug Sharp, through the bulkhead separating the nose from the pilot compartment. I later found out that after we bailed out, Sgt. Malok emerged from the bomb bay and advised the pilot that he had extinguished the fire. They then began to throw everything movable off the plane to lighten the load. Eventually, after they had flown for nearly an hour, the plane was losing altitude so fast that the balance of the crew bailed out. The plane again began to maintain altitude and eventually reached what was at that period of time the border between the Japanese and the Allied forces. Thus the pilot, Doug Sharp and the co-pilot, Herbert Wunderich reached safety.

The balance of the crew, a young private, Tindell, had been killed in the plane. Al Malok, Hal Cummings, Eli Gonzales and Smith Radcliff were reunited with George and myself about four months later in Rangoon Prison. Malok, Cummings and Gonzales were killed by Allied bombs on November 29, 1943. Radcliff, George Wilson and I returned to Allied control after the march from Rangoon April 29, 1945.

The following information was obtained from POW survivor Dick Corbett's website.

J.A. Shortis, Flight Officer, RAF 82 Squadron, Mosquito.
Home City: Dagenham. Home Country: England.
Imprisonment: 12/19/44 thru 05/03/45.

On December 19, 1944, during a low-level rhubarb near the junction of Chindwin and the Irrawaddy Rivers, his Mosquito either hit the water or impacted a defensive cable strung across a waterway. The aircraft crash landed and disintegrated, but he and his pilot, RAAF Wing Commander Lionel Hudson survived their injuries and incarceration.

Joe Wilson, 1ˢᵗLieutenant, Pilot, 311ᵗʰ Bomber Group, 529ᵗʰ Bomb Squadron, P-51.
Home City: Foreman. Home State: Arkansas.
Imprisoned: 06/21/44.

On June 21, 1944 aircraft suffered engine failure during a strafing run on a railway target north of Mandaly. With his aircraft on fire, he jumped.

Clifford H. Brockman, Staff Sergeant, 7ᵗʰ Bomb Group, 9ᵗʰ Bomb Squadron, B-24.
Home City: Ione. Home State: Washington.
Imprisoned: 12/01/43 thru 05/03/45.

After bombing Insein locomotive shops near Rangoon, his B-24 was set upon by fighters in a running battle. Finally shot down north or northwest of Bassein, Burma.

John Donald Lomas, F/Sergeant, RAF 159 Squadron, B-24.
Home Country: Mytholmroyd, W. Yorks, UK
Imprisoned: 02/29/44 thru 05/03/45.

Illuminated at night by searchlights over Rangoon, the bomber was shot down from behind by 204ᵗʰ Sentai Oscar aces Hiroshi Takiguchi and Bunichi Yamaguchi.

Howard C. Edwards, Pilot, RAF 30ᵗʰ Squadron, P-47.
Home City: Wanganui. Home Country: New Zealand.
Imprisoned: 11/03/44 thru 05/03/45.

Inbound on a fighter sweep of Mingaladon airfield near Rangoon, the aircraft developed engine trouble and caught fire. I chose to force-land

and was ejected before the aircraft overturned upon hitting waterlogged ground northeast of Pathwe, Burma

Cyril Alexander Kidd, RAF 177 Squadron, Beaufighter.
Home City: London. Home Country: England.
Imprisoned: 08/14/44 thru 05/03/45.

Shot down by ground fire while patrolling the Kalewa-Ye-u-Monywa area in Burma.

Hubert A Reekes (Bill), F/Sergeant, RAF 215 Squadron, B-24.
Home City: Brighton. Home Country: United Kingdom
Imprisoned: 01/08/45 thru 05/03/45.

The 2nd pilot's error caused a complete loss of power nearing the Burma-Siam Railway target. A prepare-to-jump command was issued, and Reekes exited his turret in anticipation. When engines were re-stared, a crewman gave a thumbs-up to Reekes, positioned by the rear floor escape hatch. In the confusion, Reekes misinterpreted the communication as the signal to jump. Landing safely, he was soon captured. Post liberation he was not punished by his superiors for his errant jump.

Bernard Brodie Mearns (Barney), RAF 211 Squadron, Beaufighter.
Home City: Aberdeen. Home Country: Scotland.
Imprisoned: 08/12/44 thru 05/03/45.

Force-landed in central Burma from engine trouble after a low-level attack

Roy A. Wentz, Jr., 1ˢᵗLieutenant, 7ᵗʰ Bomb Group, 9ᵗʰ Bomber Squadron, B-24.

Home City: Springfield. Home State: Illinois.

Imprisoned: 12/01/43 thru 05/03/45.

After bombing Insein locomotive shops rear Rangoon the B-24 was set upon by fighters running battle. Finally shot down north or northwest of Bassein, Burma.

Jack Harris, F/Sergeant, RAF 159 Squadron, B-24.

Home City: Ynysybwl. Home Country: Wales.

Imprisoned: 02/29/44 thru 05/03/45.

Illuminated at night by searchlights over Rangoon. The bomber was shot down from behind by 204ᵗʰ Sentai Oscar aces. I was a crewmate of Don Lomas.

British Major Seagram

One of the almost forgotten stories from Rangoon was of a man who was behind Japanese lines in Burma. He became a famous spy who was murdered in New Laws Court Jail after he surrendered.

This officer had organized a powerful underground movement in Burma. He had interfered with all Japanese operations in the district.

He had ambushed raiding parties, blown up troop and supply trains. The Japanese were desperate to find him. They retaliated by burning villages and bayoneting every man, woman and child who tried to escape.

They never would have caught him. He decided to surrender so that no more villages would be burned or Burmese slaughtered.

He came to New Laws Court to surrender and his death could not have been an easy one.

THE WALKOUT FROM RANGOON PRISON

Date of event: April 1945

Date written: 1987-1989

Written by: N.E. Larsen, R.E. Derrington, C.R.Benedict, G.M. Etherington, N.P. Oglesby, J.C. Cochran, H.Pisterzi.

<u>**Nick Oglesby starts off the story:**</u> In late April, the Japanese became a little easier to get along with. They had passed out Red Cross packages, for example, which was the one and only time we realized that anyone knew we were there.

In addition to the twice-daily regular formations where we all formed ranks and counted off (in Japanese) so they could be sure no one had flown the coop, they held a special formation and a formal inspection, complete with several officers. They designated each of us as "well" or "sick." We were uneasy about that without knowing why, for such attention by the doctor was unusual.

Then, one day a large supply of clothes and shoes were dumped in the compound, and we were told to find clothes we could wear. The jackets were Japanese army issue and so were the pants, which resembled culottes. The shoes were sneakers, rubber and canvas, with the big toe separated from the other toes.

Late that afternoon (April 25), those of us designated as "well" were formed into columns of four and were marched out of the compound accompanied by a number of the guards with their bayonets mounted on their rifles. We had some handcarts loaded with supplies which we pulled along with us.

We marched about fifty minutes and rested ten minutes. We continued the march all through that night and were exhausted long before dawn. The Japanese guards were almost as weary as we were. (They had been fed better than we had, for sure, but I doubt that they were in much better shape to undertake this march.)

My shoes were un-wearable because my feet had swelled from being barefoot all the time. The Japanese shoes wore blisters on both heels, so they were discarded. This was not too bad while we were walking on the paved road.

The Japanese guards warned us that we might well be strafed by allied fighter planes; thus the night was the time the Japanese could move about. We used no lights, and it was an eerie sensation to be a part of a long column of marching men, in the dark, with the light of the moon providing the only illumination we had.

As best I recall, we were surprised twice by the British fighter-bomber planes while we were on the march. In each case we rolled off the road into the ditch and lay there while the planes cruised the roads, perhaps fifty to one hundred feet above.

In these two encounters, we were warned of the approaching planes and, if my memory is correct, while we were scared to death, we were not actually attacked. What was surprising to me was the absolute stillness with which the planes approached our location. It was only after they had reached us that their engine noise was heard.

In the morning, we were fed from the supplies we pulled in the carts and were sheltered from view in a wooded area. As the day wore on, we were increasingly aware of the Japanese army units moving on the roads. Many of them were seemingly in not much better shape than we were.

The military trucks all had to be started by being pushed. Many of the Japanese wounded were loaded on ox carts and, in some cases, were being pushed or pulled by soldiers. The following night we repeated the march, continuing up the paved road to the north. Since Rangoon is located on a peninsula, to get to the mainland, and to move south away from the British Army advance, we had to be moved north and then east around the bay.

I think on the third night, we were moved off the road and began following a railroad line. At that time the lack of footwear became a real problem. The gravel was sharp, and the railroad ties were spaced just wrong for walking, especially in the dark. The bottoms of our feet became cut and bruised and hurt like hell.

There were moments of humor, of course. I remember someone asking one of our Japanese guards, a fairly chubby, moon-faced short man with those Coke-bottle glasses, when we were going to stop to rest. He mopped his brow and said, "Soon, I hope!" with such feeling that we all chuckled.

There were about 400 prisoners on the march, and we were guarded by a much smaller number of Japanese guards. While I was not privy to the thinking going on with the upper ranks of our group , I believe they planned to attempt to overpower the guard detachment on a signal after we had marched as far north as we were going and before we went too far east. I believe this word had been passed to us that third night. However, before the signal had been given, we stopped shortly before dawn at a wooded village and were allowed to lie down and rest.

Soon after day broke, we were given the news the Japanese guards had left us, having given to the British Brigadier (ranking officer) a written document passing command of the prisoner detachment to him.

So, we were free! (Of course, we were free behind the Japanese lines with Japanese troops moving all around us as they attempted to get to the safety of Thailand before the British Eighth Army overran their units.) While we were certain the British knew exactly where we were, (remember spies that saw us march out of jail?) we felt we needed to pinpoint our present location so they could plan our rescue operation more easily. Therefore, large white cloth panels were arranged on the ground outside the village wooded area, stating that released allied POW personnel were here.

We had seen and heard four British fighter planes attacking other villages near us. When they came over our village and began to circle the panels we were very relieved. We felt it was only a matter of a short time before they would drop some instructions, etc. and perhaps a radio for us to use to talk with them.

It was a warm and comforting feeling to know it was all over. What a feeling! We could just taste that good food and feel that soft bed and see those wonderful, fine, upstanding Allied soldiers welcoming us.

The drone of the four circling planes, guarding us from harm was almost hypnotic. I was almost asleep, when that sound changed, rising in tone and pitch as propeller driven planes start to dive. Why were they diving??

Whatever it was, it was not good and I, and everyone, took off for any cover available. From habit. When I had first settled down before we had word that we were free and safe at last, I had mentally marked a small dugout. It was about a four man size, I think. I was fifth man in and three more piled on top of us. (Scared to death!) Those planes made several passes each, dropped bombs and strafed us with twenty millimeter cannon fire.

It still seems unbelievable but out of 400, there was only one casualty from all these passes. Brigadier Hobson was struck and killed by a 20 mm shot. No one else was hit.

When we came out of the dugout, I picked up a 20 mm slug which I still have. It was hot. (Me, too)

Talk about scared. We had been feeling so good, no longer prisoners, free at last, and protected by the beautiful British fighter planes.Now we were still behind the Japanese lines, still likely to be killed by Japanese who might not wait to read the paper given to Brigadier Hobson. It was clear the British did not have any idea we were there and would spare no horses to destroy us, if they could.

(Friendless! You ever hear of a Lonesome Polecat?)

The new Commanding officer dispersed the men throughout the whole area, to not present too attractive target. We spent the day down in small scattered dugouts the Japanese had in the fields around the village. We could see Japanese units and stragglers making their way down the road not far from us. It was a long day.

At dusk, someone had arranged for us to be fed after dark in the village. We were eating when some of us were told to form up and march to some trucks that had come to get us. The moon had not come up yet and it was black as pitch as we stumbled our way through the woods to where we did not know. Nor were we (or at least I) at all sure that this was not some diabolical trap designed to deliver us back to some vindictive Jap.

My heart stopped when I made out a machine gun pointed at us from a spot beside our path. The troops manning the gun were as black as the night and softly they called "Hello, Johnny; Hello Johnny" and I could have kissed those beautiful Bengalese.

Norman Larsen tells what he remembers of the march out: We left Rangoon jail late in the afternoon of April 25th. There were about 430 prisoners on the march. At the head of the parade strode British Brigadier Clive Hobson, walking stick under his arm and marching as erect as a West Point cadet. At his side, equally erect, strode the Japanese commandant known to Japanese soldiers and us alike as BigTai. Dragging ass at the tail end of the parade was the motley gang of Air Corp people most of who, like me, walked barefoot. We were forced to pull a couple of large, two wheeled bullock carts loaded with

Japanese equipment. A group of about 10 of us took turns pulling each cart. We were allowed to stop and rest for a few minutes every once and awhile, and everybody would immediately drop to the ground.

Everybody more or less got through the first night's march and in the morning we made camp in what appeared to be some sort of military bivouac area. We were fed a rather generous portion of rice and tea, and I thought that things aren't all that bad. Little did I know that this meal was to be the last we would have until the night of the 29th. For the next three nights and days, all we had to eat was what we could liberate from the bullock carts. This was a precarious and dangerous undertaking because if caught, the penalty would have been rather severe and permanent.

I recall Chet Paul and his buddy, Joe Levine (bombardier on Bud Meyer's crew) swiped a couple of raw onions. Somebody else got a very sweet substance which looked almost like fudge. I got a little of this. In my one attempt at pilferage, all I got for my effort was a Burmese cheroot.

In the bivouac, I had scrounged around looking for something to carry tea in. I found a small piece of bamboo and then, incredibly, found the top of an Eveready flashlight which fit in the bamboo quite well. It held a cup and a half of tea. I tied my "canteen" to my waist with the vine I was using as a belt.

The events of the following three nights of matching are somewhat blurred in my mind. There was the matter of the fat little Weary Willie, one of the guards assigned to the Air Corp group. Willie was very overweight and way out of condition. We all knew him because each one of us at one time or another had been interrogated by him. He really wasn't all that bad of a guy, and we wanted to keep him as our guard rather than get some strange roughneck Jap. He was sweating profusely, and at one point I suggested to him that he stop drinking so much tea, and maybe he would stop sweating. Then he started limping badly.

Willie was simply not used to soldiering. It reached the point where we were afraid he was going to drop out altogether so some of the guys lifted him up and put him on top of a cart we were pulling. For awhile, one of our people actually carried his gun until it was pointed out that if Japanese soldier saw him carrying a gun he would no doubt be killed. The gun was passed back up to Willie. We knew if the time ever came to revolt against the guards that we would have easy access to Willie's gun.

Early on there had been a few successful escape attempts by the people in the groups ahead of us. Many of us had formed small four- or five- man escape units and were planning to take off at an opportune moment. However, Big Tai put a quick stop to this. He passed the word back that if anyone escaped, ten people were to be picked at random from the group he was marching with and shot. The Brigadier, in order to protect our own people from being shot, passed the order that anyone who escaped would be subject to court martial. That was the end of the escapes for the time being.

As extreme hunger, fatigue and thirst took over, we were in very desperate straits. One of our guys, Lou Bishop (a P-40 pilot and long-term POW) developed a severe case of diarrhea. He was dropping further and further behind the column and was using those precious and infrequent rest periods to catch up with the rest of us. When I wasn't pulling one of the bullock carts, I dropped back to help Lou. But I found that it was more than I could do to stay with him all night. I got four or five of the other guys to take turns helping him. Incredibly, he somehow managed to get through the march.

As the nights dragged on, some of the POWs from the groups ahead of us were dropping out. We passed these pathetic-looking creatures who were sitting at the side of the road as we went by. The word was that they would be picked up by trucks and brought back to the POW camp in Rangoon. In actuality they were picked up by Japanese soldiers and immediately shot and killed.

One of the things I worried about was falling asleep during a rest period and not waking up promptly when the order came to resume marching. Several times I had slept for two or three minutes while pulling one of the carts. My buddy, Jim McGivern (bombardier on my crew), had solemnly promised to see that I was awake in time after a rest period. However, one of the people in our group (I understand he was an American major) was not so fortunate. Evidently he overslept by a minute or so, and a Japanese stuck a bayonet into his chest and killed him.

In the morning after the third night's march, our group was hiding out is a small grove of trees a couple hundred yards from the road. The sounds of aircraft were now almost constant. Flight after flight of P-51s went zooming by a hundred or so feet over our heads. It seemed like almost a miracle that they didn't spot us. I was sitting on the ground watching the plane fly by when the guy sitting next to me casually remarked that it was his squadron of P-51s overhead. He said his name was Roger something or other and that he was the CO of the Squadron. He said the planes were ranging up and down the road looking for targets of opportunity, and for this reason it was very important for us to stay absolutely motionless. He also told me that each plane was carrying two small napalm bombs. I had never heard of napalm, and he explained to me what it was and how devastating it could be. He said that if one plane dropped two bombs in our area not one of us would survive.

Later that morning we got word that the Japs were abandoning the bullock carts. This was great news, but it also created a problem for me because my shoes were tied on the back of one of the carts. P-51s or no P-51s, I had to cross an open field to get down to where the carts were hidden at the side of the road. There was no question in my mind that I had to get my shoes. If I were ever to escape, shoes could be essential, especially if we got further north and into a jungle area. I ran across the open field and got about halfway down the road when I heard the damn P-51s coming again. I had been carefully avoiding a huge ant hill on my left, but now it was the only shelter available, and I dove in back of it. I was soon covered with huge black ants. I stayed absolutely motionless until the fighter planes had passed, then got up, brushed the ants away as quickly as I could, and made my way to the cart where I was able to retrieve my shoes and get back to the grove of trees.

The events of the last night marching are somewhat blurred. The complete lack of sleep and a diet of nothing but rice and tea was pushing all of us to the very edge of complete exhaustion. How some of the weaker prisoners ever made it through that night is almost incomprehensible. Not having to pull those cursed bullock carts any longer helped a bit.

During the course of the night, we passed the remains of a Japanese truck which we assumed had been destroyed by one of our planes. There was debris all over the road, and as I slugged along more asleep than awake, I came down hard on a nail through a piece of wood. The nail was driven deep in my heel and as I hopped along on one foot, I got the guy next to me to pull the board out. It hurt like hell.

During the early morning hours we walked through the bombed-out city of Pegu. It was only a shell, and I didn't see one living creature. It was kind of eerie. At one point the column had to go around a hole in the middle of the road. In the hole crouched a Japanese soldier cradling a rather large bomb. The British later told us this was a Kamikaze booby trap. When a British tank or truck went over the hole, the Jap would detonate the bomb and blow himself and the British equipment to bits.

We walked a few miles past Pegu and just about daybreak left the road and went into this all but abandoned Burmese village. As I recall, it was Sunday morning. We could hear the sounds of gunfire and knew the front could not be too far away.

A couple of hours later I was scavenging around the village for something to eat when I noticed there weren't any Japanese guards around. Just about that time a POW came running down the path shouting "We're free. We're free. The Japs are gone." I turned to the guy nearest me, an English soldier, and we solemnly shook hands. I saw that tears were streaming down his face, and he kept repeating, "Good show. Good show. Jolly good show." A feeling of complete exhilaration swept through me. I have never again experienced a feeling quite like it.

It took me a few minutes to come down to earth and realize that our situation still wasn't all that great. There was a Japanese army between us and the British 14th Army. If the Japanese retreated back through our village, they could very easily wipe us all out. And on the other hand, the British in the mistaken belief that we were the enemy could also shell and shoot the hell out of us.

But first things first, and it was back to looking for something to eat. I and five or six other guys found a fruit tree just at the edge of the village. One of the guys reached up and picked up a fruit, tried it, and said it was delicious. It was a little tiny fruit 1" to 2" long. But they were ripe and ready for eating. In a flash, all of us were up in the tree, and we were quickly joined by about ten other guys. I managed to pick seven of the little darlings and threw them down to Jim McGovern on the ground. So we each had 3½ pieces of fruit. And I thought: Wow!! Things were sure improving. A couple of hours ago we were slaves and here we are free men and gorging ourselves on delicious fruit.

Back in the village we found that Big Tai had formally turned over command of the POWs to Brigadier Hobson. Then Big Tai gathered up his troops and ran out to fight the British. The Brigadier, a real soldier, quickly organized things in a military fashion setting up things like G-1, G-2, etc. He evidently decided that our best course of action would be to try to attract the attention of allied planes which were now almost continuously overhead and try to get a message to them that we were in this village.

A bunch of guys quickly scrounged up some red and white cloth and sewed together a large British flag. The flag was placed on the ground in a field just outside the village. In each corner of the field was a POW who had a stick which was attached to a white piece of cloth which he was waving around. There was a haystack in the field which was set on fire. And in the middle of the field was Roger, the P-51 CO who said he knew all the latest codes and how to send them. He had a piece of mirror, and he was attempting to contact the planes flying overhead. A group of B-25s saw this astounding scene and I guess decided that it was a lot of nonsense and since they had already dropped their bombs, they proceeded to go back to their base. The next reaction we had was from a group of four British Hurricane fighters. They were manned by Royal Indian Air Force pilots. They were flying at possibly 2000 or 3000 feet and saw all this stuff on the ground. They did contact their base about it. And some guy at the base said "It's a lot of baloney, it's a Japanese trick, all the POWs are back at Rangoon, go ahead and hit them." So this is precisely what the Hurricanes did.

Before the Hurricane raids started, I had heard that a first aid station had been set up underneath the Burmese basha that the Brigadier had taken over as his headquarters. The basha was built on stilts like all the Burmese huts and had a little platform extending in front of the door. It was here that the Brigadier presided. I had gone to the aid station hoping that perhaps they could do something for my heel, which by now was aching continuously. They couldn't do anything, they had nothing for it, but this was no more than I expected.

When I heard the sound of machine-gun fire, I knew we were being attacked. I dove behind a huge tree which was next to the Brigadier's basha. The bullets slammed into the tree and also hit the Brigadier killing him instantly. Bombs were crashing into the village, and I decided this was no place to hang around. So after the first wave passed, I made a dash across an open field for a bomb crater that I remembered seeing when we came to the village that morning. I got part way across the field when the fighters came around for the second pass. There was no place to hide so I just lay flat on the ground and waited for the worst to happen. A line of bullets plowed up the dirt no more than a foot away from my head. After this pass was over, I did manage to get into the bomb crater which by now was full of guys and in fact several came in on top of me which was quite comforting.

The Hurricanes made four passes and when they were gone, we drifted back into the village. We found out that incredibly, the only person who was killed in the raid was Brigadier Clive Hobson. A number of people were wounded by bomb fragments, but he was the only fatality. The Brigadier had been captured in Singapore early in 1942, had endured over three years of Japanese imprisonment and now he had been killed by his own people, a few hours after liberation.

Colonel Douglas Gilbert, an American Infantry Officer who had been attached to the Chinese Army assumed command. There was no further thought given to try to signal Allied airplanes. Now our big worry was that the Allies knew there was activity in our village and of course they did not know it was occupied by POWs. Our fear was that we could be bombed again or hit by British artillery fire. Scouts were sent out to look for a place where we could suitably regroup.

Late in the afternoon the order was passed for us to retreat in small groups to a village a mile or so to the south of our present position. We were told to stay off the road and keep a low profile. When we got to this village we found there were still some Burmese occupying it and also found to our great delight that arrangements had been made to feed us. It was fully dark when we were fed a huge meal of rice and tea. For the first time since I was captured my hunger was completely satisfied.

We learned that a couple of our people had been dressed up as Burmese and accompanied by some Burmese children, had set off down the road in an attempt to reach British soldiers. Since by now it was pitch dark and the word came that we were to scatter about the village to bed down for the night, and hopefully a rescue party would show up in the morning. I was with 10 or 12 other guys when we found a nice grassy plot off the path running through the village. I lay down and was sound asleep before my head hit the ground.

The next thing I knew, someone was shaking me hard. I sat up and to my horror, when I looked around no one was near me except the young Burmese who had awakened me. In my befuddled state of mind

I thought I had only been asleep for a matter of minutes. I should have realized that the moon was now up and shinning as bright as daylight and that some hours had passed since I had lain down. The Burmese were no friends of air people from Rangoon Jail's compound 8. Many of our POWs had been found by Burmese civilians who invariably promised to help them escape but instead turned them over to the Japanese for a few pennies. When I saw that I was alone with this Burmese I was absolutely sure that he planned to turn me back over to the Japs. I reacted violently. I hit him as hard as I could and knocked him down and then jumped on him. I tried to wrestle his knife away from him and had every intention of killing him. We were rolling around on the ground, and the Burmese was shouting something unintelligible. I guess he realized that he was literally fighting for his life. At that time two British POWs came walking down the path and quickly broke up the fight. The young Burmese ran off like a scared deer. The British guys explained that he was only trying to help me. They said the rest of our people had been rescued by the British, but that there were some stragglers left in and around the village. They told me that some of the guys had gone quite far away from the village to spend the night and as a result missed the rescue operation. They also said that they were sure that the British would send in a rescue force to pick up the stragglers in the morning. They suggested that I find an inconspicuous spot in or around the village and stay out of sight for the rest of the night.

I went back into the village and found a middle-aged Burmese who spoke a little English. He agreed to let me spend the rest of the night in his basha although he told me that he was sleeping outside. I tried to talk him out of a gun or a knife to defend myself with. He finally and rather reluctantly, gave me a small hand axe. I climbed the ladder of his hut and went into the main room. I found a mat on the floor, lay down and promptly went to sleep.

I woke up at dawn still clutching my little axe. As I stood up and looked across the room, to my complete horror, I saw a young Japanese soldier. He looked to be as completely exhausted as I was. He no longer had a gun but did have a bayonet which he quickly drew. I guess I didn't look like too dangerous a soldier. I was dressed in that Japanese army shirt, a pair of torn khaki pants and was, of course barefoot. During the air raid, I had lost the little homemade cap I had been wearing. I had a full beard and a shock of very unkempt hair. The Jap and I looked at each other for a long, long moment and then I think we both simultaneously said to ourselves "FUCK IT." He slowly backed up to the doorway and then was down the ladder and gone in a flash. I stayed in the room until I saw some activity around the village and cautiously went out to see if I could find some other people.

I came across an American, Master Sergeant Schneider, of the Chemical Warfare division. He told me that some months before he had met an observation plane pilot who was friend from his home town. They had gone for a joy ride in Northern Burma, had gotten lost and ended up running out of gas and crash landing behind enemy lines. Schneider told me that he had spent the rest of the time in cell block 5. He said the guards told him that he would be fed regular POW rations since he was not from the Air Corp. We then ran across another American, a Lieutenant from compound 6. There was also a number of British POWs in and around the village. One of the British told me that aside from my roommate, several other Japanese soldiers had been spotted in the village. He suggested that we stay out of sight as much as possible until the rescue party arrived.

Early in the morning we had heard considerable artillery fire, and it must have been about noon when we first heard rifle fire. One of the other guys and me crept to the edge of the village where we had a ringside view of the ensuing battle. We saw far across the fields a line of Gurkhas advancing and going out to meet them what later we found out to be a total of 23 Japanese soldiers. The fire fight was over very quickly and in the end the 23 Japs who had gone out had all been killed. Among those killed was my roommate of the night before.

In short order the Gurkhas, who evidently were at the point of Attack, swept past the village and continued south. They were followed by a group of English soldiers who thoroughly searched the village for Japanese stragglers. One English soldier was left to guard us. I still had that cheroot in my pocket so I gave it to him and then lit it for him with the one match that I owned and which I had been hoarding for many months. He sort of grinned and said, "Blimey, it's just like Christmas."

Later that afternoon, when I presume, the area had been cleared of enemy soldiers, a truck came to pick us up. Some Burmese villagers had gathered near us to watch our departure. I saw the man who had loaned me his hut the night before. I took off my shoes, which were tied around my neck, and went over and offered them to him. He gratefully accepted and kept repeating thanks and shaking my hand.

The truck quickly took us to what appeared to be a British forward headquarters area. Incredibly all 400 POWs who had reached there the night before were gone. We tried to find out where everybody had gone and could not get any firm answers. We did find out that at dawn an area right next to the headquarters area was leveled off and a steel runway was laid down. Shortly thereafter C-47s came in, and the POWs were gone. We were given a ration of cheese and crackers and one of the British officers promised to find out where the Americans has been taken. He did add: "Try to be patient, Gentlemen. After all we are fighting a war, you see."

The next morning we still knew nothing and were just sort of hanging around. A reporter from the New York Times came up to me and said he would like to interview me. He told me that a war correspondent had been killed by a sniper the day before, and he was waiting to attend a service for him. While he was waiting he said he would like to get my story. The story was rather lengthy and was printed in the New York Times a few days later. This is how my folks learned for the first time that I was still alive.

By that afternoon we three Americans decided we better make a move on our own, or we would be spending the rest of the war in southern Burma. We had seen some C-47s coming in and leaving. We went to the landing strip and found a pilot of a C-47 which was being unloaded. He told us that he was from a base in northern Burma and when we asked, he assured us that he would be happy to let us hitch a ride to his base. When we were airborne he called his base and told them he had on board three freed American ex-POWs. And what a fantastic reception we got when we landed! Everybody from the CO of the base on down the line was there to greet us. As we stepped out of the airplane, a great roar of welcome went up. We went down the receiving line shaking hands and we were treated as if we were real VIPs. At the end of the reception line was the base chaplain, who, with a big grin on his face, handed each of us an ice cold can of beer.

In short order we were enjoying the amenities of real civilization- a hot shower with real soap, a toothbrush and toothpaste, a towel. The other two guys had serviceable uniforms, but I was still in rags. So some of the guys on base quickly rounded up some clothes for me. I got a clean set of underwear and socks and a GI gave me a khaki shirt and a pair of pants. I offered him my Japanese army shirt as a souvenir, and he was delighted to get it. I couldn't get a pair of shoes on my swollen feet, but somebody came up with a pair of sneakers which was just fine.

A flight surgeon came to give us a quick checkup, and gave me what I presumed was a tetanus shot for the puncture wound in my heel. From there we went to the mess hall for a meal which the cooks had especially prepared for us. It was absolutely delicious, I don't think I have ever before or since eaten so much at one single meal. Among other things I remember eating a half a loaf of bread and jam on the side. When we finally reached the point where we couldn't eat another morsel of food, a major invited us to his tent for a nightcap. He said that he had been hoarding a bottle of Scotch for a special occasion, and he couldn't think of a more special occasion that this one. We sat around talking and sipping on the Scotch until it was gone. When we got up to leave for the tent we had been assigned to, somebody came in and offered us each a can of chocolate drink. I accepted and drank it. I headed for my tent, but never made it. I did make the head, however, and I have never been sicker in my life. Must have been that damn chocolate drink.

In the morning the three of us decided to push on. The night before, the flight surgeon had suggested that most likely the other POWs had gone to the 142nd General Hospital in Calcutta so we caught the first C-47 which was heading for that city. When we landed we checked with operations and told them we were three POWs from Rangoon and could he please tell us where we were supposed to go. He told us he would try to find out and to come back in an hour or so. It was getting on to lunchtime and even though I had no great interest in food after the event of the night before, I joined the other two guys and went to the officer's club for lunch. We went into the club and were met at the door by a lovely young lady whom we told we would like to have lunch. She said, "Yes sir. That will be three rupees (about 32 cents) each." We explained that we had no money because we had just gotten out of a prison camp, but we would like to have lunch anyway. She adamantly refused to let us in, and we finally asked if we could talk to the Club Officer. She brought back a captain who asked us what the problem was. We again told him that we were just freed POWs and wanted to eat. He looked at us; admittedly, we didn't look exactly like spit-and-polish soldiers. He asked if we had any identification. This was the most asinine thing I had ever heard in my life, and said so. His reply was that we could not come in unless we had identification and unless we paid three rupees. Like the other two guys, I was a little annoyed. But then the thought occurred to me that this is really great because now I finally realized that we were once again part of the United State Army Air Corps. A colonel who had listened to the conversation intervened and saw to it that we were fed.

When finished we went back to operations to try to find out again if somebody knew where we were to go. And then we had further proof that we were back in the Army. The operations officer came out and demanded to know what the hell we were doing wandering around the base when we were supposed to be in quarantine until we had been deloused. At any rate, we were bundled into an ambulance, given an MP motorcycle escort, and we were driven out to the 142nd General Hospital in style.

There I had a joyous reunion with the guys who had long since given me up for dead. And a wild period of my life had come to a quiet and peaceful finish.

<u>Bob Derrington gives us an aftermath vignette and more:</u> Word had
been passed among the prisoners that after crossing the Sittang River,
we would enter an area occupied by Karens, a Burmese tribe known
to be friendly to the Allied forces. We planned to try am escape at that
point, knowing that our chances would decrease after boarding trucks
or trains. Forty-two years later, I finally met some Karens when Joan
(my wife) and I returned to Rangoon. While searching for our prison
site, we asked our driver to take us to Judson College, the Japanese
headquarters where some of us had been detained and interrogated
when first captured. The driver thought about this for a few minutes and
then remembered that the name of Judson College had been changed
to Rangoon University. It was a Sunday morning when we visited the
campus. We stopped at the chapel and met several Burmese students
about to start a Christian service. They were Karens.

Back on that march out in the early morning in 1945, we arrived at a
small deserted village. It was here that the Japs declared us free, and they
immediately continued on their way at a much faster pace. During the
day, several more soldiers passed the village singly and in small groups,
ignoring us in their haste. We learned later that the advancing British
Army troops were rapidly nearing our position.

Somebody found a mirror, or piece of glass, and tried to signal the
fighter planes as they patrolled the area. The reflections must have
looked liked rifle fire to the pilots so they promptly attacked the village.
We were caught by surprise and could only take cover behind small trees
during the first strafing pass as the planes circled for another run, we
all jumped into foxholes and slit trenches that had been dug by natives.
I remembered two men landed on top of me. One of them still had his
rear end and legs above ground. After two or three more passes, the
aircraft went on their way, and we began to sort ourselves out again.
I returned to the small tree where I had stretched out during the first
attack. There I found the remains of a canteen that has been beside me.
It was now just a piece of tangled metal and loose bark was everywhere.
Excuse the expression, but that is where I almost had my ass shot off.
Miraculously, of the 400 men, only one was killed. He was the ranking
officer, a British General who had been imprisoned about three years.

Somehow we made it through the day. During the time, contact was made with the approaching Army. After sundown a young native boy led us in small groups through fields to meet with advance troops. I was in the first group to leave the village and we were soon stopped by a lone English officer. He very carefully checked us to verify our identity. When he was satisfied that we were escaping prisoners, he gave a signal. Just then, a bright moon broke through a large cumulus cloud formation, and we found ourselves surrounded by a squad of Gurkhas carrying their large curved knives. These fierce-looking, turbaned soldiers were a welcome sight!

We were escorted to the infantry camp and given some food and a blanket. I rolled the blanket for a pillow and fell into a deep sleep in a nearby field. The next morning I awakened to the sights and sounds of low-flying fighter aircraft, and a bulldozer was scraping a landing strip close by. Hank Pisterzi was lying next to me, and he said that the noise woke him up earlier. He was about to get up and run when he saw me still sleeping. He said to himself, "Oh, the hell with it" and went back to sleep.

A C-47 arrived and took several of us to an air base some distance to the north. I don't remember if it was Akyab or Chittagong. We reported that many more prisoners were still in Rangoon and described the prison complex so it could identified and supplies flown to them. After one more night we were flown to Calcutta and placed in the 142nd General Hospital for medical treatment and processing. Soon, those who remained in Rangoon arrived at the hospital; the rest is history! (Bob noted to MEMORIES that the date on which he wrote this was exactly 44 years after the date he and his fellow prisoners were freed.)

Bob Etherington tells more about the walkout: Shortly after the last march (those of us from 8 compound) arrived in the patch of woods about five miles beyond Pegu, the Jap Commanding Officer called for the ranking Allied officer, Brigadier Hobson. He gave the Brigadier a note saying that we were free. The Japs then all took off in a hurry eastward down the railroad, hoping to avoid being trapped by the advancing British 14th Army. WE WERE FREE---much of our fatigue suddenly almost vanished.

The exhilaration of freedom was tempered by the reality of our situation. Here we were over 400 weak, exhausted, starving men, trapped behind a battlefront with no food or supplies, no contact with either friendly or hostile troops, and no one except us and our fleeing guards knowing of our presence. A collection was made of all spare clothing which was then spread in one of the adjoining fields in the form of a message like "POWs HERE." We felt quite safe in doing this as there had been no sign of any Japanese planes since we left Rangoon. We had seen several Allied fighters and reconnaissance planes already that morning.

An hour or two later, four Royal Indian Air Force fighter planes arrived overhead. They circled our patch of forest and then started down in a series of strafing passes. I was terrified. Several of us sought what shelter we could behind a very inadequate tree. I was on the outside edge of this pile of people. On about the third pass, I was horrified to watch a stream of machine-gun bullets striking the earth in a path almost parallel to my body and only about four inches away. As that strafing pass ended, I ran from the tree and dove behind a mound of earth just as I heard the machine-gun fire of the next strafing. Unfortunately, I had, unknowingly, dived into an ant hill, and by the time that strafing pass was over, I was being attacked by numerous vicious ants about an inch long. At that point I was wearing only a loin cloth so I had no clothing to protect any part of my body. That was the last of the strafing, and I left the ant hill frantically brushing off the ants as fast as I possibly could. Their bites were painful, and many of the resulting sores did not heal for several months.

During these strafing attacks, our ranking officer, British Brigadier Hobson, who had been a prisoner for over three years, was killed and one British sergeant was wounded. Those were our only strafing causalities.

After this attack our situation seemed more uncertain and precarious. We were, however, still a military organization of sorts. Word was passed around to hide out the best you could and wait for further instructions. I wound up in the shack by the railroad with perhaps six or eight others. We could look out through the cracks in the wall to see if something was happening. More stray Jap soldiers wandered across the fields near us, but apparently were unaware of our presence. Late in the afternoon we saw a parachute drop (presumably supplies for the British troops) going down over Pegu. This was too much for one of the fellows, who grabbed our canteen and ran off down the rail tracks toward Pegu yelling "I can help."

A little later we got word that about dusk we were to go to a small village in the woods across the fields to the southwest. We were only to go in small groups and should try to be as inconspicuous as possible. About four of us in a group were making our way across the fields, crouching rather low. Suddenly two or three men with guns sprung up out of the tall grass. In the fading light it was difficult to identify them. Our hearts sank as we were about to be shot by some of the Japs we had seen earlier. As it turns out, these men were from the village to which we were heading. They had come to protect us as we crossed the open fields. What a relief! We hurried on to the village.

We were still functioning, at least in part, as a military organization. Most of us from the #8 compound, where our contacts with others had been so restricted, were less aware than some of the others about all that was going on.

An American, Major Charles Lutz, had been serving as an Adjutant to Brigadier Hobson. In this capacity, he was making some arrangements of which we were not aware. He had found someone in one of the little nearby jungle villages who could speak a little English. Through this person he got a guide to take him through the jungle to make contact with the British 14th Army. They were thus made aware of the presence of our POW group isolated behind the front lines. Arrangements were made for the British to meet us at some predetermined point that night. Arrangements had also been made for us to meet at the village about dusk, be fed, and wait for further orders. We did not know all of this when we arrived at the village that evening.

The village people had prepared some rice for us. This was certainly appreciated since we had not eaten for three days. Probably close to three hundred of us, out of the more than four hundred who had left the prison, were the guests in the village that evening. The others were fending for themselves in one way or another. The village people were very friendly and seemed anxious to help us. After eating we were told to go down a path in the jungle, sit or lie down at the first empty place and to be absolutely quiet. It was now well after dark.

Sometime later the fellow next to me whispered for me to get up, place a hand on his shoulder so I could follow him, and continue to be quiet, but whisper the message to the next fellow. We all got up and soon started to move single file down the jungle paths. In some places it was so dark that you could barely see the fellow you were following, so the hand on his shoulder was a good idea; in some other places it was quite open. We understood the need to be silent as possible as we were still traversing enemy territory.

After walking in this manner for what I think might have been four or five miles, we came out of the jungle into some open area. We had gone several hundred yards, and my heart sank again when I spotted the silhouette of a machine gun against the skyline. We quickly realized to our great relief that it was not the Japs, but rather the British who were covering us as we emerged from the jungle. We walked on another few hundred yards to where some British trucks were waiting for us. What an incredibly good feeling- REALLY FREE AT LAST!

Nick Oglesby records arrival at the hospital in Calcutta: I was on the third plane out, I think. We flew to Calcutta and there transferred to trucks to take us to the 142nd General Hospital.

When we got to the hospital, we were taken to a special ward set aside for us. We were shown our beds and given some items we would need. Our ward was one of two beside each other, and we were told we would have our own mess hall for two wards. However, that would be activated the next morning so we would need to walk to the central mess hall for dinner that night.

When we got there, we found the damnedest, biggest most delicious meal being piled on our trays by the cooks and attendants, all of who urged us to take more! (We did.) Steak and potatoes, green beans, biscuits and strawberry jam and all those great subjects of our jailhouse dreams were almost unbelievable. I ate it all. I don't know how. I do know that I ate too much for I quickly developed a horrible headache and became sick to my stomach, losing all of it after I managed to get outside the mess hall. I felt horrible. All I wanted to do was find the ward and get in that bed.

Unfortunately, the mess hall was huge and had four identical sides. I did not know which direction to start walking. So I had to go back inside and wait for the group. When I got inside, the smell of the food made me get another full tray. This time it stuck.

The next day, the processing began. We had been eating very well ever since we had that first chicken and dumplings with the British. I weighed 105 pound on the hospital scales so I have no idea what I weighed when we were trucked out by the British. I certainly was not in as bad shape as many.

That was quite a mess hall we had between our wards. We had our own cooks and attendants who fixed what we wanted and urged us to eat more. We certainly wanted to be cooperative, all of us, and we ate more and more and more. I remember one of us ate 14 fried eggs for breakfast for several days. Each meal was two eggs with a ration of bacon. He ate 7 every morning. This was the same man who, when we were in Rangoon and I was so sick with malaria and could not get my rice down, came to me and gave me a hard-boiled egg, saying he had lots of them and could get more. I still remember that was one very good egg! (I later found he had one egg previously, in his two years in jail, and I don't think he ever got another, until we were released.)

The prisoners from Rangoon who had been designated as too sick to march joined us in a few days.

Henry Pisterzi tells how he remembers the walkout: We left the prison—those of us who they determined were able to march—with supplies loaded on carts and pulled by Japs and POWs. We traveled north for two nights. Some of us felt that since we were headed north, there was a possibility of an exchange of prisoners. (The last word we had before the march was that the British 14th Army was closing in on Rangoon from the north.) However, when we changed directions and headed east, we thought maybe the Japs were trying to get us to another prison camp in Indo-China.

Near the end of the second night, some of us had planned to break up into groups of three or four and try to escape. About noon the third day the Jap commander told us we were free men. Free, Hell!! Here we were in an open field. Ahead of us were the Allied troops. Behind us were the Japs. Heavy artillery was being fired over us even before we had been turned loose.

During the march, we would have a ten-minute rest period about every hour. For me and those in our group this turned out to be anything but. When we stopped for the rest, the Japs guarding us would line us up and have us count off. They didn't trust us. We formed up probably three deep and the front row was to count off in Japanese. Somehow, it seemed that each time we were to count off, we had three or four people in the front row that couldn't count in Japanese so by the time we had been counted, the rest period was over.

While in prison, most or all of us had not worn shoes or much of any clothing, and would save these for a later need if required. My feet were so sore that I didn't think I could make another step so I could have used the ten-minute rest, but that was not to be.

All along the route, Japs were wiring the bridges we had crossed and were digging holes in the road. These holes were large enough for a bomb and one Jap. The bridges were to be blown up after they were no longer needed by the Japs. We asked what the holes were for and were told, "Bomb and Nippon in hole with hammer, when enemy comes over, Nippon hits bomb with a hammer. Boom! Hammer, Jap, bomb and enemy all blown up."

After our rescue and delivery to the hospital, we posed a problem for the hospital staff. "What do we do with these people? Set up a diet and control their eating? Or, do we turn them loose and see what happens?" They decided the latter. Without any exaggeration, I saw some of the POWs eat a dozen eggs, a dozen pancakes along with all the trimmings—all for breakfast. I recall no ill effects from this for any POWs. After getting cleaned up—showers, haircuts, decent clothes, etc.—it was not unusual to barely recognize the person you had slept next to in the prison. After a day or so, several people—Bill Rooney amongst them—arrived at the hospital to see and interrogate the men from the 40th. What a sight to see someone from your own squadron!

After our month's stay in the hospital and the 60-day furlough most of us got, I was in the process of reassignment at Ft. MacArthur. The reassignment procedure was probably half over when the war ended. Separation, if desired, was started. I was discharged out of Ft. MacArthur in August of 1945. Thus ended my military career.

Julian Cochran brings the story to an end: We were placed on normal rations immediately. We were fed too much, and we also received too much booze, but I had no complaints, and no harm was done. All, of course, received medical exams and were treated, if needed. Everyone had malaria, many had Beriberi, and some had open sores. A ranking officer visited us and asked what we wanted. We told him "watches, sunglasses and B-4 bags." We got them all. I still have mine- the watch and sunglasses are worn out, and the B-4 bag is in the basement in a musty condition. In the Officer's Club in Calcutta, I ran into a friend from my hometown, John Cross, who thought I was dead. I last saw him in the Officer's Club in Karachi when we were on the way to Chakulia.

On May 19- according to my knowledge and order No2, APO 496, dated 18 May, 1945, the first six POWs from Rangoon departed from Calcutta for the USA. Five members of the 40th were on the orders: Julian C. Cochran, Robert E. Derrington, Joseph Levine, Chester E. Paul and Norman Larsen. The other man was Harold W. Goad, outfit unknown. It is possible other 40th members departed prior to 19 May. I was always of the opinion that I was one of the lucky ones to leave with the first bunch. We were flown in C-54s across Africa to LaGuardia Field, New York.

Home in America at last. Thus was the five-month ordeal ended.

Was obtained from the 40th Bomb Group Association "Memories" Issue #37 March 1991. Letter from Nicholas Oglesby to Chris Morgan

LIBERATED PRISONERS OF PEGU

At ten o'clock in the morning of May 1st, word was flashed to Four Corps Headquarters that an unestimated number of Allied prisoners of war had been freed at Pegu, in the front lines of British advance, just north of Rangoon.

In a half-hour, Captain Julius Goodman loaded his C-64 with correspondents and Signal Corp photographers, and took off for the Pegu encampment.

The expressions on the faces that later met the planeload of Yanks made an everlasting impression.

Some of the weary relaxed inside the row of four-man tents, smoking American cigarettes and watching others, equally tired and hungry, either stumble into the queue for fresh clothing issue (British fatigues, woolen socks and sneakers). They wandered aimlessly about, talking to former cell companions. Here, along the blacktop road, four miles north of Pegu, these four hundred and twenty Allied prisoners of war were the first to be liberated in Burma and were becoming re-acclimated to a life of unrestricted freedom. Airmen clad in their battered jump suits and Chandits, wearing nothing more than Jap loincloth, still limped from their fifty five mile barefoot march from Rangoon's city prison, a veritable torture chamber.

The rescued prisoners, headed by Lt. Col. Douglas G. Gilbert, West Point, class of '33, from Washington, D.C., believed that when they set out on April 26th, their captors had planned to herd them into Indo-China. But having miscalculated the rapidity of the 14th Army's drive, the Japanese abandoned their "excess weight" two days later to make their escape to the East that much easier.

As the truckload of Americans, flown in by Capt. Goodman, drove into the area in search of men long given up for lost, the clothing queue disappeared. Even the B-24 pilot, who hadn't covered his feet in a year, said, "To hell with the shoes for now," and rushed over to a U.P.Correspondent, Hugh Crumpler, asking if he would send a message home to his wife.

Everyone's eyes strained to locate a familiar face. Suddenly, Goodman cried out, "There 'Red 'Gilmore- Hey- 'Red,' you old Santa Claus!"

Lt. Richard Gilmore, stocky 1st Air Commando fighter Pilot of Pittsburgh, Pennsylvania, had sprouted a heavy beard since he was shot down northeast of Heho on January 18th. Burmese kept him until the 20th, before turning him over to the Japs.

Alongside Gilmore stood his squadron mate, Lt. Hilton Weesner of South Bend, Indiana, chatting with Capt. Goodman and Lt. Col Bill Taylor, of Combat Cargo Task Force. Weesner's cheeks were drawn, his one-piece flying suit which had not been washed since he crashed on November 12th near Meiktila, was punched full of holes. Weesner was the first of the Group's fighter pilots lost in this year's operations. When he spoke he blurted out his words excitedly: "Guess they gave me up for dead. The rest of the flight saw my ship burn, while they circled overhead. That night after coming to, I was picked up by a Burman in an ox-cart and taken straight to the Japs. I wouldn't give them my unit's name or tell them anything about the P-47, so they beat me across the face with the flat side of a sword. Later, they transported me by truck across the Irrawaddy down to Rangoon. Occasionally, we'd hear rumors of the British advance, though the Japs never mentioned it to us. They beat the airmen with clubs continually. It seems their practice was to discriminate against air crews. They shoved us into individual cells, and placed ground troops in compounds. I had dysentery, but wasn't allowed medication. I dropped from 172 to 145 ponds."

A slender, middle aged officer rose from one of the prisoner tents and asked. "Have you heard of any Second Air Commandos being found? Pryor's my name…Major Roger Pryor; from Starkville, Mississippi… C.O. of the 2nd Fighter Squadron…Will you please notify Colonel Chase that I'm all right." At Major Pryor's mentioning of the words, "Second Air Commandos," "My God, is there a second over here now, too?" "Why sure," replied Capt. Donald V. Miller, veteran 1st Air Commando P-51 pilot, shot down north of Mandalay, on February 14th 1944, "we heard about them several month ago."

It remained for Capt. "Red" Miller, of Menonomie, Wisconsin, Cpt. John Hunt, McCleansboro, Illinois, and Lt. John T. Whitescarver of

Pittsburgh, Kansas to reveal the life endured inside Rangoon's city prison, referred to as the "lock up."

"For nine months we had no medical attention," Miller began. "Men stricken with dysentery just had to stop eating. That's all true about airmen being discriminated against. Thirty seven of the sixty four interned at Rangoon passed away. The guards used to run lotteries on the dates the different ones left to rot, would die. As the very sick began failing away. The guards would inject needles into their arms, killing them within an hour's time."

Lt. John Whitescarver, who had been a prisoner since the second of April 1944, hurriedly broke in for a moment. "When first admitted, airmen were stripped of all clothing and force to sit cross-legged in front of the bars all day. If we bent backwards or leaned forward, the guards would thrash us soundly. They'd beat us anyway, for no reason other than that we didn't understand Japanese. If we failed to salute them, they'd beat us. Nights they came in drunk they'd beat us worse than ever. For seven months we saw no sunshine. Mosquitoes were so thick that they obscure any ray of light."

"We had no place to sleep and nothing to drink except the one half cup of tea at mealtime," interrupted Hunt, a sixteen-month prisoner. "A few of the boys were beaten to death right before our eyes for trying to escape from the 'lock-up,' and until this past November, they made us bury our dead naked, wrapped in gunny sacks. Not until last fall did they give us a slab-board coffin."

"Nevertheless, we worked out a means of communicating with one another," spoke up Miller. Whenever we heard rumors of any news, we'd spell out words in the air with our fingers. Hunt lived in a cell across from mine," Miller smiled as if to say, "You see, our spirits weren't broken."

To mingle with these men was like visiting with the resurrected. Voices would cry out, "Why, sure, you're Halstead, the guy who went down back in...." and then break off, so as not to let slip the rest of the sentence, "I never thought you'd be alive."

This narrative was obtained through the courtesy of Karnig Thomasian.

Freed POWs who walked out of Rangoon Prison to Pego.
– Courtesy Pegasus Archives.

THE REUNION

I sat midst aging warriors

Shining golden in the after-glow of youth,

And my heart overflowed.

Neither those who stood at Thermoplyas,

Nor those who charged at Balaclava,

Nor those who fell at Gallipoli

Were braver than these.

For, truly they had walked "thru the valley
of the shadow of death"

And brought the gift of freedom to me.

This was so eloquently written by Virginia Humphry for the Rangoon Ramblings, a newsletter sent to the Rangoon Prisoners of War, written and distributed by Diana and Karnig Thomasian.

PART 4

Our Lives Are Ours Again?????

Prisoners of War never have their lives returned to them the same. The common thread for Prisoners of War is what their loss of freedom did to them. They relate again and again that being captured by an enemy and having your freedom taken from you, freedoms you have always known to be so basic; the ability to move, communicate and live. Now you had to depend on your enemy for everything and never knowing when or how it will end. Seeing others, as well as yourself, beaten, tortured and sometimes killed. Denied water, food and even made to lie in your own excrement. Becoming less than human, your captors demanding slave-like obedience and not knowing if or when this will ever end. Soon your only goal is to survive. Many Prisoners of War will respond if you call them hero's that they are only "survivors".…..

Along with that terrible knowledge they bring home, they also suffer from the memories of those who did not survive and the way their lives were lost. This was just one more burden they were to carry.

These men were expected to come home and continue on with their lives as if this terrible experience was only a brief interlude in their lives and that after a few months rest they would pick up where they left off. This was the expectation, not only of their families, but of themselves as well, but unfortunately it was not the case. Their experiences would change them forever.

As they were welcomed home as hero's by loving families, wives, sweethearts and friends, how were they going to explain this "dark side" feeling that they really didn't understand or were unable to control at times. Everyone expected that after a few months home they would be the same "ole guy" who left. They were not and could never be that same "ole guy." They had suffered too much both physically and mentally. They would never be the same, but they would learn to cope and in many instances begin again, but they would always be different.

The wives and families of these men also endured stress, trauma and anguish when those telegrams began arriving. Those little white flags with the blue stars that had been hanging in their windows designating that a member of the family was serving in the war, sometimes changed to gold. Now neighbors, friends and family members knew that those men had been lost. The men who had been unaccounted for, such as prisoners of war or missing in action had no designated stars. Their families, friends and neighbors just waited praying they would somehow return.

The Japanese gave little information on Prison Camps and very little information about prisoners of war. The families of those in the Rangoon Camp were never to know of their existence until they were liberated.

While waiting, the women also served in any capacity they could, hoping somehow to help. The country had enlisted every man, women and child to do their part as they were able. Victory gardens (as they were called) sprouted up everywhere to supplement dinner tables. People were issued Ration stamps on many items to make sure everyone had some of the things that they needed. Everything that could possibly be used was sent to the two war fronts both Europe and Asia. As recorded by a Japanese General as Pearl Harbor was bombed, "I am afraid we have awakened a sleeping giant."

Meat, butter and gas were rationed. Each family was allotted 5 gallons of gas per week, 1 pound of butter. Meat was in very short supply. Nylon stocking were things of the past as nylon was needed for parachutes. Ladies began painting their legs with a brown dye. Everyone saved foil, string and aluminum which they turned into neighborhood stations to be forwarded to factories to be recycled. All cooking grease was saved in large tins and taken to the butcher who would then deliver the cans to special stations where they were used in the process of making bullets.

Adults bought Savings Bonds and school children every Monday dutifully took their dimes to school for Savings Stamps. When they had acquired enough they eventually received a $25 Savings Bond. Everyone not only worked toward victory but invested their money into it.

People crowded movie theaters hoping to possibly see their loved ones in News Reels from the fronts. Pictorial magazines were scoured to get information and newspapers read from front to back.

When the fortunate men began returning, it was their wives and loved ones, with their smiles and welcoming arms who tried to make all the suffering disappear. These were the ones who took care of the ailments, the countless visits to the doctor or hospital. It was they, who dealt with the emotional and psychological behavior. The wives of these men not only had to deal with these problems, but at the same time deal with the problems of everyday living while taking care of their families. Sometimes the price for understanding was too high; sometimes stress, emotional and psychological problems experienced by those wives cost the family its unity. The war's toll was not only with the men, but with the women as well. Thankfully their families were spared the real horror and terrible trauma of war.

One woman in England, Irene Jones Beckwith, related her experiences she says: "then those seven glorious words 'It is my pleasure to inform you…' The wives who were fortunate enough to receive that cable could look forward with unbelievable joy in seeing their men return. The women who were widows were trying to cope with their grief through counseling and resolve to move on. Those with children had to find jobs, sitters and spend money very thriftily. Many evidenced damage to their own psyches, trying not to be haunted by mental visions of torture, starvation and death."

No one is the same person after being witness to dying or imprisonment. In everyday life, we were to experience moments of silence, withdrawal by the men. Hurtful outbursts, nightmares, sweats, moans in sleep, tremors. The wives became chauffeurs for countless visits to doctors, psychiatrists, and dentists and for every ailment in the book, malaria, diarrhea, limitation of movements, prosthesis for lost limbs, blood problems, diabetes, frostbite, and finally post-traumatic syndrome disorder. Medicine was administered, favorite food prepared, clothes pressed, shoes polished and hair brushed. Many women did not really understand their husbands until they died and discovered hidden diaries, photos, letters; then bitterness and resentment came to light. The ex-POW wife shared the scarring of combat and imprisonment.

Another wife, Irene Beckwith from England, relates that "in February 1942, Singapore fell and my husband's regiment was sent there to defend it. At the end of May," she says, "I received the dreaded War Office letter, my husband Joe was missing. It was ominous, especially as my Father was still missing from HMS Courageous since 1939 after enemy action in the North Sea. My mother's house took a direct hit in the first blitz on Plymouth, and I was on my own now with three small children; my son had been born physically handicapped. I moved to an old school house on Dartmoor, where we could still hear the devastation of war but far enough away to sleep in peace at night.

"On return one day from taking my son to the doctor, my friend and sister met me at the train station to tell me the Japanese had unconditionally surrendered. That was August 1945 and I sat down and wrote my husband a letter hoping, always believing him alive to tell him the news. I had been writing every week throughout those long anxious years, only to have my letters returned in bundles marked 'Addressee missing.' Daily I walked or rode on our little train to Dousland to see if there was any news for me. At long last there was. The Postmistress told me a telegram had arrived and her husband had gone on his bike to deliver it to my house. The children were with me but I ran ahead of them, heart in mouth. That day I must have been the fastest two miler on record. The telegram was from a friend of mine in Plymouth 'Come at once I have good news for you.' I spent the rest of the day calling everyone in our little village begging for a lift for us to Plymouth. The letter had arrived at my former home with my husband's name on it, but my friend was afraid to send the letter on as I was living out in the village alone with my children

"When I arrived and received the letter I opened it feverishly and saw the dear familiar handwriting. After the fall of Singapore he was interned Changi Jail and then, with thousands of others, taken in cattle trucks through the jungle into Thailand where they cleared the jungle to build the infamous Burma-Siam Railway of Death, where one man would die for every sleeper laid. So at the time of writing, my husband was in the hospital in Rangoon. A few moments later a policeman came to the door with a cablegram but I was so afraid that it was bad news, I was unable to read it, he read it for me. 'Safe in Allied hands letter following. All my love, Joe.' By some quirk the letter arrived before the cable.

"It had been decided to let some of the released men come home by sea so they could convalesce. I heard from two friends that their husbands died on the way home, and my fears mounted again. I was advised on October 27th that his ship would be docking in Southhampton. Relatives were asked to stay away so that the men could be processed quickly.

"I cleaned the house from top to bottom; put the kids in the bathtub so many times they rebelled and took themselves off to a neighbor. On the evening he was due to arrive in Plymouth, I phoned my vicar and begged him to take me to the station. 'He's not due for hours yet,' he reasoned. 'I just want to get there now, please,' I begged. So off we went fortified with rugs and a thermos jug of hot coffee to help us through the long wait at the station. We arrived in the city and the vicar went to get platform tickets, I wandered on to the dim platform, and noticed a soldier seemingly exhausted lying prone on the ground his head on his kitbag. I thought to myself 'what is he doing down there?' As I moved on, the figure rose up and called my name, we looked at each other hard. Then I was clasped in his arms but his body felt so thin and brittle that I pulled myself away, I know this fellow from somewhere, I thought, and looked into the gaunt face and sunken eyes. Could this be my husband? He took my hands in his and raised them to his cheek, a very enduring habit he had, and which I loved. Yes! It was him and we clung to each other again. When the vicar joined us, Joe tried to hoist his kitbag up to his shoulder but staggered, so taking it from him, the vicar led us to his waiting car. Inside he told us how his brother and brother-in-law had found him in Southhampton, hurried him through the formalities and got him on to an earlier train from Paddington to Plymouth. There to his delight, we had arrived early too, and found him. So Joe came back, saw his children grow up, marry and have their own children and died in peace in his own bed."

Margo Etherington, wife of Bud Etherington: "Bud and I were married at the Pratt Air Base Chapel in late February 1944, shortly after Bud left for overseas. He was involved in the disastrous December 24th mixed bomb load mission over Rangoon Burma. He was captured by the Japanese the same day. On December 27th 1944, I received a War Department telegram informing me that Bud was missing in action since December 14th in the Asiatic Area. The next few months were spent in futile attempts by the family to get more information about the circumstances of Bud's whereabouts.

"It never occurred to me that he might be a Japanese POW. Always felt that Bud would return, I resented anyone telling me otherwise. It was sad to receive all my letters back, but I never gave up.

"May 2, 1945, while my father-in law was commuting to Philadelphia, his eye caught an article in the New York Times relating to the freedom of some 429 Japanese POWs. Bud's name was listed. Excitedly, my father-in law got off the train at the next station and called his wife. She quickly got a copy of the paper to read it herself and that night she called me telling me about the article and that Bud was liberated. I called the other wives on the crew to share my good news realizing that their husbands might not have been freed. But the whole crew had survived and were liberated

"On May 4th, I received a telegram from the War Department confirming Bud's freedom. I would be allowed to send him a message not to exceed 25 words, addressed to Washington. Letters started to arrive from Bud hospitalized in India. Not knowing about his POW status, I was spared the tremendous concern about his life and well-being. We were aware of the brutal sadistic treatment by the Japanese of their POWs.

"After a few weeks Bud came home. He looked good to me getting off the train in Los Angeles though he had lost over 50 pounds and had a yellow pallor from the malaria drugs he was taking. The war with Japan ended and he opted for immediate discharge from the service. Bud had very disturbing nightmares and trouble sleeping. At times, he would fall asleep in the middle of a sentence. The POW experience had a profound influence on our lives."

Post-Traumatic Stress Syndrome was a real and serious problem. Everyone remembers the story of General George Patton's famous outburst in Europe at an Army Hospital. He was visiting the wounded soldiers when he slapped a soldier he accused of malingering because he showed no signs of injury.

For returning Rangoon Prisoners of War in 1945, this was a major problem. Beside the major health problems they suffered and with the many diseases contracted along with wounds from the beatings and torture, many also suffered from an undiagnosed illness: post-traumatic stress disorder.

In the early part of the 19th century, military doctors started to notice soldiers with exhaustion after the stress of battle. The "exhaustion" was characterized by mental shutdown due to individual or group trauma. They were also identified as shell shock, battle fatigue or traumatic war neurosis.

The true understanding of post-traumatic stress syndrome did not begin until the 1970s, when it began to be recognized by physicians and a name was found during the Viet Nam war, this was called a conflict, but it was war.

Today, all returning men and women are given a medical exam and evaluated psychologically to determine if they have any disorders or other problems. Unfortunately, this was not available in 1945. As this syndrome became recognized as a real and irrefutable fact, it began to be addressed.

One of the problems that faced not only physicians but the men themselves was the way men were characterized . Hollywood had done a good job in depicting all of our men as John Wayne. These men were trained to "suck it up." While this was great for the home front, as we were spared the real atrocities of war, it was very difficult for these men to admit to problems or even recognize them. They sometimes felt that giving a voice to this or even discussing it would somehow constitute a flaw in their manhood.

The name eventually given was "Post-Traumatic Stress Disorder." In recent years, it has been suggested that it be re-named "Post Combat Reaction." As studies emerged and treatment became available, it was finally addressed.

During combat or imprisonment there is no time for grieving over the loss of a friend or a horror you have witnessed. Now also your own survival is uncertain. These traumas are deeply embedded in the brain. The younger the man, the deeper it is embedded. Those memories and responses are not something that can be turned off easily when you come home.

There are certain "triggers" that conjure up those embedded memories. Our men from Rangoon may have an emotional reaction from a few days of constant rain bringing back thoughts of the monsoons and rain forests. Sometimes tropical foliage could remind them of the jungle, sometimes a taste or a smell as these are involuntary reactions once their body reacts to some trigger, it is like a chain reaction: Trigger, physical response, emotional reaction. This can happen in a split second, and then the memories are likely to follow.

On some occasions a trigger can result in a flashback, the soldier can feel like he is actually back in prison or combat. This may only last a few seconds, but the results may leave him irritable, depressed or distracted. Nightmares are common and sometimes the returning soldier may have to sleep in a different room because of calling out, yelling and thrashing around, all of it done during sleep.

When holidays roll around they may be a trigger. The soldier may remember where he was on that particular holiday and some of those memories are very painful.

The mind is set up biologically in such a way that one of the emotion centers is located right next to one of the long-term memory centers. This enables some intense emotions to be burned into the memory. This is a protective device that nature teaches us to remember what is dangerous and to avoid it. That is why these particular horrific memories are difficult as they are burned into the memory bank.

Some of the men from the prison related that sometimes just a noise in their home, would make them involuntarily jump out of bed and stand at attention with the expectation that he had heard a guard making his rounds. He would then have to be coaxed back to bed by his wife. If the man was living alone, he would have to fight those demons alone. You can't just flip off your experiences like a light switch when you get home. You are likely to act strongly to any threat that you perceive to involve your security or safety or that of your family. Whoever said "real men don't cry" hadn't met many men who have been to war.

Dr. Daniela David, a practicing psychiatrist at the Miami Florida Veterans Hospital specializes in PTSD. She states there are definite changes in brain neurotransmitters and neurohormones with extreme stress, early trauma exposure, PTSD and depression. These changes can be significant and are the topic of extensive research at present, as well as the target of treatment interventions.

Cognitive Processing Therapy (CPT) and Prolonged Exposure (PE) are evidence-based talk-therapy interventions that have been shown to improve PTSD symptoms. They address traumatic memories, thoughts and feelings. Many of these veterans attend weekly or monthly groups.

Individuals who experience PTSD often "re-experience" traumatic events through vivid memories and dreams. Sometimes this triggers intense emotions such as grief, guilt, fear or anger. Sometimes this could be so intense that the individual thinks the memory is really occurring. This could not only be frightening to the individual but also children or anyone witnessing them. When children see this, they do not understand what is happening and begin to fear that the parent will be unable to care for them. A high of anxiety and arousal may manifest in high irritability with exaggerated concern for their own safety and the safety of their loved ones. For the children who witness this behavior of soldiers modeling anger, hyper vigilance or emotional detachment, it can come with its own problems. Some of these men might not experience full blown PTSD for years or even after retirement. The men who came home and those who didn't, 67 years later are referred to as "The Greatest Generation."

Standing, left to right:	**Kneeling, left to right:**
Dudley W. Hogon, Jr.	Ferrell Majors
Norman Larsen	Julian Cochran
Robert Derrington	Gus Johnson
Henry E, Pisterzi (Hank)	Richard Montgomery (Monty)
Joseph Wells	Joseph Levine
Galpin (Bud) Etherington	Daren Engel
Karnig Thomasian	F.R. Edwards (Bud)
Grady M. Farley	
Richard D. Moore	
Marion Burke	
John H. McClosky (Jack)	
Lionel F. Coffin	

Personal signatures of POWs at a POW Reunion

EPILOG

This book would not be complete without knowing something of what happened to some of the Emperor's men after their surrender.

Edward Leary, a Chicago Sun Reporter, came home with the rank of Captain in the Intelligence section. He located twenty-three Japanese Officers and Prison Guards who were at New Laws Court and Rangoon Jail. He was aided by Harry Suzakawa (a Japanese American) who later served as a court reporter at that trial. These men of the Emperor beat, murdered and tortured Allied soldiers and Airmen. They were brought to trial. Some were hanged and others imprisoned.

Captain Leary was able to find them from lists supplied to him by prisoners through descriptions and names as well as nick names they were given such as Tarzen, Moose Face, The Nose, Sparrow, Hollywood etc. In those lists their Japanese names were spelled phonetically.

"Tarzen" was sought first and Captain Leary was determined to find him. He was one of the cruelest guards at the Rangoon Prison. We heard the men also called him Limpy and Wano. Thanks to Sgt. Suzakawa, we found a name that sounded like the name that the prisoners had spelled phonetically. The name was Ueno: there were many Ueno's in the area. We rounded up all the Uenos that we could find and finally identified Superior Private Koigetsu Ueno. He admitted he was a guard in cell block 5 where American Airmen were held in solitary. He also admitted he was called Tarzen. He said he had beaten every American in his charge until he was unable to lift his club anymore. We also found witnesses who identified him. He was sentenced to hang.

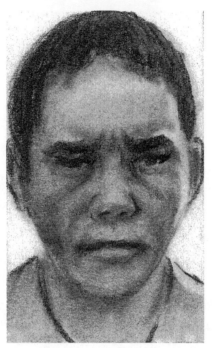

"Tarzen", a cruel and vicious guard remembered by all the men
and drawn from memory by Karnig Thomassian.

General Kimura: This was the General in command of Burma and was the one who gave the orders for abandoning Rangoon. He was the first one to flee to safety by air to Moulmein. He was convicted as a war criminal and dressed in US Army fatigues with no insignias of any kind, was hanged. At the time of Pearl Harbor, he had been a Vice Admiral directly under Tojo.

Major Maeda Hiroshi: An intelligence officer who interrogated the captured men. In 1987, he was found living a quiet life in a garden like home in Tokyo.

Tamura Mastataro: Third Sectary in the Japanese Embassy at the time of the evacuation of Rangoon. In 1985 at age 76, he was still angry at General Kimura who he thought should have defended Rangoon until death. He felt the General's betrayal was from his fear of being captured by the Allies. He said that if the Allies had not hanged him the Japanese Government should have for his treachery of abandoning Rangoon and not fighting until death.

Haros Ito: Chief Officer for the Rangoon Jail. In 1985 Mr. Ito was Counselor for the Kikko Food Corporation, Auditor of Mann's Wine Ltd., Counselor Japan Amateur Association, Chairmen Hitotsubashi University's Rowing Assoc. and President of the Japan Oarsmen Club. When asked about Captain Tazumi Motozo who had been commandant of the goal before he took over, his reply was:"I don't know what happened to him as I never met him." (This statement does not sound credible.)

As some still debate the dropping of the atomic bombs on Japan, ask any man who fought that war and you will find that they will agree that decision saved many Allied lives. They experienced the tenacity and determination of the Japanese population. Their vow to fight until death. To the horror of American soldiers, sailors and airmen who experienced Kamikaze attacks and suicides of not only soldiers but in some cases women carrying their children to death.

Japanese Definition of Kamikaze: The kamikaze, the wind of the gods, is the name for the typhoon which saved Japan from an invasion by Kublai Khan and his Mongolian hordes late in the 13th century. It destroyed the great Kahn's armada. They looked for the great wind to protect them from all enemies. They said "At the last stage of the battle, the kamikaze will blow." In 1945 the great wind never came.

Rangoon Prison Jail: After being deemed as unfit for human habitation in the 1930s, it is still in use today and called **"Insein Prison."**It is notorious worldwide for its continuing inhumane and dirty conditions. They still use abusive techniques along with mental and physical torture. It is used largely to repress political dissidents. The only difference is that the Japanese are gone.

Burma (Myanmar): Still looking for peace and Democracy.

ACKNOWLEDGEMENTS

This book could not have been written without the help and encouragement of the following people. My sons, Bob and Edward Newland. They both read and critiqued my manuscript. Edward pointed out the need for me to explain some details that while I thought everyone was aware of, his generation and younger ones were not. Bob, who also read my manuscript and was kind enough to draw a great rendition of the prison camp. My sister, Betty Blanton, for her encouragement and support with publishing this book. Stephen Siegel, one of my earliest advocates who helped me with understanding some of the nuances of writing. Many thanks to Julie Chase, who helped me format the book. Carlos Romero who was my computer guru. My dear friend Reva Hurtes who edited my book. She had more than she bargained for to overcome my inexperience. To Sam Burton, his daughter Diane, and her husband Steve Gershenson, my gratitude for sharing with me those great stories about the Hump pilots but also sharing with me their copies of the banquet speeches made in China and their experiences on their return trip there.

And last but not least Karnig and Diana Thomasian for their generosity in sharing their copies of Rangoon Ramblings, of which they were the editors and driving force of that publication. Also giving me compete access to Karnig's book, Then There Were Six. His gracious invitation to their home in New Jersey where he shared his memories of my Uncle who was not only his crewmate but his cellmate. I am eternally grateful to him for his blessing on this endeavor. It was important to me that these men were remembered. Karnig also designed the cover of the book duplicating exactly the cell door he remembered.

BIBLIOGRAPHY

KarnigThomasian. Then There Were Six: The True Story of the 1944 Rangoon Disaster. Bloomington, Indiana, Authorhouse, 2004.

Col. K.P. MacKenzie. Operation Rangoon Jail.London, England, C. Johnson, 1954.

Wilbur H. Morrison. Point of No Return; The Story of the Twentieth Air Force. New York, New York, Times Books, 1979.

Lionel Hudson. The Rats of Rangoon; the inside story of the "Fiasco" that took place at the end of the war in Burma. London, England, Leo Cooper, 1987.

United States. 40th Bomb Group History. Nashville, Tennessee, Turner Publishing, 1988.

Donald Nijboer, Steve Pace. B-29 Combat Missions; First-Hand Accounts of Superfortress Operations Over the Pacific and Korea. New York, New York, Metro Books, 2011.

Barbara W. Tuchman. Stillwell and the American Experience in China, 1911-45. New York, New York, MacMillan, 1971.

Charles Balaza. Life as an American Prisoner of War of the Japanese. Published by the author, 2002.

John Boyd with Gary Garth. Tenko! Rangoon Jail; the Amazing Story of Sgt John Boyd's Survival as a POW in a Notorious Japanese Prison Camp.Nashville, Tennessee, Turner Publishing, 1996.

Anne Freund. Taming the Fire Within; Life After War. Gainesville, Florida, Bravehearts Books, 2011.

Burma Star Association. London, England. Available at: http://www.burmastar.org.uk

Made in the USA
Lexington, KY
20 December 2012